Teacher Learning with Classroom Assessment

Heng Jiang · Mary F. Hill
Editors

Teacher Learning with Classroom Assessment

Perspectives from Asia Pacific

 Springer

Editors
Heng Jiang
National Institute of Education
Nanyang Technological University
Singapore
Singapore

Mary F. Hill
The University of Auckland
Auckland
New Zealand

ISBN 978-981-10-9052-3   ISBN 978-981-10-9053-0   (eBook)
https://doi.org/10.1007/978-981-10-9053-0

Library of Congress Control Number: 2018937323

Printed on acid-free paper

This Springer imprint is published by the registered company Springer Nature Singapore Pte Ltd. part of Springer Nature
The registered company address is: 152 Beach Road, #21-01/04 Gateway East, Singapore 189721, Singapore

Foreword

Learning is the common theme underlying both teacher learning and classroom assessment. These two topics represent currently developing fields, and this volume investigates them in tandem in the context of education in the Asia Pacific region. Readers will discover that simultaneously considering teachers as learners and examining the assessment practices teachers use to help students learn creates a kaleidoscope of colors.

The Ground upon Which This Volume Builds

While both classroom assessment and teacher learning are developing fields, teacher learning is at present a much larger presence in the scholarly literature than classroom assessment. However, much still remains to be learned, especially about the thinking of learners in regard to assessment, whether those learners are teachers or the students they serve.

There is a large research literature about teacher education (for current summaries, see Clandinin and Husu 2017; Cochran-Smith et al. 2008). When the topic narrows to how teachers learn about assessment, the literature becomes more sparse. Campbell (2013) pointed out that much research on teacher learning in assessment has evidence of short-term outcomes (for example, pre-service course assignments or the short-term results of professional development), not the quality of actual teacher assessment practices and products over time. Also, teacher learning about summative assessment has a much longer history (Wise 1993) than teacher learning about formative assessment (Scheider and Randel 2010).

The classroom assessment research literature is not as vast as the teacher education literature. However, and importantly for this volume, the field of classroom assessment has undergone a radical shift recently. Under older transmissionist views of learning, classroom assessment was understood as a way to measure how much of the information teachers transmitted to students was retained. Under more modern cognitive and constructivist views of learning, classroom assessment is now understood as a way to help students and teachers gather evidence of how students are thinking (Andrade and Brookhart 2016).

Learning theory is what unites these two topics, teacher learning and classroom assessment, both in this book and more broadly. Teachers must construct their own understanding of assessment, and students must use classroom assessment to help them construct their own understanding of their lesson content. The case studies in this book layout example after example of how this works in a variety of contexts, all within the Asia Pacific region. In Chap. 1, the editors offer three stances (training, practice, and inquiry) through which these case studies can be viewed, contributing to that kaleidoscope.

Learning from This Volume

The chapters in this book are overflowing with rich patterns, textures, and colors. Every reader will approach the book from a different perspective and take something different away from the experience of reading it. In this foreword, I offer three big insights that I gained from this volume, knowing that there are many others. After all, one can look through a kaleidoscope for hours and never see the same view. Nevertheless, I have chosen these three things because I believe they are at least part of the lasting contribution this volume will make to the fields of teacher learning and classroom assessment.

First, and consistent with most current learning theory, teachers must experience high-quality classroom assessment, and especially formative assessment, themselves if they are to really understand effective assessment practices and be able to break out of the transmissionist views and practices that they learned through the apprenticeship of observation as students themselves. That is, teachers not only need to see high-quality classroom assessment modeled, it must be modeled on them. This volume is not the first place that this idea has surfaced (e.g., Willis 2015), but it is the first place I have seen this principle illustrated from so many sides. Dixon and Hawe (Chap. 4), for example, show how explicitly modeling desired assessment practices help teachers make the difficult transition from conventional practices of classroom assessment to practices based on more current learning theory. Zhao, Yan, Tang, and Zhou (Chap. 5) show how Chinese teachers' learning about classroom assessment must begin from the traditional school experiences that have shaped their prior understandings of learning and assessment.

A second contribution of this book is that it expands the discourse about diversity in classroom assessment. The diversity encompassed in the case studies in this volume is broader than much that is written in the name of "diversity" in classroom assessment. The Asia Pacific region itself encompasses great cultural diversity. Some of the cultural and educational traditions represented in this volume derive from Asian sources (for example, China and Japan), although even within

"Asian sources" the diversity is great (for example, China is not like Japan). Some of the cultural and educational traditions represented in this volume derive from Anglophile sources (for example, Australia and New Zealand). Other educational systems represented in this volume derive from a mixture of both Asian and Anglophile sources (for example, Hong Kong, India, and Singapore). The result is a description of a wider variety of approaches to and understandings of classroom assessment, and teacher learning about assessment, than is available in most other sources.

Finally, and stemming from the previous point about diversity, this volume begins to describe a longer learning progression for classroom assessment than many current writers in the field envision. Research on assessment literacy—what it is and how teachers acquire it—tend to describe a learning trajectory that begins with mastering a set of knowledge and skills, then honing those skills to a level of fluency and effectiveness, and finally incorporating this assessment literacy deeply into one's instruction and who one is as a teacher (e.g., Xu and Brown 2016). The case studies in this volume suggest that this learning progression may be artificially truncated because it is based on research done in countries where some progress in classroom assessment has already been made. The descriptions in this book cause me to envision a longer progression: from viewing learning as memorization (Ratnam and Tham, Chap. 7), which positions classroom assessment as recitation; through viewing learning as conventional acquisition of knowledge produced by others, analogous to the training stance described by Jiang and Hill (Chap. 1) or the understandings of some of the teachers described by Leong (Chap. 9), which positions classroom assessment as a set of conventional methods; through viewing learning as more cognitive and replete with learners' "stumbles" (Ishii, Chap. 8), which positions classroom assessment as a more responsive set of methods and practices; and through viewing learning as a journey each learner may take in a slightly different way, which positions classroom assessment as a window on student thinking (Willis and Klenowski, Chap. 2). In fact, this top end of the progression is difficult to reach. When I read in Chap. 4 (Dixon and Hawe) that at first, New Zealand teachers thought that Learning Intentions and Success Criteria were the whole of Assessment for Learning—showing how their understanding was incomplete—my own response was that I would be delighted if I heard as much from many of the U.S. teachers I work with.

These three contributions—descriptions of the value of experience in learning classroom assessment; illustrations of very diverse contexts, teachers, learners, and classroom assessment practices; and a wider perspective on the learning progression for assessment literacy—together make something remarkable.

Pittsburgh, PA, USA   Susan M. Brookhart
                                                                   Duquesne University

References

Andrade, H., & Brookhart, S. M. (2016). The role of classroom assessment in supporting self-regulated learning. In D. Laveault & L. Allal (Eds.), *Assessment for learning: Meeting the challenge of implementation* (pp. 293–309). Switzerland: Springer International Publishing.

Campbell, C. (2013). Research on teacher competency in classroom assessment. In J. H. McMillan (Ed.), *Sage handbook of research on classroom assessment* (pp. 71–84). Thousand Oaks, CA: Sage.

Clandinin, D. J., & Husu, J. (Eds.). (2017). *International handbook of research on teacher education*. London: Sage.

Cochran-Smith, M., Feiman-Nemser, S., McIntyre, D. J., & Demers, K. E. (Eds.). (2008). *Handbook of research on teacher education* (3rd ed.). New York: Routledge.

Schneider, M. C., & Randel, B. (2010). Research on characteristics of effective professional development programs for enhancing educators' skills in formative assessment. In H. L. Andrade & G. J. Cizek (Eds.), *Handbook of formative assessment* (pp. 251–276). New York: Routledge.

Willis, J. (2015). Learning through feedback loop metaphors. *Curriculum Matters, 10*, 193–212.

Wise, S. L. (Ed.). (1993). *Teacher training in measurement and assessment skills*. University of Nebraska-Lincoln: Buros Institute of Mental Measurements.

Xu, Y., & Brown, G. T. (2016). Teacher assessment literacy in practice: A reconceptualization. *Teaching and Teacher Education, 58*, 149–162.

Acknowledgements

We acknowledge with gratitude all the contributors to this volume for their wonderful contributions that enrich this book with diverse perspectives about teacher learning and classroom assessment in unique Asia Pacific contexts. We especially thank Susan Brookhart who gave generously of her expertise and insights at a critical time. Thanks too, to Kim Schildkamp and Anil Kanjee for their special insights, looking from their different worldviews. We are grateful for Hilary van Uden, our copy editor, who is always there for us with a better phrase, a perceptive comment, and a word of encouragement. Very special thanks are due to Lawrence Liu, our editor at *Springer*, whose patience, unflagging good spirit, and concern for quality made him much a joy to work with.

We are also deeply beholden to our family members, who cheered us on, just by being who they are.

Contents

Editors and Contributors

About the Editors

Heng Jiang is an Assistant Professor at the Curriculum, Teaching, and Learning Academic Group at the National Institute of Education, Nanyang Technological University, Singapore. Her research interests include teacher learning and professional development in a comparative and international perspective, with a focus on using high-leverage teaching practices, such as assessment, to improve the quality and equity of the teacher preparation for underrepresented populations.

Mary F. Hill is an Associate Professor in the Faculty of Education and Social Work at The University of Auckland, New Zealand. Her work is grounded in the context of contemporary schooling and teacher education and the contribution that quality teaching makes to a socially just society. Her research interests include educational assessment, assessment education for teaching, practitioner inquiry, and the use of complexity theory and critical realism as explanatory theory for rethinking teacher education for equity.

Contributors

Helen Dixon is an Associate Professor in the Faculty of Education and Social Work at The University of Auckland, New Zealand. Her teaching and research interests are focused on the development of assessment literacy and capability both within the schooling sectors and in higher education. She also has a particular interest in teacher beliefs, including their efficacy beliefs, and how these influence assessment practice.

Eleanor Hawe is a Principal Lecturer in the Faculty of Education and Social Work at The University of Auckland. Her main area of teaching and research, Assessment for Learning (AfL), encompasses primary, secondary, and higher education, across a range of disciplinary areas. A guiding imperative in her work is identification of problems of practice regarding teachers' assessment literacy and capability (e.g., teachers' beliefs, self-efficacy, knowledge bases, and professional learning) with particular reference to AfL and discussion of ways forward. In 2015, she was the recipient of a national Ako Aotearoa Tertiary Teaching Excellence award.

Terumasa Ishii is Associate Professor of the Graduate School of Education at Kyoto University. In his doctoral dissertation, he studied the development of theories on educational objectives and assessment in the United States: (1) the Revised Bloom's Taxonomy developed by L. W. Anderson, (2) the Dimensions of Learning developed by R. J. Marzano, and (3) the Structure of Knowledge in Understanding by Design developed by G. Wiggins. He then went on to show how these frameworks improved the Tyler Rationale and Bloom's Taxonomy. He has also conducted action research toward school reform around lesson study.

Anil Kanjee is a Research Professor and Coordinator of the Postgraduate and Research Programme in the Department of Primary Education at the Tshwane University of Technology in South Africa. He also serves as a Research Fellow at the University of Oxford, and at the Centre for International Teacher Education (CPUT). Previously, he was an Executive Director at the Human Sciences Research Council, where he headed the Centre for Education Quality Improvement. He has worked as a technical advisor to education ministries in Africa, Asia, and the Middle East, and to several national and international organizations including JET Education, NECT, UNESCO, and UNICEF. His current research focus is on addressing the challenge of improving education quality and equity; enhancing teachers' use of assessment to improve learning and teaching; developing effective models of teacher professional development; monitoring and evaluation of education systems, programs, and projects; and the development of a national reporting framework for large-scale assessment studies.

Valentina Klenowski is an Adjunct Professor in the Faculty of Education at the Queensland University of Technology. She has researched curriculum development and assessment practice internationally at all levels from early childhood through to higher education. She is particularly interested in teachers' classroom assessment practices and the interrelationship with learning, curriculum, and pedagogy.

Ricky Lam is Associate Professor and Programme Director of Master of Education in the Department of Education Studies at Hong Kong Baptist University. He has been working in the field of English language teaching for 23 years. His publications have appeared in *Assessing Writing, Language Testing, TESOL Quarterly*, and other international journals. His research interests are assessment for learning, portfolio assessment, and second language writing assessment.

Wei Shin Leong is Assistant Professor with National Institute of Education (NIE), Nanyang Technological University (NTU), Singapore. He currently teaches undergraduate, graduate, and executive leadership and Ministry of Education (MOE) courses on curriculum planning and implementation, basic and advanced assessment literacy, formative assessment, and reflective practices. As the focal contact person for NIE of the Network on Education Quality Monitoring in Asia

Pacific (NEQMAP), he has been invited by UNESCO to be their assessment specialist representative and guest speaker on formative assessment and alignment of curriculum, assessment, and teaching.

Tara Ratnam is an independent teacher educator and researcher based in Mysuru, India. She fosters teacher learning and change in reflective communities of inquiry by focusing on the sociocultural forces that mediate their thinking and practice. She is also keenly interested in the issue of diversity and in providing socially sensitive learning support to the culturally diverse student populations. Her theoretical perspective is interdisciplinary and includes the works of theorists such as Mikhail Bakhtin (Philosophy of Language), Lev Vygotsky (Cultural Historical Psychology), William Perry (Adult Development), and Paulo Freire (Critical Pedagogy) among others.

Penelope Serow is an Associate Professor, as one of the project leaders of Nauru Teacher Education Project (NTEP) at the University of New England in Nauru. She comes from a background of prior association with Nauru where she was instrumental in the development of the Nauruan Mathematics Syllabus (2012). Penelope teaches mathematics education to pre-service and in-service teachers within primary, secondary, and postgraduate programs and she fondly looks back on her days teaching in rural New South Wales and brings many of these experiences to her research directions. These directions include ICT as a teaching tool in the mathematics classroom, mathematics curriculum development in developing countries, assessment, and building local teacher capacity in Pacific Island countries.

Kim Schildkamp is an Associate Professor in the Faculty of Behavioural, Management, and Social Sciences of the University of Twente. Her research, in the Netherlands but also in other countries, focuses on data-based decision-making and formative assessment. She has been invited as a guest lecturer and keynote speaker at several conferences and universities, including AERA (American Educational Research Association), the University of Pretoria in South Africa, and the University of Auckland in New Zealand. She is the president-elect of ICSEI (International Congress on School Effectiveness and Improvement), and she is chair of the ICSEI data use network. She has won awards for her work, and she has published widely on the use of (assessment) data. She developed the datateam® procedure, and she is editor of the book *Data-Based Decision Making in Education: Challenges and Opportunities*, published by Springer.

Dianne Smardon is one of the University of New England in-country lecturers working closely with students in the delivery of the Nauru Teacher Education Project (NTEP). Her background is in assessment for learning where, for 9 years, she led the Assess to Learn (AtoL) Project for the University of Waikato, New Zealand (NZ). This project provided long-term (up to three years), school-based teacher professional development, as well as short courses and workshops for teachers in specific aspects of classroom assessment. Her NZ experience with the consequences of deficit practice through the colonizing of curriculum has informed this research which has been conducted in the face-to-face setting, alongside the mediated curriculum of the Moodle site.

Kelvin Tan is Associate (Practice) Professor, and Head, of Curriculum, Teaching and Learning at the National Institute of Education of Singapore, Nanyang Technological University. His teaching, research, and advisory areas revolve around formative assessment for learning, teacher reflection, phenomenography/variation theory, and critical perspectives of assessment.

Liwei Tang is a Lecturer at College of Educational Sciences, Inner Mongolia Normal University in China. She received her doctoral degree in educational leadership from School of Education, Fayetteville State University. Her research focuses on educational leadership and administration. She is also interested in studying the management and professional development of teachers.

Jacob Tharu is a former university teacher of educational measurement who was engaged largely in in-service work with teachers of English and the development of English language tests. His continuing activities relate to professional support for teachers, program (curriculum) evaluation oriented toward enhanced inclusivity as cultural diversity among learners and teachers increases, and research methodology for small-scale studies in education. He has a special interest in demystifying social statistics. The evolving work of Jerome Bruner and the debates around Vygotsky's ideas were strong influences on his approach to education.

Jill Willis is a full-time Senior Lecturer in the Faculty of Education, Queensland University of Technology, Brisbane. Her research interests focus on assessment and evaluation that leads to greater learner agency, with specializations in classroom assessment and student experiences of next-generation learning spaces.

Bo Yan is a master student at Faculty of Education, Beijing Normal University in China. Her research focuses on educational evaluation and educational administration.

Decheng Zhao is an Associate Professor and Doctoral Supervisor at Faculty of Education, Beijing Normal University in China. His research focuses on educational evaluation, teacher appraisal, and policy analysis. He also has a particular interest in human resource management in the field of education.

Yao Zhou is a master student at Faculty of Education, Beijing Normal University in China. Her research focuses on educational leadership and classroom assessment.

Chapter 1
Teacher Learning and Classroom Assessment

Heng Jiang and Mary F. Hill

Abstract In this chapter, we introduce the dual themes of teacher learning and classroom assessment, and describe three stances (*training stance, practice stance, and inquiry stance*) to examine the relationships between these two themes. We then situate the case study chapters in the Asia-Pacific contexts and map out the structure of the book.

Keywords Classroom assessment · Inquiry · Learning and teaching
Practice · Teacher learning · Training

We have dual themes interplaying through this book: teacher learning and classroom assessment. Teacher learning refers to an ongoing process of engagement in outcome-based activities that result in changes in teacher practices and changes in teacher beliefs regarding teaching and learning (Putnam and Borko 2000; Russ et al. 2016). Classroom assessment is "a broad and evolving conceptualization of a process that teachers and students use in collecting, evaluating and using evidence of student learning for a variety of purposes, including diagnosing student strengths and weaknesses, monitoring student progress towards meeting desired levels of proficiency, assigning grades, and providing feedback to parents" (McMillan 2013, p. 4). Classroom assessment is an integral part of teaching and learning (Earl 2013), and teachers use it every day. They adapt the assessment practices to their curricula and instruction, examine and react to student work, and change instructional practices to foster student learning. Teachers learn to develop classroom assessment tools, experiment with new initiatives, and test them with assessment results. They use classroom assessment as the "vehicle to understand the interconnection of classroom teaching

H. Jiang (✉)
National Institute of Education, Nanyang Technological University, Singapore, Singapore
e-mail: heng.jiang@nie.edu.sg

M. F. Hill
Faculty of Education and Social Work, The University of Auckland, Auckland, New Zealand

© Springer Nature Singapore Pte Ltd. 2018
H. Jiang and M. F. Hill (eds.), *Teacher Learning with Classroom Assessment*,
https://doi.org/10.1007/978-981-10-9053-0_1

and group learning experiences with individual psychology and individual learning" (Brookhart 1997, p. 162). They also learn how to collect information from these classroom assessment practices, analyze, and interpret it for future changes in their teaching practices. Hence, although classroom assessment has often been associated with summing up and reporting student learning, it also plays an important role in how much teachers can learn from their everyday experiences.

On the one hand, researchers have suggested that teacher learning and professional development in classroom assessment can help teachers acquire the necessary assessment skills for the purpose of improving student learning and performance (Black and Wiliam 1998; Brookhart 2017; Hattie and Timperly 2007; Heitink et al. 2016; Hill 2016; Koh and Luke 2009; Shepard 2016; Wiliam 2011). Teachers' judgments based on teacher-made classroom assessment can overlap and converge with the standardized test scores in rating student achievement in mathematics, but this level of convergence varies across different classrooms with different teachers and students (Martinez et al. 2009). The implication of this complements as well as resonates with the dominant theme in most discussions of classroom assessment, which has been the external control of assessment quality and teacher assessment literacy. That is, what teachers should assess, how to ensure that they assess student learning with reliable and valid assessment practices, and how they are held accountable to the standards set by the external educational experts and assessment specialists. As a result, the responsibility for and effective use of classroom assessment have been treated as issues to be resolved outside the classroom, primarily under the charge of policymakers, school administrators, and researchers. Teachers, in turn, have been deemed to lack the assessment skills to produce trustworthy measures of student learning (Duckor and Perlstein 2014), and in need of training to ensure that they learn about and carry out the institutionally settled requirements for assessing their students effectively. As we will elaborate in this chapter, we are with Shepard (2000) in that teachers may need support to develop effective classroom assessment. But the development of the classroom assessment is not the end in itself. It needs to be adapted, implemented, mediated, and interpreted by the teachers as they gradually learn about their students, curriculum content, and teaching in their specific contexts.

On the other hand, arguments that classroom assessment can foster teacher learning in terms of building knowledge and strengthening practices (not limited to practicing classroom assessment strategies) have also been advocated in a few studies (Conderman and Hedin 2012; Falk and Ort 1998; Goldberg and Roswell 2000; Laguarda and Anderson 1998; Wilson and Sloane 2000; Young and Kim 2010). Indeed, as Wilson (2004) suggested, teachers build common understandings of assessment tools, a professional language for assessment practice, and opportunities for reflection on practice and student learning. Students learn most when teachers continuously learn from their teaching. Teachers acquire knowledge and skills for teaching through observation, practice, and constant feedback from experienced others and reflection upon their own teaching (Ball et al. 2014; Lortie 2002). Once they have achieved a certain level of expertise, they can attempt to teach through established teaching routines (Kennedy 2005) supported with tacit knowledge internalized in practice, which is understandable considering the complex and demanding classroom settings they have to cope with (Jackson 1990). But to support and max-imize student learning, it is important for teachers to reflect upon the routinized teaching, learn from feedback on their teaching, challenge themselves with ongoing evidence of student progress, and use this information to feedback to student learning and teaching practices. Classroom assessment can provide the means and informa-tion for teachers to examine the outcome and process of their teaching, and can, hence, hold the potential to have teachers learn to work with students and curriculum content in different ways (Darling-Hammond and Falk 2013; Jiang 2015; Little et al. 2003; Nolen et al. 2011).

Both teacher learning and classroom assessment have been influenced by con-ceptions of learning rooted in educational psychology. Early educational psychol-ogy based on Edward Thorndike and Charles Judd's work influenced educational research, which sought to conduct behavioral, experimental, and statistical analyses. The focus was on the accurate measurement of specific behaviors and learning out-comes (see Bayles and Hood 1966). "It was a science dedicated to control rather than to making sense of the forms and processes of schooling and teaching" (Doyle 1992, p. 489). This view had a substantial impact on the delineation of what assessment is, how it can be conducted, and its significance for teaching in the classroom. In contrast, Dewey saw education as a process in which teachers bring the child and the curriculum together in natural settings (Dewey 1902; Kliebard 1986). In this view, teachers need to develop their own knowledge to solve practical problems rather than being constrained by the prescriptions of scientific claims of education devel-oped by people outside the classroom contexts. Following from these two lines of thought, shifts in the prominence of ideas about the nature of cognition, learning, and teaching can be traced—weaving together behavioral, cognitive, and sociocultural views. These theories have been accompanied by parallel shifts in ideas about assess-ment (Penuel and Shepard 2016; Shepard 2000) as well as about teacher learning (Feiman-Nemser and Remillard 1995; Borko et al. 2010; Russ et al. 2016).

Linking the two strands of classroom assessment and teacher learning together, we argue that studies related to these two themes can be described through three "stances" (Bruner 1986; Cochran-Smith and Lytle 2009; Cochran-Smith and Vil-legas 2015) for positioning both strands in relation to each other: (1) *the training stance* for teachers to apply particular classroom assessment strategies in their teach-ing (Gearhart et al. 2006; Goldberg and Roswell 2000; Parr et al. 2007); (2) *the stance of practice* for teachers to adapt, negotiate, and practice their classroom assessment strategies informed by the external resources (Box et al. 2015; Jiang 2015; Pedder and James 2012; Poskitt 2014); and (3) *the stance of inquiry*, which is the exten-sion of the stance of practice, to unify the structural and programmatic request and teacher agency through, as we call it, the notion of reciprocity of teacher learn-ing and classroom assessment via teachers' critical inquiry. This stance claims that teacher learning and classroom assessment are both the medium and outcome of each other in an inquiry process (Cochran-Smith and Lytle 2009; Hill 2011; Nelson et al. 2012; Wyatt-Smith et al. 2014). Bruner (1986) sees "stance" (p. 50) as a point of view about the use of the mind in relation to the things and events in the world. As he described and differentiated the scientific and humanistic stances, "we know the world in different ways, from different stances, and each of the ways in which we know it produces different structures or representations, or, indeed, 'realities'" (p. 109). Classroom assessment, as the means to work with the world of teaching and learning in classrooms, not only refers to the techniques of assessment and the information to be found, the content, but also marks the stance of the teacher, how they use their own mind and understanding in relation to such techniques and information. Further, learning is not a process of achieving higher and higher levels of understanding of abstract ideas, but about "becom[ing] increasingly adept at seeing the same set of events from multiple perspectives or stances and at entertaining the results as, so to speak, alternative possible worlds" (Bruner 1986, p. 109). Thus, although studies show that teachers mediate assessment results with impressionistic information (Cizek et al. 1995/1996; Goertz et al. 2009), the teacher learning process is not teachers simply taking in whatever information is provided, but also keeping a distance from the process to examine "why" and "how" they have to make the changes. Such a process of teacher learning involves "objectifying" different stances, including the theoretical stances underlying the proposed/imposed learning tools and theories as well as those implicit stances adopted by teachers in their daily practices. This is achieved by expressing stances and inviting counter-stances and, in the process, leaving space for reflection and for metacognition (Bruner 1986, p. 129). Hence, teasing out the three stances of teacher learning in relation to classroom assessment does not only reveal the underlying rationale for teacher learning and classroom assessment but also reflect the ways in which we learn about these two connected topics.

The training stance assumes that classroom assessment is scientific, generalizable, often decontextualized, and uses an objective set of tools. Furthermore, in this view, teachers are sometimes assumed to implement classroom assessment in routine ways, due to lacking skills and knowledge to improvise classroom assessment. From this perspective, teachers may need training to acquire and apply assessment skills and to use tools and techniques devised by experts. Out of good intentions to help teachers to make sense of classroom assessment tools and data, the approach to teacher development usually takes the form of short-term workshops for teachers to acquire knowledge and skills for using classroom assessment strategies and tools. Such an approach can be beneficial for assisting teachers to improve their assessment practices while also learning more about classroom assessment and the subject they are teaching. In this regard, Parr et al. (2007) describe a carefully designed 5-day workshop on crafting writing assessment tools that intended to enable teachers to use rubrics to assess children's writing with accuracy and consistency. As the authors point out, at that time, teachers only had broad descriptions of expectations for students' progress in written language and there were "no formalised tools for helping teachers to understand how to assess students against the achievement objectives of the national curriculum" (p. 71). The research team developed a diagnostic writing assessment tool as part of a project developing assessment tools for teaching and learning in New Zealand. As a result, the teachers appreciated the use of the rubrics, began to use the scoring rubrics efficiently and reliably, and reported that they benefited from such training experiences in regard to their knowledge of writing, students, professional work, their beliefs, and their actual classroom practices.

However, a training stance is not always successful in promoting specific classroom assessment strategies. For instance, in one study, Maryland teachers participated in brief training on scoring students' performance-based assessments (Maryland School Performance Assessment Program) but did not implement practices consistent with the provided training in spite of explicit guidance. The teacher learning process was described as "scoring training tak(ing) place over a 2- to 3-day period, during which all readers must reach 70% exact agreement with pre-established 'true scores' on one or more qualifying sets of student responses" (Goldberg and Roswell 2000, pp. 259–260). This training experience seemed to be detached from classroom teaching, and discrete, and an accurate application of what was learned in the workshop was expected. The unsatisfying result of studies like this may be due to the fact that we cannot separate teachers from the daily teaching contexts they help to constitute. As a matter of fact, teachers strategically improvise their classroom assessment strategies with greater or less creativity, commitment, dexterity, and grace (Smardon and Serow this volume).

As well as learning to use tools produced outside the classroom, practices of classroom assessment are both produced and reproduced at the level of teaching (Ratnam and Tharu this volume). But the meso- (school) and macro- (national even global) levels of schooling still set constraints for teachers' agency in applying, modifying, and adjusting their classroom assessment strategies (Hill 2011; Lam this volume; Smardon and Serow this volume). So we have to put teachers back into co-constructing the classroom assessment process without neglecting the larger structures that enable and constrain their actions. In contrast with some instances of the training stance, *the practice stance* describes the intention to incorporate teacher agency—the teachers' ability to act upon and change their own classroom practices. This stance usually situates teacher learning and classroom assessment within classroom practices. Drawing on multiple learning resources, teachers try out, adjust, and scrutinize their own teaching in relation to student learning. In this view, while assessment tools can be incorporated, classroom assessment does not rely solely upon externally designed tools to gauge student learning, but is transferred, constructed, and co-constructed in the process of teaching and used in a specific context.

For example, Jiang (2015) studied how a group of preservice teachers in China learned how to teach students from low socioeconomic backgrounds through practicing classroom assessment strategies guided by their mentor teachers. The standardized test items were used formatively to help the teachers (including the mentor teachers and the preservice teachers) to identify the nexus between curriculum content, the student thinking, and the teaching approaches. However, she also found that such classroom assessment practices were limited, depending on the teachers' espoused beliefs about assessment and about the students.

Another study also shared similar findings. Box et al. (2015) conceptualized the complex interactions between teachers' beliefs, knowledge, and practices that are based on personal experiences (as a student or parent) and practical experiences in teaching that "influence their decisions about the purpose of assessment activity" as "personal practice assessment theories" (Box et al. 2015, p. 960). The authors studied three science teachers' self-reported formative assessment practices in classroom and claimed that their personal practice assessment theories influenced their approaches to practicing classroom assessment, which are also mediated by the layers of internally constructed, and external, contextual elements. One of the participants, Phoebe, was consistent with the principles of formative assessment and adjusted her instruction based on the assessment-elicited evidence. The other two, however, were guided by their "folk pedagogy" generated in the contexts, which diverted them away from the uttered rationale of formative assessment to emphasize the summative assessment in classroom. All three participants were engaged in reflections upon their assessment practices. Phoebe's reflection, combined with the trial of the formative assessment tools, helped her to use the formative assessment effectively for student learning. But the other two participants, Mary and Monica, could not get past their original assessment practices in their reflection and saw no need to modify the process.

Thus, the practice stance may be constrained by the implicit power of the teaching routine that teachers either develop from repetitive daily practice or internalize from the structural and institutional requirements. On the other end of the spectrum, the word "training" in the training stance implies that the teacher's role is one of conforming their practice to a set of more or less formal external requirements, plans, or approaches. The emphasis on the quality of classroom assessment bears the assumption that some teachers need to improve their assessment practices and later enhance the quality of the information they use to judge and foster student performances. The idea of "practice" strengthens the teachers' need to exercise their professional discretion in making use of classroom assessment. Such practices are deeply rooted in teachers' daily teaching routines and personal practical knowledge—"the experiential, moral, emotional, embodied knowledge teachers hold and express in their classroom practices" (Clandinin et al. 2009, p. 141). Without a critical inquiry into these practices, the tacit knowledge, beliefs, and values may be a hindrance to teacher learning rather than affordances when appropriating classroom assessment.

In the middle between the training stance and the practice stance, the inquiry stance, furthermore, suggests the continuing appropriation of various resources and the reconstruction of the forms in which teachers represent and evaluate knowledge in classrooms, in collaboration with students, as they critically reflect upon the evidence for student learning and their teaching. The inquiry stance can be viewed as one type of teacher "learning", but it highlights the need for teachers to reflect on and conduct inquiry into their own teaching practices when negotiating the use of the classroom assessment tools. It is not only an individual action but also a "disciplined inquiry" endorsed by professional learning communities, which "investigate and take action to progress learning in systematic ways through establishing goals or priorities, gathering evidence, reflecting on that evidence in light of the planned goals and taking action to move towards goal achievement" (Hill 2016, p. 773).

Here, classroom assessment is not so much an implementation procedure as an experimental process for pedagogical improvement. The third stance, *the stance of inquiry*, is both "world view, a critical habit of mind, a dynamic and fluid way of knowing and being in the world of educational practice that carries across professional careers and educational settings" (Cochran-Smith and Lytle 2009, p. 120) and a "data process…involving exploration, collection, analysis and implications" (Nelson et al. 2012, p. 6). It is a continual dual process of "making current arrangements problematic; questioning the ways knowledge and practices are constructed, evaluated, and used" (Cochran-Smith and Lytle 2009, p. 121), and an iterative research cycle in which teachers critically examine their own teaching with the collected evidence about student learning. In this dual process, the tacit knowledge and assumptions about students, learning, content knowledge, and teaching are subject to the scrutiny of practitioners, individually and collectively, based on the evidence from classroom assessment (Harrison 2013; Marsh et al. 2015; Willis and Klenowski this volume).

In light of this stance of inquiry, both classroom assessment and teacher learning are negotiated processes at interplay to improve teaching and learning. For instance, Nelson et al. (2012) developed a framework to examine the challenges teachers face when working with student learning data in a 3-year mathematics–science professional development model in the United States. This framework analyzed the collaborative teacher group's inquiry both from an epistemological stance about classroom assessment data and regarding the nature of the teachers' dialogue when using the data in their inquiry process. The authors found that the inquiry stance the teachers adopted to analyze the student classroom assessment data as a group helped teachers to be aware of the gap between student thinking and their own thinking. The authors found that the inquiry process tended to occur during "negotiation" (p. 25) when cognitive conflicts are surfaced and willingly explored by the group members in the conversations about interpreting student learning data. Based on such an inquiry process, the teachers learned to rethink about student data rather than "prov[ing] strengths in their practice by using data to show student learning gains" (p. 17). The stance of inquiry empowers teachers and emphasizes the transformative potential of the individual teacher as well as teacher groups to make use of classroom assessment to inform teaching and learning. Introducing such a stance to teachers and school leaders, however, is complex and requires a cultural shift and structural adjustments to facilitate the collaborative inquiry that suits particular school and societal contexts (Hill 2011).

Still, research shows that the three stances may co-exist and complement each other. For instance, Sato et al. (2008) found that teachers benefited from the teacher professional development training programs as well as the informal learning events in practice, and especially pointed out that the nature of both the training and the informal learning offered teachers opportunities to engage in critique and inquiry into their practices. Sato et al. compared the mathematics and science teachers' classroom assessment practices in a group certified by the National Board for Professional Teaching Standards (NBPTS) and the non-NBPTS groups in California. The authors observed major changes in the variety of classroom assessments used and the way the teachers used assessment information to support student learning in the NBPTS certified group in 3 years, compared to the non-NBPTS group. They also found that not only did the formal NBPTS training process influence the teachers, but the informal job-embedded learning opportunities helped teachers, including both the

NBPTS group and the non-NBPTS group, to closely examine and reflect upon their classroom assessment practices and beyond. These informal learning opportunities included the activities of the support group that the researchers helped to establish for teachers to continuously sustain their classroom assessment skills in practice, the collegial analysis, reflection, constructive critique of videotaped lessons, sharing of teaching ideas with teachers from different schools and districts, and participation in the research project. When examining the nature of the useful teacher learning opportunities along with classroom assessment, the authors pointed out that teachers were given chances to "engage in reflection and analysis of their teaching practices using rigorous standards as 'tools for critique,' …[which] guide teachers as they seek to enact the standards in specific classroom practices and give them feedback about what they are doing and how well" (Sato et al. 2008, p. 696).

To summarize, understanding the reciprocal relationship between teacher learning and classroom assessment is not straightforward. It requires the comparison of varied stances across these two research areas. Delineating the stances through which teachers learn about, and to work with, classroom assessment provides a set of lenses to view both processes at interplay. From our perspective, while the provision of assessment tools and professional training can be very helpful, teachers also need scope and support to learn together and to use their own agency in implementing classroom assessment with an inquiry stance into their classroom teaching. To adopt a reciprocal relationship between teacher learning and classroom, assessment would have three important implications. First, there seems to be a need for greater explicitness by both assessment experts and teachers about the stances for both classroom assessment and teacher learning. Our sense is that these stances may be implicit in practice and underspecified so that the professional development and learning activities pertaining to the classroom assessment seem to lack the situated understanding. Second, enactment of certain classroom assessment strategies needs a mutually collaborative process between the teachers and the assessment experts and researchers that is grounded deeply in the classroom contexts. Finally, it is vital that the research skills and tools are provided to help teachers to develop the inquiry stance and capture the use of classroom assessment suitable for their teaching and student learning.

Contexts in the Asia-Pacific Region

In this book, we claim the mutually reciprocal relationship between classroom assessment and teacher learning described above and show how it plays out in a range of very different classroom contexts. We show how the process of in-depth teacher learning about teaching needs classroom assessment in the making to provide the information teachers need in order to interpret student learning and construct follow-up practices to improve student learning. We situate this argument in the unique and varied contexts of the Asia-Pacific region.

Here, the Asia-Pacific region refers to Asia, Australia, New Zealand, and the Pacific Island nations. Many individual nations within this region have experienced rapid growth in economic development and educational reforms over the past two decades. The trend of educational reform across this region can be read as a combination of re-establishing national vision, educational aims for accountability and the decentralization, and school-based management at the local level, coupled with the endeavors to ensure teacher quality through teacher professional development, use of new technology, and paradigm shifts in learning, teaching, and assessment (Cheng 2003; Klenowski 2009). It is, however, rather challenging, in practice, to discuss the nature of these trends in practice across the Asia-Pacific region. This is because this region includes a wide variety of education systems that draw from very different cultures and histories.

Historically, the expansion of public education systems in many parts of the Asia-Pacific region was undertaken by the colonial powers. Nevertheless, many countries of the Asia-Pacific region already had established education systems before these influences from Western countries arrived, and in postcolonial times still maintain longstanding traditions and indigenous educational practices. For example, importing assessment and accountability from Western Europe started policies of "payment by results" in the Asia-Pacific region (for example, see Hearn 1872, cited in Mohandas et al. 2003). Western influences have also affected the public examination systems in different countries at different times during the twentieth century. But the use of examination to regulate teaching and learning has been a tradition for over a thousand years in China and some countries in the Confucian culture sphere (Biggs 1998). Surviving changes in governments and educational reforms, the examination system, and assessment practices have remained one of the constants of education in East Asia and act as a major mode of accountability for countries in the rest of the Asia-Pacific region, including Australia, Thailand, New Zealand, and India.

We are also using the term "Asia Pacific" as an analytic construct that refers to a diversity of unique yet connected histories and contexts, communities, and cultures (Wilson and Dirlik 1995). Important, as well, is the amalgam of diverse and indigenous ideas that mix with globalized discourses about educational reforms and practices in the Asia-Pacific region. Even though Western influences have introduced many changes and produced a global trend in educational reform nowadays, there has been a rise of "the hybrid cultures, histories, and discourses,…posing new, different, and highly volatile material conditions" (Nozaki et al. 2005, p. 3) for educational practices in the Asia-Pacific region. Much earlier work, partly influenced by comparative education and Western "area studies", studying educational practices in the Asia-Pacific region, has tended to label the Asia Pacific as "other" contexts with exotic and foreign practices in the field of education. However, such an approach has been challenged by the complex analyses from the postcolonial and indigenous perspectives, and the intricate studies with "inside out" empirical, local documentation, and critical analysis coming from scholars in this region (for example, Gopinathan 2007; Mok and Chan 2002).

With a rich history and diverse traditions, the Asia-Pacific has been an exciting context for studying the reciprocal relationship between classroom assessment and teacher learning, but also a complex setting because of the different powers dominating the discourses in this region. While specific uses of classroom assessment, and teacher learning, in particular contexts have faced different challenges in implementation in Asia-Pacific countries, all deserve research attention and critical reflection on the underlying theoretical paradigms preoccupied with Western perspectives and enriched with indigenous practices.

Structure of the Book

Assessment may look very different in classrooms across the Asia-Pacific region; for this reason, we have left these details to the case study chapters later in the book. The key issue of what should count as classroom assessment and how teacher learning relates to it is the one that all contributors to this book address as they examine the diverse contexts for teachers practicing classroom assessment in the Asia-Pacific region. In this first chapter, we have sought to renegotiate the interplay between the learning paradigms to support teacher learning and those underpinning classroom assessment. In so doing, we frame a central challenge faced by those attempting a critical study on the connections between teacher learning and classroom assessment, and propose the stance of inquiry for studying teacher learning in nexus with classroom assessment. This challenge involves the repositioning of the teacher's role as avoiding an uncritical adherence to training that leans toward the technicization of classroom assessment. At the same time, we are also aware that a shift to practice stance can leave teachers struggling with a large amount of classroom assessment data all by themselves, and that this might discourage them from making sound judgments about their teaching and student learning.

The need to empower teachers to critically reflect on and inquire into what is imposed about classroom assessment strategies and learn to utilize it in a specific classroom context, and the use of classroom assessment to foster teachers' professional growth, run across the case studies in this book. Specifically, the case study chapters respond to three inter-related questions: (1) How do Asia-Pacific teachers practice classroom assessment? (2) Why do they practice such classroom assessment strategies? (3) What do teachers learn from practicing classroom assessment? Some also begin to tackle a fourth question, how do students benefit from these forms of classroom assessment in the Asia-Pacific region? These chapters, collectively, through examples from various locations, provide a sustained focus on the challenges that educational practitioners and researchers face when implementing classroom assessment in response to educational reforms and policies, along with the situative responses to those challenges via teacher learning and professional development. In Chap. 2, Jill Willis and Valentina Klenowski draw on two cases from Queensland schools to study teacher agency in using approaches to classroom assessment in the Australian context of informed professionalism and intelligent accountability. The first case, situated in a Queensland primary school, concerns Year 2 teachers (of students 6–7 years old) navigating how national achievement standards in the new state curriculum and assessment packages could be incorporated and combined with their existing classroom assessment practices. In the second case, in a Queensland senior high school, the teachers were planning the final summative classroom assessment pieces for their Year 12 (17-year-old) students. It is found that teachers are assessment learners negotiating meaning and actively shaping the varied contexts at work. The authors analyzed the findings within the ongoing debates around the Australian Curriculum, which requires teacher learning about how the latest changes influence their classroom assessment practices and correspond to three perspectives of teacher agency: (1) pragmatic, the ecological perspective of agency; (2) agency as a dynamic social process; and (3) personal response. The authors suggest providing cultural and structural support for teachers to collaboratively inquire into their teaching via classroom assessment, and include students in the process of such critical inquiries.

In Chap. 3, Dianne Smardon and Penelope Serow focus on Nauruan teachers' views of how classroom assessment is understood in the context of their Pacific pedagogy. Like Chap. 2, the authors also found that teachers exercise agency to extend their understanding and use of classroom assessment to inform student learning. In a centralized education system in the Republic of Nauru, teacher-made tests are administered midway through and at the end of the year in the primary schools. This chapter studies the experiences of two teachers' professional learning in the Nauru Teacher Education Project (NTEP) program, which was supported by the Australian Department of Foreign Affairs and Trade and New Zealand Aid, and their 2 years in classroom practice after the program. It reveals the participants' opinions about how they use (and adjust) Australian-based classroom assessment strategies in their daily teaching in Nauru, learn from the process about student-centered pedagogy and constructivist approaches to the classroom assessment, and what they think students benefit from regarding their classroom assessment practices. In it, the authors delineate the process of how the participant teachers worked as "cultural brokers", actively responding to the varied discourses of classroom assessment, and how they navigate the pedagogical differences between their Australian-based content in the NTEP program and their Nauruan contexts.

While the process through which classroom assessment is implemented always requires careful discretion, teacher professional development as a supporting scheme of practice deserves scholarly attention in its own right. In a recent review by Brookhart (2017), the profound transformation in teachers' practices in incorporating formative assessment in classroom, which she terms a "sea change", are reported "in the context of teacher learning communities and other ongoing professional development programs where the kind of long-term learning required for changes in beliefs can happen" (p. 938). Teacher professional development implemented as one-off training workshops does not always have a substantive influence upon teachers' beliefs and practices. When teacher learning is contextualized in a community of learning, using the very assessment practices, the teachers are learning about may help to impact their practices and beliefs when working with classroom assessment. In Chap. 4, Helen Dixon and Eleanor Hawe explain their design of a course for teachers which deliberately has teachers experience Assessment for Learning (AfL) as learners, while concurrently learning about AfL. Based on the analysis of interviews with 21 participant teachers, the authors found that the experiential and collaborative learning opportunities provided helped the teachers to change their understanding of AfL. These learning opportunities were modeled by the experienced teacher (the course instructor) and mirrored those expected of students in classrooms, and hence supported both teacher reflection-in-action and reflection-on-action about the construct of assessment for learning.

The learning opportunities for Chinese teachers to acquire new classroom assessment strategies (and other instructional innovations) were located in a school-based teaching and research activity as a job-embedded professional development for teachers. In Chap. 5, Decheng Zhao, Bo Yan, Liwei Tang, and Yao Zhou reveal the demands of teacher learning about the new assessment practices in response to the New Curriculum reforms in China since 2001. Drawing upon interviews and observations of 18 teachers from primary and junior high schools in Beijing, the study found changes in the teachers' classroom assessment were in accordance with the New Curriculum reform, and the teachers had started to focus on the diagnosis, feedback, motivation, and improvement functions of classroom assessment. These changes emphasize the developmental nature of assessment, strengthen diagnostic assessment before instruction, stress formative assessment during instruction, and motivate students to participate in class actively. Although challenges remain for teachers, the teacher research activities embedded within school-based professional development provided spaces for teachers to learn and change their classroom assessment practices.

In Chap. 6, Ricky Lam also deals with school-based teacher learning about classroom assessment. His work identified the school-related contextual factors as experienced by secondary-level English writing teachers in Hong Kong. Drawing on two cases based on teacher interviews, classroom observations, and narratives, this study reveals that teachers strategically chose approaches for implementing the portfolio in their writing class. One of the participants, Willy, opted to simplify what is learned in the training session and put it "in practice for achieving a quick-fix approach to change." Whereas the other participant, Winifred, used a "transferring" approach to adapt what is learned in the staff development seminars to suit her own classroom assessment practices to promote student learning. Their strategic choices were interpreted against three contextual factors in schools that constrain or facilitate the implementation of portfolio assessment by the participants: teacher evaluation systems, school cultures, and opportunities for collaboration. The author suggests more teacher-initiated professional development endeavors backed by collegial school culture are needed for teachers to learn to use portfolio assessment.

Similarly, in Chap. 7, Tara Ratnam and Jacob Tharu illustrate how Indian teachers chose to restructure what is expected for classroom assessment, advocated by the Continuous and Comprehensive Evaluation (CCE) scheme, and fit in their original ways of practice, in the context of implementing the educational reforms scripted in the National Curriculum Framework 2005. Based on questionnaires, interviews, and classroom observations involving 57 teachers from 16 schools in Karnataka State, the authors found that teachers were able to articulate the new vocabulary of formative assessment according to CCE, but not really practice it as intended. Further investigations about the school contexts helped the authors to interpret the gaps between what the teachers say and what they do. Their analysis shows how the following contextual factors restrained teachers from practicing the classroom assessment strategies they had learned about: teacher overload, overambitious plans for the teacher training program, and a lack of conceptual clarity at all levels.

Indeed, implementing classroom assessment strategies developed outside the classroom is a complex issue for teachers, as classroom teaching is deeply contextualized. In Chap. 8, Terumasa Ishii is particularly concerned about responsive and emergent assessment as a tradition in Japanese classrooms. As the author points out, the debate about educational measurement and assessment has historically moved from outside the classroom to inside it, and from relying on testing specialists to teachers, and even students, in Western countries. In Japan, however, teachers, especially elementary school teachers, have worked hard to understand children and to generate learning moments through creative whole-class teaching that reveals and facilitates student thinking through classroom discussions. With two vivid examples of how teachers orchestrate whole-class teaching through turning stumbles in students' understanding of the academic content into opportunities for learning, this study highlights how the act of classroom assessment is fundamentally integrated, indigenous, and a natural part of the teaching process, embedded in the Japanese culture of teacher community learning processes.

In Chap. 9, Wei Shin Leong also focuses on teacher learning juxtaposed with classroom assessment by examining, in depth, the case of one teacher in Singapore. Pei Pei, a lower secondary music and English teacher, deemed assessment as only standardized tests and was unaware of her natural assessment practices in the classroom. Probed by the researcher's interview questions, she reflected upon her own classroom assessment practices and realized the limits of her professional knowledge and skills. This process of learning helped Pei Pei to consciously learn more about, and refine, her classroom assessment practices on her own. This case corresponds to the earlier chapters about teachers' agency in actively learning about, interpreting and implementing classroom assessment within immediate social, epistemic, and cultural contexts.

In addition to the case chapters, we also invited two commentary chapters, one from a European/Dutch perspective, and the other from the South African perspective. The commentary by Schildkamp points out the opportunities and challenges classroom assessment has in Europe/The Netherlands in regard to the issues of accountability pressure, the use of formal and informal assessment data, data literacy, student involvement, and professional development in the form of teacher collaboration. Kanjee's commentary resonates with the issues about assessment professional development initiatives challenged by the regular external testing in the context of curriculum reforms in South Africa, and argues for the need to better prepare and support teachers in their classrooms. All these correspond to what has been discussed in the cases in Asia-Pacific contexts. Both commentary chapters highlight that the issues addressed in the abovementioned case studies in the Asia-Pacific areas are not unique, but have international relevance.

Chapter 12 includes an overview of the content and focus of previous chapters according to themes, and acts as a concluding chapter for the book. The authors tease out a continuum of classroom assessment practices delineated across the included case studies, ranging from relatively formal teacher-implemented assessment tasks to interactive formative assessment processes. Along this continuum, the authors discuss the major purposes of classroom assessment in relation to teaching and teacher learning as manifested in the cases: making judgments, monitoring progress; diagnosing learning status to plan teaching; and, informing learning and teaching through assessment as an embedded process. Further, this chapter highlights the historical, societal, and cultural contexts when unpacking the duplex of teacher learning and classroom assessment, and in relation to international trends.

Taken together, the chapters in this volume suggest the complexity and intricacy of teacher learning in nexus with classroom assessment. Teacher learning, when carefully crafted, can facilitate the implementation of effective classroom assessment to promote student learning. In this process, teachers also learn to choose appropriate strategies for classroom assessment to examine the student learning data closely, interpret their practices in particular contexts, and adjust their teaching accordingly. However, such practices tend to stand in relation to diverse cultural traditions and practices in the Asia-Pacific region. The cases here might appear not as readily amenable to Western theories and practices about teacher learning and classroom practices, but the key issues evident in these cases are not unique to the Asia-Pacific area. The authors provide cases from their particular contexts demonstrating nuanced understandings and explanations about teachers' agency. Many of these demonstrate how teachers can struggle to apply classroom assessment strategies designed by external agencies often influenced by the Western discourses in education. Together, they do not only reframe issues of teaching, teacher learning, and classroom assessment for educational researchers and practitioners in the Asia-Pacific, but also open up further discussions on the critical issues of teaching quality, assessment, and accountability in a global context.

References

Ball, D. L., Ben-Peretz, M., & Cohen, R. B. (2014). Records of practice and the development of collective professional knowledge. *British Journal of Educational Studies, 62*(3), 317–335.

Bayles, E. E., & Hood, B. L. (1966). *Growth of American educational thought and practice*. New York: HarperCollins.

Biggs, J. (1998). Learning from the Confucian heritage: So size does not matter? *International Journal of Educational Research, 29,* 723–738.

Black, P., & Wiliam, D. (1998). Assessment and classroom learning. *Assessment in Education: Principles, Policy and Practice, 5*(1), 7–74.

Borko, H., Jacobs, J., & Koeliner, K. (2010). Contemporary approaches to teacher professional development. In P. Peterson, E. Baker, & B. McGaw (Eds.), *International encyclopedia of education* (Vol. 7, pp. 548–556). Oxford: Elsevier.

Box, C., Skoog, G., & Dabbs, J. (2015). A case study of teacher personal practice assessment theories and complexities of implementing formative assessment. *American Educational Research Journal, 52*(5), 956–983.

Brookhart, S. M. (1997). A theoretical framework for the role of classroom assessment in motivating student effort and achievement. *Applied Measurement in Education, 10*(2), 161–180.

Brookhart, S. M. (2017). Formative assessment in teacher education. In D. J. Clandinin & J. Husu (Eds.), *International handbook of research on teacher education* (pp. 927–943). London: Sage.

Bruner, J. (1986). *Actual minds, possible worlds*. Cambridge: Harvard University Press.

Cheng, Y. (2003). Trends in educational reform in the Asia-Pacific region. In J. Reeves & R. Watanabe (Eds.), *International handbook of educational research in the Asia-Pacific region* (pp. 3–16). Dordrecht: Kluwer Academic.

Cizek, G., Fitzgerald, S., & Rachor, R. (1995/1996). Teachers' assessment practices: Preparation, isolation, and the kitchen sink. *Educational Assessment, 3*(2), 159–179.

Clandinin, D. J., Downey, C. A., & Huber, J. (2009). Attending to changing landscapes: Shaping the interwoven identities of teachers and teacher educators. *Asia-Pacific Journal of Teacher Education, 37*(2), 141–154.

Cochran-Smith, M., & Lytle, S. L. (2009). *Inquiry as stance: Practitioner research for the next generation*. New York: Teachers College Press.

Cochran-Smith, M., & Villegas, A. M. (2015). Framing teacher preparation research: An overview of the field, Part I. *Journal of Teacher Education, 66*(1), 7–20.

Conderman, G., & Hedin, L. (2012). Classroom assessments that inform instruction. *Kappa Delta Pi Record, 48,* 162–168.

Darling-Hammond, L., & Falk, B. (2013). *Teacher learning through assessment: How student-performance assessments can support teacher learning.* https://www.americanprogress.org/wp-content/uploads/2013/09/TeacherLearning.pdf. Accessed May 21, 2017.

Dewey, J. (1902/1990). The child and the curriculum. In *The school and society and the child and the curriculum* (pp. 181–209). Chicago: The University of Chicago Press.

Doyle, W. (1992). Curriculum and pedagogy. In P. W. Jackson (Ed.), *Handbook of research on curriculum* (pp. 486–516). New York: Macmillan.

Duckor, B., & Perlstein, D. (2014). Assessing habits of mind: Teaching to the test at Central Park East Secondary School. *Teachers College Record, 116*(2), 1–33.

Earl, L. (2013). *Assessment as learning: Using classroom assessment to maximize student learning* (2nd ed.). Thousand Oaks, CA: Corwin.

Falk, B., & Ort, S. (1998). Sitting down to score: Teacher learning through assessment. *Phi Delta Kappan, 80,* 59–64.

Feiman-Nemser, S., & Remillard, J. (1995). *Perspectives on learning to teach.* https://www.education.msu.edu/NCRTL/PDFs/NCRTL/IssuePapers/ip953.pdf. Accessed August 7, 2017.

Gearhart, M., Nagashima, S., Pfotenhauer, J., Clark, S., Schwab, C., Vendlinski, T., et al. (2006). Developing expertise with classroom assessment in K-12 science: Learning to interpret student work. Interim findings from a 2-year study. *Educational Assessment, 11*(3&4), 237–263.

Goertz, M., Olah, L., & Riggan, M. (2009). *Can interim assessments be used for instructional change?* CPRE Policy Brief RB-51. Philadelphia: Consortium for Policy Research in Education.

Goldberg, G., & Roswell, B. (2000). From perception to practice: The impact of teachers' scoring experience on performance-based instruction and classroom assessment. *Educational Assessment, 6,* 257–290.

Gopinathan, S. (2007). Globalisation, the Singapore developmental state and education policy: A thesis revisited. *Globalisation, Societies and Education, 5*(1), 53–70.

Harrison, C. (2013). Collaborative action research as a tool for generating formative feedback on teachers' classroom assessment practice: The KREST project. *Teachers and Teaching, 19*(2), 202–213.

Hattie, J., & Timperly, H. (2007). The power of feedback. *Review of Educational Research, 77*(1), 81–112.

Hearn, W. E. (1872). *Payment by results in primary education.* Melbourne: Stillwell and Knight.

Heitink, M. C., Kleij, F., Veldkamp, B., Schildkamp, K., & Klippers, W. (2016). A systematic review of prerequisites for implementing assessment for learning in classroom practice. *Educational Research Review, 17,* 50–62.

Hill, M. F. (2011). 'Getting traction': Enablers and barriers to implementing assessment for learning in secondary schools. *Assessment in Education: Principles, Policy & Practice, 18*(4), 347–364.

Hill, M. F. (2016). Assessment for learning community: Learners, teachers and policy makers. In D. Wyse, L. Hayward, & J. Pandya (Eds.), *The Sage handbook of curriculum, pedagogy and assessment* (Vol. 2, pp. 772–789). London: Sage.

Jackson, P. (1990). *Life in classrooms.* New York: Teachers College Press.

Jiang, H. (2015). *Learning to teach with assessment: A student teaching experience in China.* Singapore: Springer.

Kennedy, M. (2005). *Inside teaching: How classroom life undermines reforms.* Cambridge: Harvard University Press.

Klenowski, V. (2009). Assessment for learning revisited: An Asia-Pacific perspective. *Assessment in Education: Principles, Policy & Practice, 16*(3), 263–268.

Kliebard, H. (1986). *The struggle for the American curriculum: 1893–1958.* Boston: Routledge & Kegan Paul.

Koh, K., & Luke, A. (2009). Authentic and conventional assessment in Singapore schools: An empirical study of teacher assignments and student work. *Assessment in Education: Principles, Policy & Practice, 16*(3), 291–318.

Laguarda, K., & Anderson, L. (1998). *Partnerships for standards-based professional development: Final report of the evaluation.* Washington: Policy Studies Associates.

Little, J., Gearhart, M., Marnie, C., & Kafka, J. (2003). Looking at student work for teacher learning, teacher community, and school reform. *Phi Delta Kappan, 85*(3), 185–192.

Lortie, D. (2002). *Schoolteacher: A sociological study* (2nd ed.). Chicago: The University of Chicago Press.

Marsh, J., Bertrand, M., & Huget, A. (2015). Using data to alter instructional practice: The mediating role of coaches and professional learning communities. *Teachers College Record, 117*(4), 1–40.

Martinez, J., Stecher, B., & Borko, H. (2009). Classroom assessment practices, teacher judgments, and student achievement in mathematics: Evidence from the ECLS. *Educational Assessment, 14*(2), 78–102.

McMillan, J. H. (2013). Why we need research on classroom assessment. In J. H. McMillan (Ed.), *Sage handbook of research on classroom assessment* (pp. 3–16). Thousand Oaks: Sage.

Mohandas, R., Wei, M., & Keeves, J. (2003). Evaluation and accountability in Asian and Pacific countries. In J. Reeves & R. Watanabe (Eds.), *International handbook of educational research in the Asia-Pacific region* (pp. 107–121). Dordrecht: Kluwer Academic.

Mok, J. K. H., & Chan, D. K. K. (2002). *Globalisation and education: The quest for quality education in Hong Kong.* Hong Kong: Hong Kong University Press.

Nelson, T. H., Slavit, D., & Deuel, A. (2012). Two dimensions of an inquiry stance toward student-learning data. *Teachers College Record, 114*(8), 1–42.

Nolen, S., Horn, I., Ward, C., & Childers, S. (2011). Novice teacher learning and motivation across contexts: Assessment tools as boundary objects. *Cognition and Instruction, 29*(1), 88–122.

Nozaki, Y., Openshaw, R., & Luke, A. (2005). Introduction. In Y. Nozaki, R. Openshaw, & A. Luke (Eds.), *Struggles over difference: Curriculum, texts, and pedagogy in the Asia-Pacific.* New York: State University of New York Press.

Parr, J., Glasswell, K., & Aikman, M. (2007). Supporting teacher learning and informed practice in writing through assessment tools for teaching and learning. *Asia-Pacific Journal of Teacher Education, 35*(1), 69–87.

Pedder, D., & James, M. (2012). Professional learning as a condition for assessment for learning. In J. Gardner (Ed.), *Assessment and learning* (2nd ed., pp. 33–48). London: Sage.

Penuel, W. R., & Shepard, L. A. (2016). Assessment and teaching. In D. H. Gitomer & C. A. Bell (Eds.), *Handbook of research on teaching* (5th ed., pp. 787–850). Washington: American Educational Research Association.

Poskitt, J. (2014). Transforming professional learning and practice in assessment for learning. *The Curriculum Journal, 25*(4), 542–566.

Putnam, R. T., & Borko, H. (2000). What do new views of knowledge and thinking have to say about research on teacher learning? *Educational Researcher, 29*(1), 4–15.

Russ, R. S., Sherin, B. L., & Sherin, M. G. (2016). What constitutes teacher learning? In D. H. Gitomer & C. A. Bell (Eds.), *Handbook of research on teaching* (5th ed., pp. 391–438). Washington: American Educational Research Association.

Sato, M., Chung, R. R., & Darling-Hammond, L. (2008). Improving teachers' assessment practices through professional development: The case of national board certification. *American Educational Research Journal, 45*(3), 669–700.

Shepard, L. A. (2000). *The role of classroom assessment in teaching and learning* (Technical Report 517). Los Angeles: Center for the Study of Evaluation, National Center for Research on Evaluation, Standards, and Student Testing, and Center for Research on Education, Diversity and Excellence, University of California, Santa Cruz.

Shepard, L. A. (2016). Testing and assessment for the good of education. *Educational Researcher, 45*(2), 112–121.

Wiliam, D. (2011). What is assessment for learning? *Studies in Educational Evaluation, 37,* 3–14.

Wilson, S. (2004). Student assessment as an opportunity to learn in and from one's teaching practices. In M. Wilson (Ed.), *Towards coherence between classroom assessment and accountability* (National Society for the Study of Education Yearbook, Vol. 103, Part 2, pp. 264–271). Chicago: University of Chicago Press.

Wilson, R., & Dirlik, A. (Eds.). (1995). *Asia-Pacific as space of cultural production.* Durham, NC: Duke University Press.

Wilson, M., & Sloane, K. (2000). From principles to practice: An embedded assessment system. *Applied Measurement in Education, 13,* 181–208.

Wyatt-Smith, C., Klenowski, V., & Colbert, P. (2014). Assessment understood as enabling. In C. Wyatt-Smith, V. Klenowski, & P. Colbert (Eds.), *Designing assessment for quality learning* (pp. 1–20). Dordrecht: Springer International.

Young, V., & Kim, D. (2010). Using assessment for instructional improvement: A literature review. *Education Policy Analysis Archives, 18*(19), 1–36.

Chapter 2
Classroom Assessment Practices and Teacher Learning: An Australian Perspective

Jill Willis and Valentina Klenowski

Abstract This chapter draws on empirical evidence to explore the purposes and the approaches to classroom assessment used by some Australian primary and secondary teachers. Insights into how teachers learn in the development of classroom assessment for formative and summative purposes, and the strategies they employ to address student learning needs, are described and critically analyzed. The importance of teacher agency when learning about classroom assessment to enhance validity, consistency, and equity is addressed.

Keywords Assessment learning · Classroom assessment · Informed professionalism · Teacher agency

Introduction

Classroom assessment in Australia has historically relied on teacher informed professionalism. Classroom teachers design assessment for both formative and summative purposes as part of their daily practice alongside some common summative assessment tasks provided for senior school certification purposes, and national census testing in literacy and numeracy. Classroom assessment ranges from informal conversations and questions, to projects and timed tasks evaluated by criteria and standards, all designed to gather information that can inform improvements in student learning and teaching. Teachers draw on their knowledge of the students, curriculum, pedagogy, and assessment principles of validity, consistency, and equity within systems coordinated by a relevant educational authority. Teachers evaluate and moderate the classroom assessment outcomes, and strategically adjust their

J. Willis (✉) · V. Klenowski
Queensland University of Technology, Brisbane, Australia
e-mail: jill.willis@qut.edu.au

© Springer Nature Singapore Pte Ltd. 2018
H. Jiang and M. F. Hill (eds.), *Teacher Learning with Classroom Assessment*,
https://doi.org/10.1007/978-981-10-9053-0_2

assessment designs for future learning. Through this emphasis on teachers as agents who are responsible for classroom assessment, a diverse and distributed system of intelligent accountability to students, parents, peers, school leaders, systems, and state and federal governments has evolved.

Intelligent accountability in schooling systems occurs when there is public trust in teachers, and a community takes collective responsibility for students to achieve valued outcomes (Sahlberg 2010). O'Neill (2002) argues convincingly that such accountability is achieved through systems of self-governance within a framework of reporting, where professionals provide an account of their practice to experienced others, rather than by greater control over professionals through increasing accountability, conformity, and audit. Informed professionalism occurs when there is an expectation that teachers will engage as agents in active inquiry into ways to enhance student learning and ethical judgement making. Teachers respond to the emerging needs of their learners through their design of curriculum, pedagogy, and assessment—a description of best practice professional learning (Timperley et al. 2008).

In Australia, principles of informed professionalism and intelligent accountability reflect historically persistent values of equity and pluralism, state and federal balance of responsibility, and state and private schooling choices. Such a system depends on teachers as assessment agents and assessment learners who are "adaptive experts, alert to situations where previous routines are not working well and seeking different kinds of solutions" (Muijs et al. 2014, p. 248). In Australia, this historical tradition of trusting teachers as assessment designers is changing. One purpose of this chapter is to provide an overview of some of the changes that have prompted renewed attention to teacher learning about classroom assessment practices in Australia.

Rapid educational changes in education accountability in recent years in Australia have led to the structural reorganization of Australian curriculum, assessment, and pedagogy. There has been a neoliberal cascade of changes for educators (Connell 2013), which include the introduction of audit instruments (Queensland Government 2016), teaching and learning audits (Masters 2009), and school audits (Marshall 2014). Such changes have led to a greater focus on the collection of data and have, to some extent, led to constraints on teachers in designing classroom assessment. Teacher professional learning increasingly focuses on efficiency and development within agreed, audited frameworks. Yet even with greater prescription, teachers are still able to actively engage in making decisions about classroom assessment. Teachers are simultaneously meeting national, state, system and school agendas, and also working in incredibly diverse geographic locations, and a variety of sociocultural contexts. As criteria for good teaching change rapidly in response to new assessment agendas, teacher agency is also taking multiple forms. The second purpose of this chapter is to understand how teachers engage in their agentic work as classroom assessors.

Two case studies of teachers learning to enhance their classroom assessment are outlined, the first involving junior primary teachers and the second involving teachers of senior high school students. They are then analyzed, drawing on a number of theoretical perspectives of teacher agency (Archer 2003; Bernstein 2000; Emirbayer and Mische 1998). The aim is to focus on "the particular" in each case (Simons 2009), not to homogenize the concept of teacher agency and informed professionalism. From these cases, two principles, which add to the body of teacher learning about classroom assessment, are proposed.

How Do Australian Teachers Practice Classroom Assessment?

It is challenging to characterize an "Australian" approach to classroom assessment, with multiple geopolitical influences evident in Australian classrooms. Each state and territory in Australia has their own curriculum authority that is responsible for setting and monitoring the quality of learning, meaning that there are slightly different traditions for classroom assessment in each state and territory. Within each state and territory, there are different systems of schooling, with the state government providing fee-free state education for all students, and parents being able to choose to pay various fees for schooling through either the Catholic schooling system or other independent schools with both religious and non-religious affiliations. These systems promote different professional practices and provide advice or interpretations of quality for classroom assessment. There are also geopolitical differences in the approaches to teacher classroom assessment learning. While Australia is situated within the Asia Pacific region, the strongest influences over classroom practices have been from the Anglophone traditions with increasing influence of off-the-shelf pedagogic packages such as Marzano's (2007) *Art and Science of Teaching* and Hattie's (2008) *Visible Learning*. While there are signs of shifts in global reference societies toward Asia, with Australian schools looking toward Singapore and Shanghai as high performing systems (Lingard and Sellar 2016), this chapter acknowledges that teachers learning to practice classroom assessment interpret these multiple influences through varied sociocultural contexts.

This section highlights some of the influential changes to assessment and curriculum in Australian education. Common assessment practice across the six states and two territories was previously described by Cumming and Maxwell (2004). The themes identified at that time were:

(1) a strong curriculum base influencing assessment, (2) the incorporation of school-based assessment in all certification, (3) preference for standards-referenced assessment, (4) respect for teacher judgement, (5) increasing vocational education delivery within schooling, (6) multiple pathways to future study and careers, (7) school-based assessment in the compulsory years of schooling, (8) moves towards outcomes-based frameworks, (9) issues relating to national benchmark data, and (10) equity issues. (p. 89)

In 2016, much has changed with the introduction in 2008 of the National Australia Program—Literacy and Numeracy (NAPLAN) which introduced national testing of all students in Years 3, 5, 7, and 9 (Australian Curriculum, Assessment and Reporting Authority [ACARA] 2013). In 2010, test results for individual schools were released publicly through the media, and the MySchool website was established, enabling "like" schools to be compared across the country. The comparisons prompted intense data scrutiny and a backwash toward more scripted curriculum and pedagogic responses in many schools (Klenowski and Carter 2015). Such an increase in the competitive nature of the testing has intensified the demands on teachers and schools. Noticeably, there has been a shift in the enacted curriculum in Australia with a focus on literacy and numeracy, as these are the subjects and skills that are tested. Schools are now involved in more measurement and comparison than ever before with persistent concern about the preparation for standardized testing which has led to excessive test practice with a focus on results (Klenowski and Carter 2015).

In 2012, another major change took place when ACARA (2013) became responsible for the progressive implementation of the first National Curriculum and Achievement Standards. Curriculum content for the Foundation to Year 10 levels, for English, mathematics, science, history, and geography, was endorsed first. By 2014, other curricula for the arts, health and physical education, technologies, civics and citizenship, and economics and business had been developed but had not yet been fully endorsed by all states and territories. Languages, other than English, were the last learning area to be developed. The development of a senior (Years 11 and 12) curriculum followed. Seven general capabilities were included to assist students to "become successful learners, confident and creative individuals, and active and informed citizens" (Ministerial Council on Education, Employment, Training and Youth Affairs [MCEETYA] 2008, p. 7).

In 2014, the Australian Government conducted a review to evaluate the development and implementation of the Australian Curriculum and to ensure that Australia was performing well in the international context (Donnelly and Wiltshire 2014). It was found that "the Australian Curriculum privileges a combination of a utilitarian, a 21st century, a personalised learning, and an equity and social justice view of the curriculum and the purpose of education, it undervalues introducing students to the conversation represented by 'our best validated knowledge and artistic achievements'" and that "the Australian Curriculum … fails to do full justice to the Melbourne Declaration's belief that the curriculum has a vital role to play in the moral, spiritual and aesthetic development and wellbeing of young Australians" (Donnelly and Wiltshire 2014, p. 31). The review of the Australian Curriculum identified that a consensus model of decision-making had led to an overcrowded curriculum. It was therefore recommended that ACARA "reduce the amount of content to a narrow core required to be taught, especially in the primary years. Foundation to Year 2 should focus on literacy and numeracy" (Donnelly and Wiltshire 2014, p. 245). The ongoing debates around the Australian Curriculum require that teachers engage in continual learning about how the latest changes impact on their classroom assessment.

Additionally, new Australian Professional Standards that outline "what teachers should know and be able to do" (Australian Institute for Teaching School Leadership [AITSL] 2014, para. 1) were introduced in 2012 and have increasingly regulated teacher daily practice. Through the standards, teachers are exhorted to focus their professional learning and growth toward practices that impact student learning (AITSL 2015). These professional standards have been critiqued as a form of covert control of teachers (Bourke et al. 2015) and, alternatively, a recognition of the importance of teacher agency within system improvement (Biesta et al. 2015). In the following section, three perspectives about teacher agency drawn from Bernstein (1999), Emirbayer and Mische (1998), and Archer (2003, 2007) are introduced before a nuanced analysis of teacher learning in changing contexts of classroom assessment.

Teachers Exercising Agency in Classroom Assessment

Teachers exercise agency when they engage with the changing structures to make informed professional judgments about the design, practice, and consequences of classroom assessment with their learners. Teacher agency is broadly defined as "their active contribution to shaping their work and its conditions" (Biesta et al. 2015, p. 624). By focusing on teacher agency, teacher learning is acknowledged as more than a process of acquiring or receiving approved assessment knowledge. Agentic teachers may productively engage in implementing and amplifying student learning through new ways of assessing. Equally agentic teachers may actively resist assessment reform, or misunderstand or be overwhelmed by conflicting demands. Teachers as assessment learners negotiate meaning and actively shape the varied social, political, and cultural contexts in which they work.

Paying attention to what teachers prioritize through their classroom assessment, what they leave out, how they communicate purposes to students, and the activities and practices that they plan, enables the ways that teachers design classroom assessment to be understood. As teachers make these choices, they are recontextualizing knowledge, and it involves both vertical discourses of official or schooled knowledge, and horizontal discourses of local knowledge that are "context dependent and specific, tacit, multi-layered" (Bernstein 1999, p. 159). The process of recontextualizing between and across the multiple layers of assessment policy occurs as part of the daily learning and assessment work of teachers.

The significance of the social context is also emphasized within ecological understandings of agency so that agency is understood as a "quality of the engagement of actors with temporal–relational contexts-for-action, not a quality of the actors themselves" (Biesta et al. 2015, p. 626). This pragmatic, ecological perspective of agency is based on the work of Emirbayer and Mische (1998) who define agency as dynamic interplay of "habit, imagination, and judgement" (p. 970) that enables structures to be transformed through the actions of the actors. Teacher learning occurs through purposeful dialogue with teaching peers that is supported when teachers have the space to maneuver (Charteris 2016; Charteris and Smardon 2015). In this perspective, agency is always a social process. This perspective also enables teacher learning about classroom assessment to be considered in light of historical and future actions.

Teacher agency is also a personal response. According to Archer (2003), corporate agents are both shaped by, and shape, their collective contexts depending on how they activate the personal, structural, and cultural emergent properties that are available. The properties are emergent, as what may be experienced as constraining for one person may be experienced as an enabling factor by another. For example, a requirement by a school leader to submit weekly assessment data updates may be regarded as unwanted surveillance and workload, or alternatively a teacher may enjoy having their assessment work recognized by the school leader. This perspective of agency acknowledges the sociocultural context, but also the way that an individual teacher actively makes sense of emerging change through balancing their experiences with a desire to live a professional life worth living. The individual agent decides on his or her next action through a process of individual reflexivity that "actively mediates between our structurally shaped circumstances and what we deliberately make of them" (Archer 2007, p. 16). These three perspectives on teacher agency all share a concern with the interplay of sociocultural contexts as well as positioning teachers as capable actors who can intentionally shape their practices. Two case studies of teacher assessment learning are now introduced before these three perspectives are explored to see how they may offer different insights into teacher learning from classroom assessment.

Purposes and Approaches

The first case was situated in a Queensland primary school, where Year 2 teachers of students aged 7 and 8 were navigating how national achievement standards, integrated into new state curriculum and assessment packages, could be reconciled with their existing classroom assessment practices. The second case was also in Queensland, in a senior high school. The teachers were planning the final summative classroom assessment pieces for their Year 12 students (aged 17 years).

Case Study One

Rebecca and Cathy taught Year 2 children from diverse cultural backgrounds and home language groups in a state primary school in an inner-city suburb of Brisbane. They had recently experienced significant curriculum and assessment change with a rapid introduction of the new national curriculum in maths, English, and science in 2012 using scripted support materials known as *Curriculum into the Classroom* or *C2C* (Queensland Government 2013). Initial implementation strategies across Queensland were prescriptive before principals encouraged staff to adapt and adopt the materials. Some teachers approached the changes positively (Mills and McGregor 2016), while others experienced a sense of de-professionalization and engaged in covert resistance (Barton et al. 2014). The context required teachers to engage as agents who could prioritize new curriculum and assessment texts for their context and reconcile historical and emerging national, state, and local practices.

   The teachers engaged in conversations facilitated by researchers, to discuss their assessment practices and how they related to curriculum, as well as what evidence of learning and achievement might look like in response to the new national and state expectations. Previously, the teachers each had responsibility for planning one part of the curriculum and assessment for the rest of the team. While this was time efficient, there was no time to engage in deep conversations together about the assumptions behind the curriculum and assessment designs. Differences in assessment beliefs were often avoided or glossed over. The researchers probed and explored assessment ideas with both teachers in ways that were supportive and enabled the teachers to treat differences of opinions as moments for inquiry and reflection (Adie and Willis 2014; Willis and Adie 2014).

During a professional planning meeting, the teachers used the new national assessment standards to articulate their expectations about what evidence would distinguish a high-quality and satisfactory quality classroom assessment response. The teachers then recorded their ideas as annotations on the classroom assessment task to preserve the discussed ideas for future learning. Some of the significant moments of teacher learning about assessment included:

- How to work together when some of their assumptions about assessment differed;
- Identifying the relationships between national assessment documents and system expectations;
- Developing a shared language of assessment;
- How to record observations about assessment standards and expectations about what evidence of assessment might look like as annotations on student samples of work;
- Designing curriculum plans to enable students' opportunities to demonstrate the quality of the expected assessment standard;
- Realizing the benefits of clarifying assessment standards and expectations prior to planning teaching;
- Realizing that students were more capable than either teacher had imagined.

Reaching agreement about specific evidence in student work that might distinguish it as a high-quality response was challenging work, as teachers were imagining how their students might respond, navigating between state and national texts, as well as articulating some of their own latent expectations of quality criteria (Wyatt-Smith and Klenowski 2013). It involved sharing provisional understandings with colleagues and being open to having their ideas or assumptions challenged or changed. For example, when a teacher tried to explain why one student response was an example of high quality, but not the highest quality she would expect, she realized that she expected an answer to a literal comprehension question to begin with some of the words from the question. Further, she realized that she had never explicitly taught this to her students before and felt distressed at the realization. Questioning assumptions was emotional work that required teachers to take risks with one another. It also took a few hours of sustained conversation about student work before teachers began to see new shared understandings develop (Willis and Adie 2014). After teachers began to develop a shared understanding of what qualities they were expecting for different assessment standards, they moved quickly to plan for ways to share this specific knowledge about their expectations for assessment evidence with students.

The teachers later reflected that their students' assessment performances improved dramatically in a range of curriculum areas that they had discussed. Cathy had shared her new assessment understandings with her students by collaboratively annotating some examples of the assessment task with her students: "They knew exactly what I was looking for. Everything that I had showed them was what I marked them on. There was nothing else." Rebecca commented that the quality of the written work from her students, after she had taught them more explicitly the skills she was expecting, was significantly beyond the quality she had expected: "I was blown away by the results…who would have believed this was the work of 7- and 8-year-olds?" While Rebecca had initially felt guilty for not providing students with an annotated high-quality example, as this had been a suggestion from the researchers in order to share expectations of quality with students, in the end she was pleased. She reflected, "Maybe if I had shown an A exemplar, maybe my standard would have been less because I didn't think they would be able to achieve this high standard." The iterative cycle of teacher learning continued as Rebecca reflected on the student work and adjusted her expectations for future learners, and a new round of teacher conversations began. While the conversations prior to teaching had been time consuming, the teachers identified that the process of reaching deep and shared understandings about the expected quality of student work, and expectations about evidence prior to teaching, "saved time" in planning, prioritizing their teaching time, and in assessing and moderating.

Case Study Two

The senior English teachers at this regional, secondary school had been involved in a 3-year university–school partnership project that explored how achievement data could be used for formative assessment purposes to achieve equity in a context of increased, high-stakes accountability (see Klenowski and Ehrich 2016). They identified that many students had become over-reliant on teacher feedback when writing summative assignments. They wanted students to participate in more social formative assessment to negotiate meaning through dialogue and discourse with others (Murphy 2009). They decided to engage the students in the practice of formative assessment using peer review.

The teachers collaborated with the information technology coach to engage the students in the formative assessment of their peers' work using Turnitin, an Internet-based plagiarism review tool. This process of peer review allowed students to receive timely critical feedback and to learn how to self-assess to improve the quality of their own written work. First, the teachers worked together and critically reviewed the previous assessment task design. They redesigned the task so that it was more authentic and rigorous in terms of the quality of critical argument, and consulted with a student to improve the clarity of the questions and instructions. The task was "chunked" into several smaller stages, so that students could produce two paragraphs, and then give anonymous peer reviews to others. This left time for each writer to receive their reviews and make timely adjustments before the next round of peer review. Skills in giving feedback and making suggestions for improvement were explicitly taught and reinforced.

Turnitin allowed students to upload their written paragraphs and have them assigned to a number of other students for anonymous reviews. Each student received several peer ratings of 1–5 against specified criteria, as well as general comments about how to improve the quality of the writing. Students were able to complete 2–3 peer reviews during one class lesson. During the process of peer review, teachers and peers were able to engage in clarifying conversations with one another about the meaning of specific criteria, and about strategies for suggesting improvements. Students were also able to make five-minute appointments with their teacher for further advice, on the understanding that the students had prepared specific questions and could demonstrate how they had responded to previous peer feedback. Teacher feedback was differentiated, depending on student learning needs, with some students preferring recordings of oral feedback, while other students preferred to make notes from face-to-face consultations. The process of peer-reviewing paragraphs continued for each of the sections of the complex task.

The teachers learned about classroom assessment by adopting an inquiry stance and problematizing their current classroom assessment practice. New insights often came from their discussions with students about their learning. These teacher impressions were confirmed when researchers interviewed eight of the secondary students from this cohort, finding:

- Students found it easier to self-assess and improve their own work;
- In providing feedback to others, they questioned whether they had actually followed their own advice;
- By reading multiple examples on the same topic and seeing the range of writing styles and interpreting the criteria, students developed an understanding of what constitutes quality writing;
- Peer feedback was thought to be easier to understand than teacher feedback, however, having the teacher in the room when peer feedback was being generated was valued, as teachers could provide clarification immediately. This aligned with previous findings (Stobart 2008);
- Students judged the quality of peer feedback, deciding which comments or ratings had greater validity;
- Students were able to ask more informed questions and became more involved as the connections between classroom instruction and formative assessment became clearer, and they could see teachers responding to their learning.

Importantly, every lesson involved discussion, which meant greater opportunity for students and the teacher to talk about their learning. Engaging students in the formative assessment process via peer review allowed the teachers to establish a discourse about learning in which the learners and their teachers engaged routinely in negotiating future learning (Murphy 2009).

Enacting such a shift in pedagogy and assessment was not without its technological and cultural challenges, as exemplified by the fact that the technology did not always work smoothly. In terms of cultural change, students needed time and support to adjust to the new role of peer reviewer. Significantly, the students wanted the peer-feedback process embedded into the learning "so it is not seen as something additional to learning." By engaging students in the process of peer review, they had increased student agency and responsibility within a supported learning process. As a small team, these teachers were able to work and learn together, about how to redesign assessment tasks so that students were more active and involved. Teachers were becoming aware that they were enacting several principles that they now identified as high-quality assessment practices.

Why Do They Practice Such Classroom Assessment Strategies?

Teachers design and adapt classroom assessment strategies constantly, in response to student learning, their own learning, new curriculum, new leaders, changes in policy or resourcing, and other levers for change. The three theoretical perspectives of teacher agency (Archer 2003; Bernstein 1999; Emirbayer and Mische 1998) can be seen as complementary. They each provide a slightly different analytic framing of how teachers are both constrained and enabled in their learning to enact formative assessment responses within the structural, social, and cultural conditions of summative classroom assessment.

Recontextualizing Diverse Assessment Policies

The teachers were learning new classroom assessment practices as they responded to top-down system assessment policies. They were knowledge actors who were actively recontextualizing official policy into pedagogic discourses, as each knowledge agent "selectively appropriates, relocates, refocuses, and relates other discourses to constitute its own order and orderings" (Bernstein 2003, p. 175). However, the spaces within which the teachers could take action had already been shaped by the way that these policies had come to their attention. In both cases, the policies had been recontextualized multiple times before the teachers enacted these policies. The intended assessment practices were filtered through syllabus committees, school leaders, curriculum and textbook writers, and website designers, each prioritizing and interpreting assessment advice before it reached the teachers. With each layer of recontextualizing, there are "backward and forward relational movements from the condensed code of policy speak to the imagined particularistic codes of everyday school and classroom talk" (Singh et al. 2013, p. 469). These imagined codes shape the work of teachers in ways that are mostly unseen as the process is diffuse and difficult to trace. The process of recontextualizing, while distributed, is not neutral, as it is a "site of struggle and appropriation" of the symbolic control of power, knowledge, and consciousness (Bernstein 2004, p. 181). This theoretical perspective enables a close look at how teachers interpret and reconcile multiple policies for themselves and then how the meaning of the knowledge is represented to others, such as students.

In case one, the teachers were simultaneously trying to balance national assessment standards, assessment tasks, school-based expectations as well as the more abstract, and specialized discourse of the subject (Willis and Adie 2014). The teachers identified that some of the assessment policy texts, such as school-based reporting documents, national online examples of student work, and their locally produced school plans, seemed to provide conflicting assessment guidance. In response, they decided which texts they deemed would have greater authority over their work, and which could be treated as less important. The facilitated dialogue with peers and assessment researchers enabled the teachers to "step outside" of their current conceptual framework in readiness to think and act differently (Muijs et al. 2014). After the project with the researchers had finished, the teachers did not continue to critically reflect on their assessment pedagogic approaches together to extend their learning to meet their goals to help students to take on greater roles as knowledge agents. Instead, they consolidated their own learning by sharing it with other teachers. Professional learning is an iterative process involving learning new knowledge, trying things out in practice, refining, and trying again. Sustaining this process of ongoing inquiry without the assistance of others is "rare" (p. 248). The teachers first had to learn how to make sense of the policy change before they could extend their knowledge into new pedagogic processes with students. Case two exemplifies how teachers sustained their learning to include students.

In case two, the students were positioned alongside their teachers as knowledge agents who were translating the official assessment criteria into feedback for their student peers. As students were able to read a range of work from their peers, they could make connections between the assessment purposes, classroom instruction, and the expected assessment standards. They had to integrate their understanding of the processes for completing the assessment task, and their understanding of the discourses within the subject discipline in their analysis of their peers' responses, and then recontextualize that understanding into effective, actionable, and supportive feedback. Through this process, the students began to ask more informed questions, and share responsibility for advancing the understanding of the whole class. While this process enabled students to be positioned with greater symbolic control of power and knowledge, the change in power brought other learning issues to the surface. Some students were fearful of peer reviews, thinking others would make fun of their work. There were also mixed messages for senior students within the school culture. A consistent message from the school was to focus on competing with one another to achieve the best senior overall assessment result, yet this particular class was promoting peer feedback and helping others. Students identified that this mixed message was "weird". They expressed preferences for more structured peer feedback in earlier year levels and more subject areas. Teacher agency in classroom assessment was leading to student agency that had potential for changes in assessment practices to ripple upward from students, as well as down from centralized policy changes.

Activating Personal, Social, and Material Properties Through Personal Reflexivity

Archer's theoretical perspectives (2000, 2003, 2007) emphasize the way in which individuals reflexively activate the personal, social, and material properties available to them in different ways. Reflexivity is an inner conversation with the self that is a process of considering what matters and what to do next. Agents shape a *modus vivendi* or (professional) life worth living through a constant process of navigating, prioritizing, or subordinating their competing concerns. The individual person acts reflexively to effect changes to the social and material conditions of their context, or to reproduce them (Priestley 2011). Rather than a dialectic relationship of structure *or* agency, Archer's work acknowledges how agency is mediated through the structural and cultural properties available to individuals and groups.

In case one, Rebecca and Cathy engaged in reflexive conversation as they navigated the multiple policy discourses, yet they each activated the knowledge in different ways in their classroom by drawing on familiar social and material resources. Rebecca responded by designing practice tests for her students so that they could learn the skills she had identified as being valued. In her agentic response, she was reproducing the material assessment conditions of testing while trying to open up the social resources of understanding achievement standards for her students to access. Cathy sought to involve students in understanding the summative achievement standards by involving them as a whole class in annotating some example answers. Students were accessing assessment discourses in new ways. However, Cathy recognized that in replicating an adult practice with her young students, she had subordinated her concern to make learning and assessment engaging for students. Her agency was constrained as she did not have ready access to personal, social, or material properties, to help her envisage an alternative pedagogic approach, as the research partnership had concluded, and, as an innovator, she was working ahead of her school assessment culture. Teacher agency that enables longer term social and material change therefore ideally involves ongoing dialogic reflexivity. Reflexivity with others can support teachers to balance competing concerns and identify additional social and material resources.

In case two, the material and social conditions combined to prompt teacher agentic action. Constraints within the syllabus required that there would be minimal teacher guidance, prompting the exploration of peer feedback. The material properties of the computer program enabled the multiple rounds of anonymous peer review to be facilitated easily by the teacher. Yet not all students found the ICT structures enabling, as they had limited access at home, or did not have access to a computer at school and had to wait until they were at home to upload their work or do the peer review, putting strain on their mobile data plans. Students also commented that dividing the task into smaller sections for ongoing feedback meant that it was challenging to fit their assessment essay drafting in around part-time work commitments. Such new social or material assessment practices can impose new or alternative constraints.

Teachers need to commit to ongoing reflexive examination of how students navigate, prioritize, or struggle with the material and social assessment resources available to them if they change assessment systems.

Integrating the Past and Imagining a Future

The teachers in these cases were also actively integrating their past assessment experiences with an imagined future for their students, through practical judgments in the present. This temporal relationship was proposed by Emirbayer and Mische (1998) and elaborated by Biesta et al. (2015). Agency is not seen as an individual capacity that a teacher or student might have, but is an emergent phenomenon within the ecology of the contexts that provides the opportunity or space for agents to maneuver (Priestley 2011). Teacher agency is therefore informed by the ecology of the present and the professional histories of the teacher, and short-term and long-term goals in the future (Biesta et al. 2015).

This was evident in case one when Cathy realized her historical experience as a student had constrained her teaching practice: "when I was coming through school that they never showed us marks until we were older and we understood what the marks meant." Working with the researchers to learn a new assessment practice provided a space for alternative action. However, she recognized that she was having difficulty imagining how she might alter her practice further to meet her goal of sharing an understanding of assessment standards with students. Agentic action in changing her classroom assessment had disrupted her ecology of practice in ways that opened up further significant areas for ongoing learning and dialogue with peers.

Imagining the future of the Year 12 students at university and drawing on their own recent past experiences of being post-graduate students at university were powerful prompts for assessment change for the teachers in case two. They spoke together about the uncertainty of being writers and receiving feedback, and the simultaneous trepidation and reassurance of seeking peer feedback. When they shared these feelings with one another, they also imagined how students would need to be prepared to seek out peer support. They were able to share these stories with students.

The teachers were also able to integrate their past experience in collective, self-reflective inquiry supported by researchers in the larger project. Supportive leadership, support from external experts, and self-regulated learning are acknowledged criteria for successful teacher professional learning (Timperley et al. 2008). Continuing their cycles of inquiry into assessment enabled the teachers to support equity and the improvement of student learning for all students.

What Do Teachers Learn from Practicing Classroom Assessment in These Ways?

The multiple lenses for understanding teacher agency in assessment learning reflect the multiple ways by which Australian teachers learn how to enact classroom assessment. Teachers reconcile what are often competing policies and practices in ways that are both pragmatic and idealistic. The teacher learning in these two case studies occurred through processes of critical inquiry with peers and students. These Australian teachers found the spaces in the high-stakes accountability context to engage in critical inquiry—underpinned by a democratic ethic. They worked within communities to generate local knowledge through making problematic their current classroom assessment practice. By making previously taken-for-granted judgment and feedback practices more visible, they could engage in reform in terms of validity, consistency, equity, and ethics.

Two principles that were evident in both case studies confirm and add to the established understandings of how teachers learn about classroom assessment. First, critical inquiry with peers is challenging intellectual work that requires cultural and structural support. Second, teacher learning was extended when students were part of the critical inquiry process.

Classroom Assessment Is a Site for Critical Inquiry with Peers

The teachers were committed to enhancing their learning about classroom assessment as part of their continuing responsibility for assessment in their day-to-day roles. Within the schooling system, these teachers were positioned as agents who were engaging in important intellectual work at the intersection of official assessment discourses and local practice, that is a "meeting point of order and disorder, of coherence and incoherence; it is the crucial site of the 'yet to be thought'" (Bernstein 2003, p. 182). A critical inquiry process requires teachers to be reflexive, search for insights and adapt their own practices. Ideals about innovative assessment approaches were adapted to fit within inflexible, whole school reporting systems. Facilitating student peer feedback challenged teachers to be more responsive and less directive in their teaching plans. A critical inquiry process also involves preparedness to work through periods of incoherence and disorder as the teachers have to search for language to articulate knowledge that has previously been tacit, and negotiate the implications within school assessment cultures and changing system requirements (Willis and Adie 2013). When students raised concerns about the messages they were receiving around collaboration and competition, they were highlighting competing tacit cultural norms in the school culture. The teachers did not have the language, the forum, or the micropolitical power to resolve this tension throughout the school. Instead, they engaged in pragmatic reasoning with students within their own subject area.

Peers provided support, stimulated critical questioning, and accountability as the teachers justified their pragmatic adaptations with one another. Peer inquiry also involved epistemic tensions as teachers re-examined their beliefs about how knowledge is created and the role of assessment in learning (Adie and Willis 2014). These cases contribute to a growing international awareness of the conditions needed to support teachers in classroom assessment learning.

To engage in this type of unsettling critical inquiry, teachers need to have "the intellectual space to think" (Charteris and Smardon 2015, p. 121). Structural resources through professional readings, and time to discuss, create, and share (Wilson 2008), are needed alongside cultural resources such as conditions that enable substantive discussions and allow teachers to voice their doubts (Haigh and Dixon 2007). Teacher learning that is situated within a subject department or teaching team can lead to collective teaching repertoire development (Wong et al. 2010). More positive outcomes for teachers and students occur when the professional learning is not imposed on teachers, and the leaders respond flexibly to enable sustained critical reflection (Hargreaves 2015). Dialogue and trust between the system level, school leaders, teachers, and students is a further cultural resource that enables the learning to be adapted to the local context and a shared language to develop (Hopfenbeck et al. 2015; Sach 2015). In both of these cases, the critical inquiry into classroom assessment was extended when the teachers sought to involve students in the critical inquiry process.

Critical Inquiry with Students Leads to Renewed Assessment Learning for Teachers

Dialogue with students enabled the case study teachers to interrogate the relationship of classroom assessment to the ongoing learning experienced by the students. The student responses affirmed the teachers and also provided additional avenues for ongoing learning. This finding was similar to those by Haigh and Dixon (2007), who concluded that classroom assessment inquiry that was grounded in the teachers' own classrooms, in their own discipline and involved their own students, led to teachers "gaining insight into students' conceptions [which] appeared to stimulate teachers' professional curiosity" (p. 373). In case two, the teachers included students in evaluative activities, seeking student review of classroom assessment tasks before they were distributed, and seeking feedback on their teaching through individual consultation sessions with students. As Hawe and Parr (2014) noted, involving students in critical inquiry about the classroom assessment "requires fundamental changes to entrenched understandings, attitudes and behaviours regarding teacher and student roles and relationships" (p. 230). Students in case two questioned the mixed messages they were receiving within the school culture, had concerns about equity issues to do with accessing digital resources, and made suggestions for curriculum changes throughout their schooling trajectory, to extend the innovation. Extending the critical inquiry to acknowledge these issues as areas for action also has the potential to extend the agency of students as knowledgeable partners in assessment and learning.

How Does What Teachers Learn from Their Classroom Assessments Impact Their Teaching and Students' Learning?

In schooling systems that rely on informed professionalism and intelligent account-ability, teacher agency is essential. However, to maintain public trust and enable high-quality practices to circulate throughout a system, teachers as professionals also need to give an account of their work to others with more experience (O'Neill 2002). In both of the cases in this study, the teachers engaged in critical inquiry into student learning through classroom assessment and gave an account of their practice to one another and also to researchers who acted as critical friends. With their peers, the teachers carefully monitored the impact of their classroom assessment practices.

In both cases, the teacher learning had positive impacts on student learning. The teachers validated their classroom assessment innovations by noting the improved quality of student work, and promoting the consistency of their judgments through confirmation by peers in social moderation. As the teachers had been able to critically inquire into the assumptions underpinning their practices, there was consistency in the design of assessment activities and tasks, and the principles underpinning their enacted assessment practices. The consequential validity, that is whether their assessment practices enabled all students to access learning successfully, was a focus of ongoing inquiry. In case one, the teachers continued to think about how they might involve students in more engaging ways in their assessment. In case two, the teachers continued to inquire into ways that they could enhance the social and material access students had identified as barriers to their full participation. This focus on the equity within classroom assessment is an ongoing focus of teacher learning, particularly when students are invited to genuinely share their perspectives about how classroom assessment might further enhance their learning.

Teachers learn about classroom assessment as they actively contribute to shaping their work and its conditions. The multiple perspectives of teacher agency that have been explored in this chapter confirm that teacher assessment learning is always contextualized. The two case studies identified contexts of complex system change; personal, cultural, and material resources that were available; and how teachers made decisions within the practicalities of the present, as well as historical experiences and imagined educational futures. Collaborative critical inquiry with peers and aca-demics led to positive classroom assessment innovations that have the potential to inform system innovation. Mills and McGregor (2016) note that top-down pressures focusing on a quick fix, and measurement in an audit society, can erode the teacher professionalism that is required to enact equitable and valid classroom assessment in local contexts. In Australia's pluralistic educational system, with the cascade of top-down change, teachers need cultural and structural support to find less turbulent spaces to support critical inquiry into their own and students' learning. Without these calmer waters, there is a danger that the bedrock of principles of informed professionalism and intelligent accountability may get swept away.

References

Adie, L., & Willis, J. (2014). Using annotations to inform an understanding of achievement standards. *Assessment Matters, 6,* 112–136.

Archer, M. (2000). *Being human: The problem of agency.* Cambridge: Cambridge University Press.

Archer, M. (2003). *Structure, agency and the internal conversation.* Cambridge: Cambridge University Press.

Archer, M. (2007). *Making our way through the world. Human reflexivity and social mobility.* Cambridge: Cambridge University Press.

Australian Curriculum, Assessment and Reporting Authority. (2013). *Australian Curriculum.* http://www.australiancurriculum.edu.au/. Accessed July 22, 2016.

Australian Institute for Teaching and School Leadership. (2014). *Australian professional standards for teachers.* http://www.aitsl.edu.au/australian-professional-standards-for-teachers/standards/overview/organisation-of-the-standards. Accessed March 18, 2016.

Australian Institute for Teaching and School Leadership. (2015). *Statement of intent.* http://www.aitsl.edu.au/docs/default-source/board-of-directors-resources/statement-of-intent-july-2015-final.pdf?sfvrsn=2. Accessed April 12, 2016.

Barton, G. M., Garvis, S., & Ryan, M. E. (2014). Curriculum to the classroom: Investigating the spatial practices of curriculum implementation in Queensland schools and its implications for teacher education. *Australian Journal of Teacher Education, 39*(3). http://dx.doi.org/10.14221/ajte.2014v39n3.9.

Bernstein, B. (1999). Vertical and horizontal discourse: An essay. *British Journal of Sociology of Education, 20*(2), 157–173.

Bernstein, B. (2000). *Pedagogy, symbolic control, and identity: Theory, research, critique.* Lanham, MD: Rowman and Littlefield.

Bernstein, B. (2003). *Class, codes and control: Applied studies towards a sociology of language Vol. 2.* Abingdon: Routledge.

Bernstein, B. (2004). *The structuring of pedagogic discourse.* London: Routledge.

Biesta, G., Priestley, M., & Robinson, S. (2015). The role of beliefs in teacher agency. *Teachers and Teaching, 21*(6), 624–640. https://doi.org/10.1080/13540602.2015.1044325.

Bourke, T., Lidstone, J., & Ryan, M. (2015). Schooling teachers: Professionalism or disciplinary power? *Educational Philosophy and Theory, 47*(1), 84–100.

Charteris, J. (2016). Envisaging agency as discourse hybridity: A Butlerian analysis of secondary classroom discourses. *Discourse: Studies in the Cultural Politics of Education, 37*(2), 189–203. https://doi.org/10.1080/01596306.2014.943156.

Charteris, J., & Smardon, D. (2015). Teacher agency and dialogic feedback: Using classroom data for practitioner inquiry. *Teaching and Teacher Education, 50,* 114–123. https://doi.org/10.1016/j.tate.2015.05.006.

Connell, R. (2013). The neoliberal cascade and education: An essay on the market agenda and its consequences. *Critical Studies in Education, 54*(2), 99–112. https://doi.org/10.1080/17508487.2013.776990.

Cumming, J., & Maxwell, G. (2004). Assessment in Australian schools: Current practice and trends. *Assessment in Education: Principles, Policy and Practice, 11*(1), 89–108. https://doi.org/10.1080/0969594042000209010.

Donnelly, K., & Wiltshire, K. (2014). *Review of the Australian Curriculum: Final report*. Canberra: Australian Government.

Emirbayer, M., & Mische, A. (1998). What is agency? *The American Journal of Sociology, 103*(4), 962–1023.

Haigh, M., & Dixon, H. (2007). 'Why am I doing these things?': Engaging in classroom-based inquiry around formative assessment. *Journal of In-Service Education, 33*(3), 359–376. https://doi.org/10.1080/13674580701487000.

Hargreaves, E. (2015). Assessment for learning and teacher learning communities: UK teachers' experiences. *Teaching Education, 24*(3), 327–344. https://doi.org/10.1080/10476210.2012.713931.

Hattie, J. (2008). *Visible learning: A Synthesis of over 800 meta-analyses relating to achievement*. New York: Routledge.

Hawe, E., & Parr, J. (2014). Assessment for learning in the writing classroom: An incomplete realisation. *The Curriculum Journal, 25*(2), 210–237. https://doi.org/10.1080/09585176.2013.862172.

Hopfenbeck, T. N., Florez Petour, M. T., & Tolo, A. (2015). Balancing tensions in educational policy reforms: Large-scale implementation of assessment for learning in Norway. *Assessment in Education: Principles, Policy & Practice, 22*(1), 44–60. https://doi.org/10.1080/0969594X.2014.996524.

Klenowski, V., & Carter, L. (2015). Curriculum reform in testing and accountability contexts. In D. Wyse, L. Hayward, & J. Pandya (Eds.), *Sage handbook of curriculum, pedagogy and assessment* (pp. 790–804). Los Angeles: Sage.

Klenowski, V., & Ehrich, L. (2016). Transitioning towards ethical leadership: A collaborative investigation of achieving equity in times of high stakes accountability. *International Studies in Educational Administration, 44*(1), 41–54.

Lingard, B., & Sellar, S. (2016). The changing organizational and global significance of the OECD's education work. In K. Mundy, A. Green, B. Lingard, & A. Verger (Eds.), *Handbook of global education policy* (pp. 357–373). Chichester: Wiley. https://doi.org/10.1002/9781118468005.ch19.

Marshall, R. (2014). *School audits lead to improvement*. https://rd.acer.edu.au/article/school-audits-lead-to-improvement. Accessed July, 2016.

Marzano, R. J. (2007). *The art and science of teaching*. Alexandria, VA: ASCD.

Masters, G. (2009). *A shared challenge: Improving literacy, numeracy and science learning in Queensland primary schools*. http://education.qld.gov.au/mastersreview/pdfs/final-report-masters.pdf. Accessed February, 2016.

Mills, M., & McGregor, G. (2016). Learning not borrowing from the Queensland education system: Lessons on curricular, pedagogical and assessment reform. *The Curriculum Journal, 27*(1), 113–133. https://doi.org/10.1080/09585176.2016.1147969.

Ministerial Council on Education, Employment, Training and Youth Affairs. (2008). *Melbourne declaration on educational goals for young Australians*. Melbourne: The Curriculum Council.

Muijs, D., Kyriakides, L., van der Werf, G., Creemers, B., Timperley, H., & Earl, L. (2014). State of the art-teacher effectiveness and professional learning. *School Effectiveness and School Improvement, 25*(2), 231–256. https://doi.org/10.1080/09243453.2014.885451.

Murphy, P. (2009). *Applying a sociocultural approach to assessment theory and practice: Issues for summative and formative assessment*. Brisbane, Australia: Lecture presented at Queensland University of Technology.

O'Neill, O. (2002). *A question of trust: The BBC Reith Lectures 2002*. Cambridge: Cambridge University Press.

Priestley, M. (2011). Schools, teachers, and curriculum change: A balancing act? *Journal of Educational Change, 12*(1), 1–23. https://doi.org/10.1007/s10833-010-9140-z.

Queensland Curriculum and Assessment Authority. (2016). *Core P–10 Australian Curriculum: A report to the Minister for Education from the Board of the QCAA, June 2016*. https://www.qcaa.qld.edu.au/downloads/publications/p-10_aust-curriculum-report-minister-education.pdf.

Queensland Government. (2013). *Introducing C2C for parents*. http://mediasite.eq.edu.au/mediasite/Play/c411f7c65eeb430495a666c46a81b1a41d. Accessed February, 2013.

Queensland Government. (2016). *Teaching and learning audits*. http://deta.qld.gov.au/about/induction/eq/leadership-team/principals.html. Accessed August 7, 2016.

Sach, E. (2015). An exploration of teachers' narratives: What are the facilitators and constraints which promote or inhibit 'good' formative assessment practices in schools? *Education 3–13, 43*(3), 322–335. https://doi.org/10.1080/03004279.2013.813956.

Sahlberg, P. (2010). Rethinking accountability in a knowledge society. *Journal of Educational Change, 11*(1), 45–61. https://doi.org/10.1007/s10833-008-9098-2.

Simons, H. (2009). *Case study research in practice*. London: Sage.

Singh, P., Thomas, S., & Harris, J. (2013). Recontextualising policy discourses: A Bernsteinian perspective on policy interpretation, translation, enactment. *Journal of Education Policy, 28*(4), 465–480. https://doi.org/10.1080/02680939.2013.770554.

Stobart, G. (2008). *Testing times: The uses and abuses of assessment*. London: Routledge.

Timperley, H., Wilson, A., Barrar, H., & Fung, I. (2008). Teacher professional learning and development: Best evidence synthesis iteration. Wellington, New Zealand: Ministry of Education. http://educationcounts.edcentre.govt.nz/goto/BES.

Willis, J., & Adie, L. (2013). Negotiating the meaning of achievement standards in the Australian Curriculum. *Curriculum Perspectives, 33*(1), 52–62.

Willis, J., & Adie, L. (2014). Teachers using annotations to engage students in assessment conversations: Recontextualising knowledge. *The Curriculum Journal, 25*(4), 495–515.

Wilson, N. (2008). Teachers expanding pedagogical content knowledge: Learning about formative assessment together. *Journal of In-Service Education, 34*(3), 283–298. https://doi.org/10.1080/13674580802003540.

Wong, P., Leung, P., Chow, A., & Tang, S. (2010). A case study of teacher learning in an assessment for learning project in Hong Kong. *Professional Development in Education, 36*(4), 621–636. https://doi.org/10.1080/19415250903554087.

Wyatt-Smith, C., & Klenowski, V. (2013). Explicit, latent and meta-criteria: Types of criteria at play in professional judgement practice. *Assessment in Education: Principles, Policy and Practice, 20*(1), 35–52. https://doi.org/10.1080/0969594X.2012.725030.

Chapter 3
Nauruan Perspectives of Assessment Learning Through Assessment Use

Dianne Smardon and Penelope Serow

Abstract The focus of this chapter is on Nauruan teachers' views of how classroom assessment is understood in the context of their Pacific pedagogy. The discussion focuses upon how they use classroom assessment strategies, how they respond and learn from this, and how they believe students benefit from their practices. The Republic of Nauru offers a centralized education system where teacher-made tests are administered mid and end of year across year groups in the primary sector. This small case study incorporates teachers' commentaries about how this assessment information is used to both inform their learning about their students and as part of their day-to-day planning and teaching.

Keywords Classroom assessment · Nauru · Pacific pedagogy
Teacher agency

Introduction

Recognizing how classroom assessment actions influence children's learning, and how this impact can cause teachers to modify their teaching actions as they also learn, is central to changes in teacher practice. Some education stakeholders view classroom assessment as simply measuring student achievements. In contrast, others understand classroom assessment to be a means of enabling teachers to view students' understanding, provide feedback, assist in making informed decisions concerning the next steps to take in the teaching/learning sequence, or as a component

D. Smardon (✉) · P. Serow
Nauru Teacher Education Project, Yaren, Nauru
e-mail: diannesmardon@gmail.com

D. Smardon · P. Serow
University of New England Armidale, Armidale, NSW, Australia

© Springer Nature Singapore Pte Ltd. 2018
H. Jiang and M. F. Hill (eds.), *Teacher Learning with Classroom Assessment*,
https://doi.org/10.1007/978-981-10-9053-0_3

within the sequence of classroom activities. In this chapter, we show how some teachers in Nauru have been learning to move from the first perspective toward the latter one. In other words, rather than seeing classroom assessment as a summative process conducted through tests and exams following a teaching sequence or period of time, some teachers in Nauru have had the opportunity to extend their understanding and use of assessment into more formative approaches. These include eliciting students' prior knowledge about curriculum topics, engaging students in ways that encourage questioning and peer evaluation, and using assessment information collected prior to teaching a topic to differentiate teaching for differing needs. We consider these pedagogical activities to constitute classroom assessment and explore through Nauruan teacher perspectives, how they are using such practices in their teaching, and learning about them, assisted by professional development and undertaking new teaching qualifications.

At the turn of this century, the *Education for All* (UNESCO 2000) review rated the need for teacher education and appropriate teaching qualifications as a first priority for Nauru. Prompted by this, the Republic of Nauru Department of Education performed a review of their system and national educational needs. As a result, the Nauru Department of Education called for tenders for a university partnership to assist in upgrading teacher qualifications, resulting in the Nauru Teacher Education Project (NTEP) in 2013. In establishing NTEP, "The Government of the Republic of Nauru provided funding for the establishment of a local initial teacher education program, with support from the Australian Department of Foreign Affairs and Trade and New Zealand Aid" (Sullivan et al. 2017, p. 40) through the University of New England (UNE) in Australia.

Available only to Nauruan citizens, NTEP is a collaboratively designed and governed project that provides an Associate Degree in Teaching (Pacific Focus) aligned with the Nauru Department of Education syllabi. Both in-service and pre-service Nauruan teachers can complete this associate degree and it also provides a pathway to a Bachelor of Education (Pacific Focus) through UNE. Thus, in this chapter, the case study teachers were also students who have recently completed the associate degree. The blended delivery approach to study occurred through online units and intensive ongoing face-to-face support from two in-country and two online full-time UNE support lecturers. There were also supplementary visits from some of the UNE unit coordinators. The units of study included learning, teaching and assessment theory, specific subject content and pedagogy, e-learning, and bilingual education.

This chapter first describes the Nauru context, the Nauruan educational setting, and the NTEP project before moving to explore perspectives of assessment in schooling. The case study research context and approach is then described, followed by the major findings: teacher's views of classroom assessment, the actions that the teachers have taken as a result of their professional learning, and the teacher's perceptions about the consequences of their actions. The chapter concludes with a discussion of key considerations.

The Nauru Context

The Republic of Nauru is a Micronesian island nation with a local population of 10,084 (Secretariat of the Pacific Community 2011), including 3340 enrolled, Nauruan school-aged children. Compulsory schooling begins at age 5. Six hundred and twenty-two students aged between 5 and 7 are enrolled at either one of the four government infant schools for their pre-school or prep classes, or the nongovernment Catholic school (catering for students from pre-school through to year 8). Four schools provide for the following year levels:

1. Years 1–3—973 enrolled students,
2. Years 4–6—766 enrolled students,
3. Years 7–9—578 enrolled students,
4. Years 10–12—361 enrolled students (Nauru Department of Education 2016, p. 1).

There is also a school for 40 children with special needs. The focus of the case study reported in this chapter is on the practices of primary teachers in Year 1–6 classrooms.

As a nation, Nauru has a unique history of occupation by German, Japanese, British, Australian, and New Zealand nationals, all wishing to capitalize on the strategic positioning of the country and, in particular, the mining, processing, and exporting of phosphate, a substance which has greatly influenced the country's economic foundations. The highs and lows of the economic impact can be read elsewhere (Anghie 1993; Davidson 1968). What remains today is a comparatively small-scale mining operation that exists within a ravaged island interior, and the ongoing legacy of colonization. Nauru is also an overseas processing center for people seeking asylum in Australia, so, more recently, there has been a small change in the school population as refugee and asylum-seeker children entered the schooling system.

The impact of colonization is evident in the continuance of ongoing educational aid projects, generally from Australia and New Zealand and, since the 1980s, the presence of expatriate teachers in the classrooms. As Serow et al. (2016) identified, "education, and especially teacher education, is understood as a key cultural strategy in sustaining Pacific Island culture" (p. 18). Therefore, it follows that the nature of teacher education can act to strengthen cultural identity and, in doing so, ameliorate the ongoing effects of colonization. Thompson (2013) argued that "educational interventions of any kind would stand the greatest chance of success if they had undergone a systematic form of 'cultural translation' from source to target settings" (p. 53).

While culture can be defined in many ways, we draw upon the words of Pacific researchers who describe culture as "a shared way of life of a group embracing knowledge, understanding, skills, values, histories, myths, art and dance – expressed through language" (Pacific Islands Forum Secretariat 2009, p. 16). The centrality of language to the preservation and maintenance of culture is undeniable. The challenges this presents in Nauru are articulated in the Pacific Education Development Framework (Pacific Islands Forum Secretariat 2009) which acknowledges that there is a need to "develop language policies that both enable all students to progress through the education system and provide a framework and mechanism for the maintenance and expansion of Pacific languages" (Pacific Islands Forum Secretariat 2009, p. 16).

Nauruans speak in a vernacular and there is not an accepted format for written language (Barker 2012). The search for consistency is ongoing in Nauru, resulting in a lack of an accepted Nauruan language dictionary. Until this occurs, children in Nauruan primary schools learn to write and read in English, while speaking Nauruan. As a result of a local teacher shortage, many classes have expatriate teachers, so the reality is that schooling has occurred in English medium for many children. The *Nauru Language Syllabus, Prep-Year 10* (Nauru Department of Education 2012) documents that in infant school, the language of instruction will be 90% Nauruan and 10% English. As each year of schooling progresses, the language of instruction in Nauruan decreases, so in Year 1 this changes to 80%, Year 2 to 70%, Year 3 to 60%. Then, in Years 4–6 the language of instruction is 50% Nauruan and 50% English, in Years 7–9 it is 20% Nauruan, and in senior secondary schooling, Years 10–12, the language of instruction is 100% English.

Nauru has a Nauru Quality School Standard Framework 2011–2020 (Nauru Department of Education 2011), developed in collaboration with an aid-funded ministerial adviser. It is against this that schools are assessed. The framework is viewed as strategic in enhancing and facilitating continuous improvement of student achievement and the performance of schools through a process of review (Nauru Department of Education 2011). This framework has four standards: quality school governance, positive school environment, effective school management, and quality learning outcomes (Nauru Department of Education 2011). This fourth standard "relates to an assessment of the quality of the educators and the education process that operates within the school to achieve an improvement of learning for each and every student" (Nauru Department of Education 2011, p. 37). Each standard is then divided into four components, in the case of Standard Four; these specific components are

1. Teaching and learning,
2. Teacher professionalism,
3. Assessment, and
4. Curriculum.

These four components are then further elaborated into four indicators. For example, Standard Four (Quality Learning Outcomes), Component 3 (Assessment) indicators are provided below:

Indicator 4.3.1   The school has a program and process to identify the learning outcomes across the whole school;

Indicator 4.3.2   Each teacher implements effective classroom assessment and evaluation techniques and processes;

Indicator 4.3.3   Effective reporting of all student's learning outcomes exists in the school;

Indicator 4.3.4   Student learning outcomes and results are used to inform whole of school strategic learning focuses (Nauru Department of Education 2011, pp. 42–43).

Each indicator has a list of evidence statements against which teaching practices are assessed and reviewed. A challenge in this context is that these standards and indicators have been largely derived from Western education systems. For example, evidence statements for indicator 4.3.2 describe aspects of practice which are considered by the Department of Education (2011) to support child-centered teaching and learning. But, as Schweisfurth (2011) identified, child-centered education can be a demanding change for teachers:

> because of the profound shifts required in teacher–learner power relations ... Policy rhetoric and implementation plans consistently belie the magnitude of the task at hand, and the *Realpolitik* of governments' desire to be making visible, positive, modern changes drives policy forward at a pace which practice cannot match (Jansen 1989; Dello-Iacovo 2009). (Schweisfurth 2011, p. 427)

In addition, Dimmock (2000) explained how it is "largely Western (Anglo-American, Australian, New Zealand) ... ideas, policies and practices which have come to dominate the globalization process ... with professional development ... assuming a Western perspective" (p. 12). Underlying this Western perspective is the assumption that the educational practices that are promoted will be "equally relevant to other ... very different cultures" (p. 12). Dimmock identified the paradoxical situation that occurs as "the more that education policy becomes globalized, the more important it becomes to take cognizance of each society's culture" (p. 13). As Alexander (2000) pointed out, "cultural borrowing happens" (p. 508), and it is sometimes difficult to explain why some educational ideas and practices become embedded in new cultural settings while others do not.

It is within this globalized education context that the NTEP project is situated. NTEP enabled teachers to gain an internationally recognized teaching qualification whilst remaining in their community. The opportunity to study in their home country, through the NTEP project, afforded a major advantage for the pre-service and in-service teachers as they continued with their busy home and community lives. As teachers commenced the program they studied part-time, however, after the first trimester they were released from their classroom teaching responsibilities to study full-time and complete their associate degree in seven trimesters. As part of their study in education, the teachers undertook practicum days with other teachers in Nauru. They were also offered an additional 20-day practical experience in schools in Armidale, NSW, to learn alongside Australian supervising teachers and see the theory, about which they had been learning, in action.

The Pacific focus aspect of the teachers' associate degree study takes into account the complex interplay of home, school, and community life that forms the Nauruan identity. Brown-Jeffy and Cooper (2011) recognized this connectedness, stating that it "demonstrates the value of cultural and social capital that students bring with them" (p. 68). During their professional learning, the teachers are challenged to bring their Nauruan knowledge and values to make their own meaning of concepts that are introduced. "Such intentional inclusion of students' backgrounds becomes a direct demonstration of the distinction between difference and deficiency. In other words, difference does not imply nor translate as deficit" (p. 68). The NTEP approach enabled teacher agency. Although NTEP was the conduit of particular approaches that may be different from those the teachers are familiar with, their contextual knowledge of Nauruan cultural practices was activated when they reinterpreted their learning to implement classroom actions. Smith (2016) reinforced this perspective as, for these teachers, "learning takes place in a specific context created by the culture, the history of that culture and of the learner, and other participants" (p. 741).

Thaman (2009) has long called to the people of the Pacific to maintain the integrity of their own cultures amidst the influences of colonization and globalization. She stated that

> As cultural mediators, Pacific teachers occupy an important but culturally ambiguous position. Whilst their professional training commits them to the rationale and practices of a Western-derived school curriculum, their personal identities, together with those of their students, are rooted in their own cultures and traditions. (p. 3)

Classroom teachers are charged with the responsibility of delivering local curriculum through pedagogy that reflects the cultural basis of the students' community. While their planning and preparation reflects the content prescribed in national syllabus documents, they make responsive decisions, moment-by-moment, regarding the focus and direction of their classroom interactions. As Charteris and Smardon (2015) argued, "teacher agency is fundamental to processes of teacher learning" (p. 115) and, in this context, agency involved teachers' capacity "to critically shape their own responsiveness to problematic situations" (Emirbayer and Mische 1998, p. 971).

The case study explored in this chapter is concerned with the professional learning of teachers participating in the NTEP program and we align with Mockler's (2013) description of professional learning as "the processes that teachers engage in when they expand, refine and change their practice" (p. 36).

In the course of their NTEP studies, teachers designed and planned assessment for different purposes, with an emphasis on assessment for learning. We follow Klenowski's (2009) description of assessment for learning (AfL) in that it "is part of everyday practice by students, teachers and peers that seeks, reflects upon and responds to information from dialogue, demonstration and observation in ways that enhance ongoing learning" (p. 264). In describing the role of the teacher in classroom assessment, we align with Booth et al. (2016) in that this involves teachers in using "their curricula, pedagogical, and subject matter knowledge to notice, recognize, and respond to students' learning needs as they arise" (p. 5) and, we add, in a manner that affects students' learning. In the Nauruan context, classroom assessment practices combined assessment for both summative and formative purposes. Throughout their study, teachers have been learning to prioritize assessment for formative purposes. Marshall and Drummond (2006), in discussing teacher actions that promote what they call the "spirit of assessment for learning," identified that the ways teachers conceptualize, sequence, and organize lesson tasks that students are to engage with, "affects all subsequent interactions within the classroom" (p. 147). Teachers broker policy and, as a policy conduit, are positioned agentically in their learning and classroom implementation. Having backgrounded the context of schooling in Nauru, we now turn to focus specifically upon assessment in this context.

Assessment in the Nauruan Context

Key staff in the Nauru Department of Education recognized the importance of assessment, both as a classroom practice and as a tool for scrutinizing shifts in the system. Conversations between the NTEP team and members of the department focused on the importance of the summative assessment regime the nation has developed. While it is not the intention of this chapter to discuss the summative assessment system in Nauru, it would be remiss to ignore these summative assessment mandates, as the classroom assessment practices of teachers are influenced by these requirements to the extent that teachers spend time and energy gathering the information for reporting. For our purposes here, we draw upon Sadler's (1989) description of summative assessment in "that it is concerned with summing up or summarizing the achievement status of a student" (p. 20) and tends to occur at an end point.

At the national level, Nauru has previously participated in the Pacific Islands Literacy and Numeracy Assessment (PILNA) (Secretariat for the Pacific Community 2014). This initiative was instigated by the Pacific Island Forum Ministers of Education in 2010. According to the Executive Summary, PILNA was administered in 2012 "across 14 Pacific Island countries for the purpose of setting the regional baseline as well as country positions for Literacy and Numeracy achievement of pupils in the Pacific region who have completed four and six years of primary education" (Secretariat for the Pacific Community 2014, p. 4). Nauru elected not to participate in PILNA 2015 as they had developed their own national syllabus documents and benchmark testing system, at the key transition points in schooling, which is at the end of Prep, Year 3, Year 6, and Year 9. This benchmark testing is collated by each school, then cumulatively by the Department of Education. The results enabled the achievement of respective cohorts to be examined, meeting summative purposes as opposed to influencing classroom practices. There was a prevalence of testing, with formal written testing a key part of primary schooling, where each year group had mid and end of year exams, designed by the teachers in those year groups. These predominantly served summative purposes and were used for twice-yearly reporting to parents.

However, both the department and the NTEP team also recognized the place of day-to-day classroom assessment practice as part of the learning and teaching process. This understanding is also documented in the *National Quality School Standards Framework, Republic of Nauru 2011–2020*. Standard Four: Quality Learning Outcomes, Component 3, Indicator 4.3.2 states that "each teacher implements effective *classroom assessment* [emphasis added] and evaluation techniques and processes" (Nauru Department of Education 2011, p. 42). Thus, it was within this context that the case study teachers were working as they were also learning about and trying to implement AfL classroom practices.

Inquiry Methods

The data for this chapter were collected through two different processes. First, to set the scene for teacher learning, Department of Education staff and teachers were invited to talk about their expectations for classroom assessment in schools and classroom assessment practices. One Department of Education staff member and four teachers agreed to participate, allowing their contributions to be shared. Over a 12-month period, when Nauruan teachers were participating in professional development workshops that explored student-centered teaching and assessment for learning in mathematics classrooms, the authors talked with these teachers about their assessment understandings and practices. This process is congruent with indigenous traditions of storying in Nauru. As Clandinin and Connelly (1996) note, "stories are the closest we can come to experience, as we and others tell of our experience" (p. 29). Stories involve multiplicities of layered meanings. Geelan (1997) adds to this, cautioning that "stories, too, highlight some facets and hide others - a process of selection is involved" (p. 561). This selection exists here, first, in the choices that the speakers make as they respond in an interview situation and, second, in the choices that the writers have used to share the stories.

Subsequent to these informal conversations, in 2015/2016, two classroom teachers, Myrna and Anne (pseudonyms), were invited to participate in a small case study to assist us to understand more about teacher assessment learning in the Nauruan context (UNE ethics approval granted). Both had just completed the Associate Degree in Teaching (Pacific Focus) over the previous 2 years and had returned to classroom teaching in a school near to the NTEP study center, and this accessibility was the reason for their selection. Myrna teaches children at the Year 1 level, while Anne teaches a Year 3 class. Both teachers have over 40 students in their classes. While both studied for their degree through an Australian context, they were challenged to recontextualize the content to their Nauruan classroom, culture, and community.

The process of data collection included the following:

1. An initial recorded and transcribed interview where the teachers talked about their beliefs and classroom assessment actions, including what they were now implementing in their classes.
2. A classroom observational visit where teachers' talk and actions were recorded in the form of field notes to support the subsequent interview.
3. A second recorded and transcribed interview immediately following the observation visit, where the teachers explained what they were doing and why, discussed the actions of the students and their responses and talked about how they had made decisions about their classroom assessment and planning. The teachers' plans for further changes were also discussed.
4. Informal follow-up conversations with the chapter authors regarding what they were noticing as a result of actions they were taking after the second interview.

Setting the Scene for the Case Studies

As described above, prior to the case studies, Mere (pseudonym), the person from the Department of Education with an overview of assessment in schools, was invited to talk about the expectations for classroom assessment in schools. She articulated these expectations as she discussed her perceptions of what happens in classrooms, highlighting the desire to shift to more student-focused learning environments yet recognizing the prevailing teaching and learning practices in schools that require modifying.

> We hope to have … teachers who have some understanding of what students need in the classroom to learn best. Because we're still used to the old-fashioned style of learning - teachers that are still putting up notes and just leaving the kids to learn from the notes. They are not challenging students enough to explore and find out more about things…We're trying to get teachers to get their students more engaged in ways that they really need to [be]. [The teachers] really need to know what it is that makes students want to learn. … They're not really getting into the students' mind and trying to find out what it is that might help them learn.

She continued, discussing concerns regarding the need for accountability in teacher practice, both in their planning preparation for teaching and their contextualizing of syllabus content to ensure relevance for the students.

> There's no accountability and I think that's where the failure is. The beauty of teaching is that you get a chance to explore what it is that students might need and you're the person who thinks "oh, if I do this, if I prepare this like this then my students will be happy to do the activities." If we get attitudes like that from teachers, I think that's where success comes in and achievement. Everybody is happy, the students are happy, the teachers are happy, the department is happy. A lot of our kids have skills. They enjoy practical things. So, because of the topics and the subjects, the teachers don't really know how to use everyday situations in their teaching. I think that's the biggest problem because then the kids go out and they can't use what they've learnt in the classroom in their everyday lives.

The four teachers also talked about the ideas Nauruan teachers saw as progressive, just prior to conducting the case studies reported in the next section of the findings. One teacher of Year 7 students (aged 12–13 years), we have called Q, shared her experiences when reflecting on end of semester common tests (those administered to all students across the year group) and compared this type of assessment with classroom-based activities with different items for different ability groups.

> The things that I teach in the classroom, that's what I assess them on when it comes to the exam. In the classroom they were happy, they really enjoyed doing the activities, cause they were always getting it correct. They were doing the right thing, but when it comes to the exam, it's a totally different thing, and when they receive their score, it's a total let down on their part and then we have to start all over again because when we start a new topic, they just have no confidence … they don't want to try the activities, but when I gave them like a topic test, I usually like a topic test with different levels. A topic that is for this level and this level and this level. They look forward to receiving that result compared to the actual standardized testing.

Year 6 teacher, R, with 6 years teaching experience, had been focused on assessment for learning as a component of her mathematics teaching/learning sequence from the first workshop she attended. R described how she provided a range of assessment items targeting an outcome at various levels of understanding. Her rationale for this approach being:

> Cause it's no use giving a test they can't do, for example, a baby who cannot chew food, give them chunk of food to chew…cause they will not be able to chew it…So it's the same as those low achievers when they see what they have no understanding of … So, I try to simplify it but I aim for the same outcome for all of the students, but theirs is in a simpler form.

When asked to describe assessment in her classroom R commented:

> Mmm, assessment. I would say that, by monitoring the students while doing the work, and evaluating their answers and how they understand the lessons…usually I give them some sort of, not all the time, a short test, but say, mental computations and on Friday morning we do short activities, a short quiz just on a recap on a week's work.

Although she did not collect work samples, she went on to explain that she was keeping some notes on her observations of the lower achieving students.

> I write notes and I keep results and a few assessments of those low achievers and, there are those special individuals that need attention.

Another teacher (S) voiced her enthusiasm for "hands-on" mathematics tasks. It is interesting to note that this teacher commented on students' development that she observed whilst they engaged in classroom activities. This teacher then trialed an activity which involved a take-home task to be completed by the students. The aim was to reinforce the learning that occurred in the classroom and as a form of communication between school and home contexts.

> I asked the students to pick any three items that will measure up to 30 centimetres and I saw that most of them could estimate that just a piece of chalk and a rubber and a pencil could … none of them got something bigger than 30 centimetres. I saw that they can now visualize the length of something in centimetres. There is another activity where I told them to go home and measure maybe three things, that one maybe 8 centimetres and other about 10 centimetres. We estimate before we went, then they went home and see if those items actually about that length.

Teacher T considered how to communicate student progress to parents through using work samples to compile a student portfolio. She saw this as a valid form of evidence for making informed decisions about students' levels of achievement.

> At the end of semester one, I thought of now getting all the activities together and the assessment tasks, thus compiling the work so that if they're not here, you have evidence [to] show the parents what their child had done in the school, this is what they've learned, you know, this and that and these evidences. So they're going to take it home with them if they're not doing it here, and for most of them it would be something that they'd be proud of it.

These discussions with Nauruan teachers during the mathematics curriculum-development process illuminated the ways in which they were changing their teaching practices over a 12-month period. Before commencing these integrated workshops, most teachers had been focused on assessment issues related to the national semester tests. The teachers were developing an understanding of the concept of formative assessment and how these assessment practices relate to the context of Nauruan schools.

Case Study

Following the 2 years of NTEP study described above, both case study teachers articulated a constructivist approach toward classroom assessment that linked to using informal classroom assessment approaches to elicit information about what their students know and/or can do in order to provide direction for their teaching.

> Anne: To me it means understanding what the child knows and does not know, like their assessments are things that you do to find out the child's strengths and weaknesses. So, in my classroom, when I [start] a new topic, I would find out first what they know about that topic.

> Myrna: It's finding out if the students have been learning from what you have been teaching them as well as finding out what they know, already know at the beginning of the term or the year and you give them a pre-assessment task. It's for the teacher to know what to teach them, what they need to learn during the year and how they are progressing throughout the year. So, to me, that's what assessment is all about.

However, Myrna also spoke of her difficulties in being able to work in the way that she wanted because of the size of her class. Due to a teacher shortage in Nauru, and no substitute teachers, classes are combined. Myrna had 60 children in her class for many weeks at the commencement of the year. With so many students present in the classroom, it was observed that Myrna found it difficult to move among them, adapting her feedback and interactions as students had to approach her. Although she had planned a sequence of writing experiences for children that would involve them working cooperatively using peer assessment strategies, the reality was that, with the resources available in her classroom and working with a large number of students, she was unable to provide the program she had planned, and had to modify this.

> The first week was supposed to be the week that they were doing a [writing] draft and then the next week, they would polish it. The week after I was going to get them to talk with each other on improving what's missing from their own reports. [Working in groups] is a challenge for Nauruan kids. It's sometimes a hassle, there are so many of them.

The teachers in the same year level had planned together at the beginning of the year so that if anyone was away they would be working at a similar place in the topics that were being taught.

> If we want the program to progress and for the students to keep going and not go back and have to repeat what they missed out. The way we plan the program or the topics is that if one teacher is missing, that that class is distributed and the other teacher is teaching the same thing.

Myrna discussed how only a few of her students were writing in English and that she supported them to construct sentences through developing a pattern in the writing routine.

> After we do the oral and sentence making in the pockets they go and write their own sentences using the word for the day, they have to use that word in a sentence.

On the classroom walls, Myrna had nouns and verbs displayed to assist the writers. She worked flexibly between explaining in Nauruan and in English to support learners' understanding, identifying that most students are having trouble with English as many of the Year 1 students had not previously attended prep or pre-school classes and this was their first exposure to learning English. To establish engagement with the children, Myrna had her students think about the writing topic.

> Usually I introduce my topic with a question. I'll get them to think about the topic.

The system required that teachers assess students in mathematics and literacy at the ends of terms two and four. Myrna described how she and the teachers at the Year 1 level had put in place a more systematic way of collecting products of student writing so that she could use this to support student learning.

> Well, I have criteria, like what we're looking for and what they would like to learn. So, I have the whole of that written out, but I'm looking for the writing of capitals, full stops, commas, question marks, things like that and the grammar and the spelling as well and the words they use.

Myrna explained how she and the students used their writing samples to inform teaching and learning.

> They have a piece of paper and a topic to write about. They check what they have there [from the criteria] there is also [time] where the students assess each other. They read to each other what they wrote and [say] you're missing that and they have to rewrite it again and present it to the class at a later time.

Anne used information that she gained from assessing students by considering what students cannot do at this point in time, and working with them at that level. She acknowledged that this may not be the expected level of work for their grade level.

> I always look at what they are unable to do. Some of my kids won't be able to do anything that has to do with grade 3 work. So, if they do not know how to identify numbers, they do that. That's a step [on] from where they are at.

The Australian-based practical experience was significant for Myrna who had previously to find her own ways of working and admits that when she first began teaching, she worked directly from the provided syllabus without recognizing the different learner needs in her classroom. She realized the need to differentiate learning for all students to progress.

> When I started I was just given syllabus to follow. This is what needs to be taught but then they didn't tell me that [and] I didn't realize that there were different levels in the one class. There is a difference between getting these people up to standard and the ones that are already up to standard that need to go up farther.

Myrna had never had the opportunity to watch other teachers and her own experiences had previously formed the basis of the approach she used in her class. She recognized that her professional learning was transforming the way she taught and had "opened her mind."

> Well, because when I started [teaching] I never got to observe anyone. I just liked to do it on my own. What I learned, I tried to get the kids to learn. So I kind of felt that with this UNE studies that I've been doing, it kind of opened my mind and it showed me some new things, new techniques, new strategies of teaching and even managing the class, I was really happy with that.

Myrna spoke of the benefits of working with other teachers, to study and share learning experiences with, during the Australian practicum. A consequence of this was that she now fostered a collaborative learning community within her school, and teachers had worked together to plan the overview of the program and events for the following term.

> From what I learnt, the overview is like what we call a timeline. Having someone who was in the same course as me, we knew what we were talking about and we had the resources as well. So, we shared that with the other teachers and we planned out the whole term, excursions and visitors and everything.

As a result of their professional learning, they have implemented a more learner-centric approach to the teaching and learning in their classrooms. In developing this approach to teaching founded on constructivist learning theory, they started with the students' prior knowledge. Myrna set up the learning environment in her class by talking with the students about what they were learning, a key tenet of assessment for learning and one that was reinforced through observing teachers in action during her Australian practical experience.

> I introduce what we are learning for that week or for that day. I tell them the topic, and why it's important to learn. Sometimes they ask questions about that too: "what ifs" and/or "why." So, I try to explain to them why they need to learn that. Like [asking] why do we need to learn numbers? They tell us that we need to count our money … when we go to the shops. So, that's a good reason: what else, why else? We need to know how many people are there, so that we can feed them, or how much money we can spend on how many things…So, I brainstorm first. I always get them to think or get them to give me what they know first.

Anne talked about how she had changed her approach using her science teaching as an example of how she set up activities for children to explore ideas in a more inductive manner. She noted that with her changed routine the children were able to provide their own definitions. As Marshall and Drummond (2006) indicated, this changed sequencing of student engagement in the task created "an environment in which learning is socially constructed" (p. 147).

> I'm trying to implement student-centred activities. For example, instead of giving students the definition they find out their own definition. For our science, we're doing animal groups, classification… My usual routine, for how I teach them animal groups, is I give them the definition for each like mammals, birds then they just find out what mammals they know. But now I've asked them to think about all the animals and how are they different. Like some animals have hair and fur. Then I write it down and some animals have feathers, beaks and

tails and then we write that. They do their own definition instead of me spoon feeding them with a definition and tell[ing] them this is a mammal and this is a bird.

Teaching in this way, where students' prior knowledge was ascertained, led to Anne being surprised about what her students already know.

Actually, they already all know them, but it's just the scientific words like mammals and carnivores and omnivores. But they know, they understand.

As a result of this learning, Anne introduced the specific scientific vocabulary and information that supported the development of the children's understanding. Likewise, Myrna identified that her teaching practices had previously been more transmission focused and that she now engaged the children in hands-on activity to support their learning.

I find that all the strategies that I've been learning about are new. To let the students do their own learning, student-centred activities. I'm more used to the transmission kind of teaching where I give the kids my knowledge. But with [my] reading and [studying] that's getting the kids to do hands-on activities, I find it's better than me doing all the talking.

The teachers articulated how their changed actions were influencing their ongoing teaching practices. In Anne's case, she realized that she knew more about the students in her class and that they had capabilities which she did not acknowledge in her previous teaching approach.

It really helped me because it makes me understand what they already know and it's also exciting for me because it's something new and when I did that to my students, oh I should have done that a long time ago, because instead of me telling them, trying to drill the concept in their minds they actually find it out themselves which is really, really good.

Like Myrna, who noted that her professional learning through her NTEP studies had "opened her mind," Anne recognized that her changed teaching practices have altered the ways in which she views her teaching and the children in her class.

It has opened up my eyes and it's, how do I say it? Like it's given me different things to do and understand [regarding] how the children learn.

Anne talked about her thinking processes and the impacts she was noticing in her changing classroom practices. She related the strategies she was implementing. Rather than responding to all student questions by providing answers, she encouraged the students to think more deeply.

I usually just expand more. If a group is finding it hard because it's a very new method that they aren't used to [and they ask] "What should I do, teacher, what should I do?" I try to give them questions, give them back the question and I say what should you do if want to, you know…? I act as a helper and help them expand their mind instead of just telling them what to do I help them up more to explore.

This changed practice, however, has consequences that Anne recognized and grappled with in her teaching context. In their Nauruan family life, children are directed in their actions and follow the directions they are given (Gaiyabu 2007). Making decisions and having autonomy in choice making is a Western education view linked closely to constructivism (Vygotsky et al. 1978) and perspectives of the child as a self-managing entity (Tabulawa 2003). Anne admitted that it was not only the teacher–learner power relations (Schweisfurth 2011) that exist in the classroom space that are affected, but also the cultural expectations that exist outside of the school gates.

> It's very hard because sometimes, I just don't know what else to say. I'm a Nauruan. I know in the community and everywhere you go, children ask what they do and you have to tell them what to do. You don't tell them, oh you find out yourself or you try and do it yourself, you know, things like that. So, it's very hard, sometimes I find it hard to, help a child to expand on their own when they keep on coming and saying, "what should I do?" … At the start, it was really hard but I think they have got the hang of what I'm like, how I teach and they understand what they should be doing now and trying out things. So, I think there is a big change.

In considering the learner-centered strategies she is implementing, Anne talked about the ongoing consequences for children in the ways they are perceived in the community and how the changed learning and teaching strategies go beyond the walls of the school.

> Honestly, I think that it will be hard for these children… the students will play two roles. When you go in the community, they cannot change because it's our cultural belief and values. You cannot talk to your parents, you have to listen. I think the children are taking up two roles, but they will make a change when they grow up and become parents themselves because they were given the opportunity, during school. So, in this time there will be no change, but they themselves will have a big change when they grow up because they get to ask questions, get to find out that thing [in that way].

Myrna talked about how she was deliberately using Nauruan stories and legends as a context for integrating the Nauruan way of life into the children's learning.

> I tell them Nauruan legends that we used to be told. Those are the ones I break up into sentence strips and they have to rearrange them, although they're in English, but the stories are in Nauruan. The characters and the names I use Nauruan and their way of behaving. It's normal for Nauruan families to have more than four kids, they get up to 10. So, they get to learn from the numbers as well, counting in English and Nauruan. … Also, to bring back the culture of respecting older people and listening to others… I tell them stories about how the Nauruan people behaved, how they looked after this place, how they lived.

In summary, both Myrna and Anne had learned through their studies, and were incorporating in their classroom assessment practice, strategies to elicit students' prior knowledge. They were using exemplars, involving children as peer assessors, and differentiating teaching based upon the information they gained. This supported them to guide student learning by adapting the curriculum, incorporating relevant contexts, and becoming more collaborative professionals. The twice-yearly assessment in literacy and numeracy seemed to sit at the periphery of classroom assessment practices. As Myrna indicated, she had sought alternative ways to collect evidence of children's day-to-day learning that would not only inform her teaching but also meet a similar purpose to the current testing regime and be used as the basis of reporting to families.

Discussion

The intention of the case study was to examine how teacher's professional learning and classroom assessment practices were influenced by their university study, how teachers applied their learning to their day-to-day classroom interactions, and how they mediated the pedagogical differences between Australian-based content and their Nauruan context. As a small, qualitative case study, it is not possible to generalize, but these findings do provide insights into the experiences, actions, and classroom assessment learning of the two teachers as they worked through a process of change. In using "narrative vignettes", we are also conscious that there is complexity of meaning, context and experience that underpins the teachers' stories. This is further elucidated by Clandinin and Connelly (1996) when they consider the source and motivation of individual's stories.

> We view these professional knowledge landscapes as exceedingly complex places with multiple layers of meaning that depend on individuals' stories and how individuals are positioned on that landscape, as well as the landscape's own narrative history of shifting values, beliefs, and stories. (p. 29)

Teachers can be agentic in their actions when they use discretion in determining what works and what to experiment with in their practice in their specific classroom contexts. Both teachers articulated that as they learnt about the students' needs from their classroom interactions, they recognized that they were modifying the classroom curriculum to meet these needs. We view these teacher practice movements as inherent to their developing classroom assessment processes in a more child-centered manner. This differs from their past practice of working from the curriculum level specific to their class year level. This also reflects their growing responsiveness to the differing needs of students as they enact classroom assessment. However, the reality of large classes, brought about by a local teacher shortage, inhibited the teachers' ability to adapt their teaching as much as they might have wished. To address these issues, the development of collaborative planning and professional learning communities became an exciting prospect. Central to the teachers' collaborative planning decisions, and in response to the teacher relief shortage, was a determination to benefit the students in their classes. As children moved between classes at the same level, they could engage in familiar content as well as benefit from the teachers' shifts toward more child-centered pedagogies.

Student-centered assessment approaches and cooperative learning strategies are new domains of practice for the two teachers in this case study, and central to their developing classroom assessment. Both teachers spoke of how they utilize questioning as an assessment strategy in ways different from their previous practice. What these teachers are negotiating in their classrooms is coherent with Nauruan documentation such as the *National Quality School Standards Framework* (Nauru Department of Education 2011). We are cognizant, however, that this document is deeply influenced by, and developed in response to, external, globalized trends. While the influence of imported Western pedagogies alongside existing Pacific pedagogy cannot be ignored, there is a danger in viewing this as a binary relationship, where the two underpinning philosophies may be seen to be mutually exclusive. Myrna spoke of the decision she deliberately made to use Nauruan stories as the context through which her young students learn and to embed mathematics and literacy, as well as cultural values, in this way.

We are also mindful of the role that teachers play as, according to Thaman (2009), they are the cultural mediators brokering the ideas and philosophies that they experience through their professional learning, with the children in their classrooms and the wider Nauruan community. The teachers were aware of the barriers and enablers that existed within the sociocultural contexts beyond the school spaces and, as Anne reflected previously, the students would "play two roles." The use of the word *play* instead of *have* may well have been accidental, yet it confirmed that these students were seen to have a future role in their culture. Are perhaps, then, Nauruan children, more than ever before, adopting the role of intergenerational cultural-change mediators, treading on the boundaries in the space between their own Pacific culture and the globalized? The challenge for Nauruan teachers is indeed the maintenance (and modification) of cultural identity within a schooling system where English is the language of instruction and Western educational ideas are strongly influencing the educational policy context.

Conclusion

Classroom assessment and teacher practices changing as a result of professional learning will always be defined by the cultural contexts, the landscapes, in which teachers exist. This is not confined to the classroom; it extends beyond to the community. These teachers had the cultural capital; they exercised agency in contextualizing the pedagogy they were exposed to through their study. They demonstrated some cognizance of the implications of the practice shifts that they made, for the children, as they moved beyond the boundaries of the school.

In the midst of perceived tensions "in" and "out" of the classroom, these teachers remained prepared for change. They viewed this as necessary if an amalgamation of student-centered learning, inclusive of assessment for learning, was to occur. To this end, one of the teachers viewed the children she taught as "change agents," and herself as the catalyst for the merging of the pedagogical knowledge acquired, into the Nauruan schooling context. While teacher resourcing and system-wide assessment regimes remained the focus of many discussions, there was also an emerging shift toward teacher collaborative learning opportunities and viewing assessment as a tool that can be used to look forward, not just to sum up learning each semester.

References

Alexander, R. J. (2000). *Culture and pedagogy: International comparisons in primary education.* Oxford: Blackwell.

Anghie, A. (1993). 'The heart of my home': Colonialism, environmental damage, and the Nauru case. *Harvard International Law Journal, 34*(2), 455–556. Retrieved from http://www.harvardilj.org/.

Barker, X. (2012). English language as bully in the Republic of Nauru. In V. Rapatahana & P. Bunce (Eds.), *English language as Hydra: Its impacts on non-English language cultures* (pp. 18–36). Bristol: St. Nicholas House.

Booth, B., Dixon, H., & Hill, M. (2016). Assessment capability for New Zealand teachers and students: Challenging but possible. *SET, 2,* 3–10. http://dx.doi.org/10.18296/set.0030.

Brown-Jeffy, S., & Cooper, J. E. (2011). Toward a conceptual framework of culturally relevant pedagogy: An overview of the conceptual and theoretical literature. *Teacher Education Quarterly, 38*(1), 65–84.

Charteris, J., & Smardon, D. (2015). Teacher agency and dialogic feedback: Using classroom data for practitioner inquiry. *Teaching and Teacher Education, 30,* 114–123. http://dx.doi.org/10.1016/j.tate.2015.05.006.

Clandinin, D. J., & Connelly, F. M. (1996). Teachers' professional knowledge landscapes: Teacher stories, stories of teachers, school stories, stories of schools. *Educational Researcher, 25*(3), 24–30. Retrieved from http://www.jstor.org/stable/1176665.

Davidson, D. (1968). Current developments in the Pacific: The Republic of Nauru. *The Journal of Pacific History, 3*(1), 145–150. https://doi.org/10.1080/00223346808572131.

Dimmock, C. A. (2000). *Designing the learning-centred school: A cross-cultural perspective.* London: RoutledgeFalmer.

Educational Quality Assessment Program. (2016). *2015 Pacific Islands literacy and numeracy assessment (PILNA): Regional report.* Retrieved from http://www.eqap.org.fj/work/Assessment.aspx.

Emirbayer, M., & Mische, A. (1998). What is agency? *American Journal of Sociology, 103*(4), 962–1023.

Gaiyabu, M. (2007). *Ekereri in the lives of teachers, parents and pupils: A path to school effectiveness and improvement in Nauru* (Unpublished doctoral thesis). University of Cambridge. Retrieved from https://www.repository.cam.ac.uk/handle/1810/252063.

Geelan, D. R. (1997). Weaving narrative nets to capture school science classrooms. *Research in Science Education, 27*(4), 553–563.

Klenowski, V. (2009). Assessment for learning revisited: An Asia-Pacific perspective. *Assessment in Education: Principles, Policy & Practice, 16*(3), 263–268. https://doi.org/10.1080/09695940903319646.

Marshall, B., & Drummond, M. J. (2006). How teachers engage with assessment for learning: Lessons from the classroom. *Research Papers in Education, 21*(2), 133–149.

Mockler, N. (2013). Teacher professional learning in a neoliberal age: Audit, professionalism and accountability. *Australian Journal of Teacher Education, 38*(10), 35–47.

Nauru Department of Education. (2011). *National quality school standards framework. Republic of Nauru 2011–2020.* Republic of Nauru: Author.

Nauru Department of Education. (2012). *The Nauru language syllabus prep-year 10.* Republic of Nauru: Author.

Nauru Department of Education. (2016). *Education management information system (EMIS) national enrolment summary 2016 for all schools.* Republic of Nauru: Author.

Pacific Islands Forum Secretariat. (2009). *Pacific education development framework (PEDF) 2009–2015: Annex A.* Suva, Fiji: Pacific Islands Forum Secretariat. Retrieved from http://www.forumsec.org/resources/uploads/attachments/documents/Pacific%20Education%20Development%20Framework%202009-2015.pdf.

Sadler, D. R. (1989). Formative assessment and the design of instructional systems. *Instructional Science, 18,* 119–144.

Schweisfurth, M. (2011). Learner-centred education in developing country contexts: From solution to problem? *International Journal of Educational Development, 31,* 425–432.

Secretariat for the Pacific Community. (2014). *Pacific Islands literacy and numeracy assessment (PILNA): Executive summary.* Retrieved from http://www.forumsec.org/resources/uploads/attachments/documents/2014FEdMM.03_Attachment_PILNA_Rpt.pdf.

Secretariat of the Pacific Community. (2011). *Republic of Nauru: National report on population and housing: Census 2011.* Retrieved from http://www.spc.int/nmdi/nmdi_documents/2011_NAURU_CENSUS_REPORT.pdf.

Serow, P., Taylor, N., Sullivan, T., Tarrant, J., Burnett, G., Smardon, D., et al. (2016). Pre-service teacher education in Nauru: Where, who and why. *Australian and International Journal of Rural Education, 26*(1), 17–26.

Smith, K. (2016). Assessment for learning: A pedagogical tool. In D. Wyse, L. Hayward, & J. Pandya (Eds.), *The Sage handbook of curriculum, pedagogy and assessment* (pp. 740–755). London: Sage.

Sullivan, T., Serow, P., Taylor, N., Angell, E., Tarrant, J., Burnett, G., et al. (2017). Supporting families: A nurturing teacher education strategy in Nauru. *Asia-Pacific Journal of Teacher Education, 45*(1), 39–52. https://doi.org/10.1080/1359866X.2015.1115821.

Tabulawa, R. (2003). International aid agencies, learner-centred pedagogy and political democratisation: A critique. *Comparative Education, 39*(1), 7–26.

Thaman, K. H. (2009). Towards cultural democracy in teaching and learning with specific references to Pacific Island Nations (PINs). *International Journal for the Scholarship of Teaching and Learning, 3*(2), article 6. Retrieved from http://digitalcommons.georgiasouthern.edu/ij-sotl/vol3/iss2/6.

Thompson, P. (2013). Learner-centred education and 'cultural translation'. *International Journal of Educational Development, 33,* 48–58.

UNESCO. (2000). *Republic of Nauru: Education for all (EFA) The year 2000 assessment: Country report, 1999.* Retrieved from http://unesdoc.unesco.org/images/0021/002194/219486eo.pdf.

Vygotsky, L. S., Cole, M., John-Steiner, V., Scribner, S., & Souberman, E. (Eds.). (1978). *Mind in society: The development of higher psychological processes.* Cambridge: Harvard University Press.

Chapter 4
Developing Assessment-Capable Teachers Through Engagement in Assessment for Learning (AfL): A New Zealand Study

Helen Dixon and Eleanor Hawe

Abstract Utilizing data generated from an interpretive, qualitative research project, this chapter outlines an approach to teacher professional learning about assessment for learning (AfL) that was by nature experiential and collaborative. We provide an illustration of the ways in which teachers were required to actively engage in a number of AfL strategies to enhance their personal learning, supported by an academic staff member who personified an AfL teacher. In doing so, we demonstrate how the act of becoming an AfL learner, taught by someone who exemplified a skilled, competent, and confident AfL teacher, activated teachers' examination of their beliefs about the roles and responsibilities of teachers and learners in learning and assessment and the apparent validity of these beliefs. Moreover, we show how teachers' personal and vicarious experiences helped build self-efficacy in relation to teachers' ability to implement AfL within their own classrooms as they recognized its importance to student learning. Overall, we argue that teachers' lived experiences contributed to their assessment literacy and their assessment capability.

Keywords Assessment literacy and capability · Content and pedagogical content knowledge · Experiential learning · Teacher professional learning · Self-efficacy

H. Dixon (✉) · E. Hawe
The Faculty of Education and Social Work, The University of Auckland, Auckland, New Zealand
e-mail: h.dixon@auckland.ac.nz

© Springer Nature Singapore Pte Ltd. 2018   59
H. Jiang and M. F. Hill (eds.), *Teacher Learning with Classroom Assessment*,
https://doi.org/10.1007/978-981-10-9053-0_4

Our Starting Point: Developing Assessment-Capable Teachers and Students Through Engagement in AfL

Assessment in New Zealand (NZ) primary schools is somewhat unique in two ways. First, while there is a universal set of standards[1] in the areas of reading, writing, and mathematics, against which student performance is judged, there is no national testing regime. Rather, teachers are expected to make judgments about student performance based on multiple sources of evidence gathered within the context of classroom learning and assessment [Ministry of Education (MoE) 2011]. Specifically, they are required to collect and utilize evidence using a wide range of formal and informal measures, *including* student voice. However, we would argue that to gain a rich, authentic, and reliable picture of student learning and achievement, teachers must be assessment literate. As such, teachers need to have a comprehensive knowledge and understanding of the principles underpinning, and methods associated with, sound assessment practice. Furthermore, teachers must be assessment capable. If students are to have a voice and hence a central and active place in learning and assessment, teachers need to possess the knowledge, skills, and volition to support them to become self-regulatory, autonomous, life-long learners (Booth et al. 2016). This aspiration is articulated in NZ assessment policy where the need for assessment-capable teachers and students is emphasized (MoE 2011).

NZ assessment policy articulates a clear vision for students to become assessment capable in that they are expected to actively participate in the assessment of their learning and recognize the significance of personal learning, including any gaps, in order to make future-orientated decisions about their learning (MoE 2011). A dual emphasis on the development of assessment-capable teachers *and* students is distinctive when compared to a number of other countries within the Asia-Pacific region. However, the realization of the assessment-capable student, encouraged by the assessment-capable teacher, is not without its challenges. As others have noted, traditionally many teachers have struggled to develop self-regulatory and autonomous learners (Black 2015; Hopfenbeck et al. 2015). NZ-based research supports such claims (Dixon et al. 2011) confirming that the assessment-capable teacher is yet to be realized on a large scale.

The NZ MoE has become a strong advocate for adoption of the principles and practices associated with AfL (MoE 2011) to support student assessment capability through the development of self-regulatory skills and behaviors. To this end, as an integral part of classroom learning and assessment, teachers are expected to promote student understanding about the goal(s) of learning and what constitutes expected performance, foster student engagement in peer feedback and self-monitoring, and encourage the taking of action to bring about desired performance. From our perspective, although itemized individually, the aforementioned AfL strategies are neither stand-alone entities nor sequential steps. Rather, they are inter-dependent, each feed-

---

[1]Introduced in 2010, National Standards (NS) describe the expected achievement of students in Years 1–8. Using a four-point scale, teachers judge whether a student is at, above, below, or well below a specified standard.

ing into and from the others in an iterative manner. It is together that they contribute to supporting and furthering student learning and capability. Hence, we hold firm the belief that the full potential of AfL can only be realized when all strategies are present, to a greater or lesser extent, within the pedagogical environment. If students are to become assessment capable, they need substantial and authentic opportunities to understand the goals of learning and what constitutes quality work, compare current performance to what is expected, and have a repertoire of strategies so they can modify performance as necessary during the production of work (Hawe and Dixon 2014; Sadler 1989).

The Challenge—AfL as a Vision yet to be Realized in Practice

Within the context of AfL, there is evidence to suggest that changes to teachers' instructional practices have proved to be modest and cursory (Black 2015). Like others with an interest in and commitment to AfL, we believe that mandated change has failed to achieve the desired outcome (Hayward 2015; Swaffield 2011). This failure has been largely due to an instrumental approach to implementation where the focus has been on the development of teachers' technical knowledge of assessment techniques at the expense of developing their assessment literacy, that is their understanding and knowledge of the principles informing, and theoretical underpinnings of, key strategies. In our mind, a lack of attention to the enhancement of assessment literacy has restricted the development of assessment-capable teachers.

In addition, a groundswell of evidence shows that teachers' beliefs are a mediating factor in regard to AfL implementation (Dixon et al. 2011; Tierney 2006). Tierney, for example, has argued that the sustained championing of particular AfL strategies and approaches will have little effect on teachers' practice if these strategies and approaches are at odds with personal beliefs about teaching and learning. Yung's (2001, 2002) work undertaken in Hong Kong, although not directly focused on AfL, illustrated how teachers' approaches to assessment implementation were influenced by their beliefs about what it meant to be a teacher, including beliefs about the teacher's role in helping students learn; the student's role in, and responsibility for, learning; the nature of the relationship between teacher and students; and how this relationship should be manifest in classroom interactions.

Within the context of teaching, self-efficacy refers to the generalized expectancy a teacher has in regard to their ability to influence students, as well as to beliefs about their ability to perform the professional tasks that constitute teaching, such as assessing student learning. However, while there have been general calls to investigate the impact of teachers' self-efficacy beliefs on curriculum and assessment innovation, research evidence about such factors is mostly absent in relation to AfL. Utilizing Bandura's (1977) theory of self-efficacy in our work (Dixon 2011) has highlighted how teachers' efficacy beliefs have been influential in regard to the nature and magnitude of changes made to their AfL practice and the amount of effort teachers have expended in moving toward mastery of specific strategies. This work has convinced us that the development of strong efficacy beliefs must be an essential component of teacher professional learning opportunities.

Self-efficacy is an expectancy belief that is goal, task, and situation specific. It pertains to an individual's belief in his/her capability to:

organise and execute courses of action required to deal with prospective situations that contain many ambiguous unpredictable and often stressful elements. (Bandura 1981, p. 200)

Comprised of two components, self-efficacy includes an efficacy expectation, which represents the belief in one's ability to perform the desired behavior, and an outcome expectation, which relates to the belief that performance of the behavior will have a desirable effect. According to Bandura (1977), efficacy and outcome expectations are either strengthened or weakened in four different ways: through personal mastery experience, vicarious experience, social persuasion, and an individual's physiological and emotional state. Of the four, personal mastery experience is considered the most powerful—I have tried and my experience tells me I can do this! Vicarious experience, in the form of social models, is considered the second most influential way in which individuals' beliefs in their capabilities to master comparable activities can be strengthened. While less influential, social persuasion, or being told that one has the capabilities to succeed, is a further source of influence. Finally, Bandura contended that people's physiological and emotional states affect how capability is determined. Given these four sources of influence, we would argue that it is essential that teachers' personal mastery and vicarious experiences related to classroom assessment engender high levels of confidence in their ability to implement specific AfL strategies, and, as well, help them to acquire the knowledge and skill to do so (an efficacy expectation). In addition, and just as importantly, teachers' experiences must help them to "see" that the use of strategies such as peer review and activities that promote dialogic feedback will have a desirable effect on student learning (an outcome expectation). Furthermore, we contend that it is only when teachers have *both* a strong efficacy and a strong outcome expectation that they will be able to persevere with the challenging task of implementing AfL in the spirit of its intent.

In summary, to date, AfL has failed to reach its potential, in part because a number of key AfL strategies are neither well understood by teachers nor well utilized in the promotion of learning (Black 2015; Hawe and Dixon 2014; Hopfenbeck et al. 2015). Many teachers are yet to commit to the development of assessment-capable students (Dixon et al. 2011; Gamlem and Smith 2013). As a counter to such findings, there have been calls from within the academy to provide practicing teachers with substantial, high-quality, professional learning opportunities that will build assessment literacy and capability.

The Context for the Study

Our Position as Teacher Educators

As teacher educators (and researchers), we have had a long-standing interest in assessment as well as a history of working with practicing teachers to support assessment literacy and capability. However, our challenge has been "to find ways in which fruitful interactions between [research] work and the world of practicing teachers" can be built (Black 2015, p. 174). Cognizant that any change to practice is dependent upon the "reflexive and discursive consciousness of teachers" (Elliot 1998, p. xiii), our work with teachers has been grounded in and informed by an experiential-based approach to learning. Specifically, we have aimed to offer teachers substantive professional learning opportunities, which promote assessment literacy and capability by:

- Expanding teachers' content knowledge in relation to theoretical ideas underpinning AfL and its associated strategies, for example, self-regulation and goal setting;
- Developing pedagogical content knowledge, through teachers' engagement in, and reflection on, AfL strategies from both a teacher's and learner's perspective;
- Facilitating an examination of teachers' deep-seated beliefs about their roles and those of students in the processes of learning and assessment to highlight the efficacy and validity of these beliefs;
- Building teacher confidence in the ability of AfL strategies to bring about desirable effects for learners, as well as confidence in their ability to implement these strategies within the classroom (their self-efficacy in relation to AfL).

The Research Impetus

Over a number of years, we have jointly taught a compulsory *assessment for learning* course in the degree program, Bachelor of Education (Teaching) Teachers' Specialization, in a university in NZ. This program has been specifically developed for practicing teachers who wish to upgrade their qualification from a diploma to a degree. While the learning objectives of the course have remained the same over time, it is fair to say that both the content and the course delivery have continued to evolve. As researchers, we have been privileged to have full access to current ideas and practices associated with AfL. In turn, as teacher educators we have had many opportunities to trial and refine our practice, as we have sought to implement the AfL strategies we have read about and discussed at length. Prior to the study reported in this chapter, course evaluations completed by teachers enrolled in the course had regularly indicated high levels of satisfaction. These evaluations, as well as informal, positive feedback received from these teachers sent us a strong message that we were on the "right track" in regard to teacher learning. Subsequently, this message became the impetus for us to develop a research project that investigated teachers' understandings and beliefs about AfL and the impact the course had on these understandings and beliefs. As with any project, ethical approval was gained prior to commencement and ethical principles and procedures were followed throughout the research.

The Teachers Involved in the Project

Although teaching in NZ is now a degreed profession, this has not always been the case. Given that up until the mid- to late 1990s teachers could graduate with a diploma of teaching, there are still teachers within the profession who do not hold a degree qualification. The 21 teachers who were part of the project reported here fell into this category—they were enrolled in our assessment course as part of their degree. While all were practicing teachers, they worked in different sectors of education, ranging from early childhood to secondary school. Three of the 21 held senior management positions in their schools. Those who had classroom teaching responsibilities worked across a range of year levels spanning Years 1 through to 10. While a majority had previously participated in some kind of AfL-related professional development, five had not. Of these five, two were early childhood teachers where professional development specifically in this area had not been available. Another teacher, recently returned to the workforce, had not had the opportunity to participate in any such programs; reasons for the other two teachers' non-participation are unknown.

The Course Content and the Delivery Modes

As teacher educators, we subscribe to the belief that social interaction and collaboration provide the impetus and context for learning. To this end, course delivery was structured in a way to create an environment and climate where students worked with each other and with the lecturer. Emphasis was placed on the development of strong, positive, respectful, learning relationships, thus providing opportunities for class members to share ideas, ask questions, and take risks as together they engaged in a multitude of in-class activities. To ensure class members could engage meaningfully with course content, course activities and tasks, including key readings, were carefully selected, scaffolding students into intended learning. To further facilitate learning, a key role for the lecturer during in-class activities was to move around the classroom, observing, listening, and interacting with class members in order to identify and respond to individual and/or class areas of confusion and misunderstanding.

Given that AfL aims to enhance learning through the development of student learning capacity and self-regulatory and autonomous behaviors (Cowie et al. 2013), Zimmerman's self-regulated learning theory was selected as the key theoretical frame informing the course. Thus, a collection of Zimmerman's works was utilized throughout the course and supplemented by scholarly pieces from seminal assessment experts such as Hattie and Timperley, Sadler, Swaffield, and Wiliam. A range of empirical studies taken from journals such "Assessment in Education: Principles, Policy and Practice" and "Assessment Matters", focused on AfL implementation were utilized to exemplify specific aspects of practice. From our perspectives, teachers' exposure to both scholarly works and empirical studies provided them with multiple opportunities to develop understanding related to the nature, purpose, and significance of:

- goal setting and its impact on performance;
- making expected learning and standards of performance explicit;
- engineering effective discussion, as well as activities including assessment tasks, that elicit evidence of learning;
- feedback, both external and internal, that advances learning;
- utilizing students as learning resources for one another;
- supporting student ownership over and responsibility for learning.

Divided into two "blocks of study," the first block of the course explored the international and NZ assessment policy context, examined the concept of self-regulation and its importance to AfL, and considered the notions assessment for teaching and assessment for learning. This block culminated in three short pieces of writing about the nature of each of these concepts/notions. The second block considered the unitary nature of AfL, exploring, in some depth, the strategies that comprise AfL including an analysis of the respective and complementary roles of the teacher and learner. This block concluded with an extended essay where course members analyzed and discussed the unitary nature of AfL with particular reference to how AfL can develop student self-regulation. Within this essay, teachers were also asked to reflect on personal areas of learning. Teachers were required to submit this essay 3 weeks after the conclusion of the course, giving sufficient time for considered, critical reflection.

Developed and refined over time, the assessment course reflected two complementary approaches. The first was a relatively traditional approach, albeit providing multiple opportunities for active and interactive learning. In preparation for a class, students were expected to read selected articles. Each article was accompanied by a prompt sheet in order to focus teachers' attention on key ideas within an article, and hence scaffold learning. Essentially, prompt sheets contained key questions related to important content, for example, key concepts, research findings, authors' arguments, or conclusions. It was expected that teachers would formulate written responses to the key questions and bring these to class for further discussion. Each 150-min session included a range of activities such as sharing responses to key readings, group brainstorming and reporting back of key ideas underlying a central concept; in-class jig-sawing of brief extracts from the literature; brief quizzes; and short PowerPoint presentations and/or summaries of central ideas. In the second approach, the strategies of AfL were deliberately infused into all class sessions where the lecturer [Eleanor] assumed the mantle of the AfL teacher, working alongside learners as she facilitated teacher–learner and learner–learner dialogic interactions. Moreover, the rationale underpinning specific strategies was explained during related class activities. In using these two approaches, our deliberate intention was for the teachers to experience AfL as learners, while concurrently learning about AfL.

The first two to three sessions of each block of study included an overview and short informal conversation about the goal or "broad horizon" (Marshall 2004) that the class was working toward. From week 2 to 6, annotated exemplars of short pieces of writing about the three central concepts, completed by teachers in previous years, were read and analyzed during class with course members subsequently debating and identifying what constituted quality work. Course members also brought their assignment-related works-in-progress to class, as time was set aside in each session to develop their evaluative knowledge and productive expertise (Sadler 1989) through in-class peer response and/or comparison of works to exemplars. During these activities, teachers were encouraged to identify and discuss instances where they engaged in self-monitoring and/or self-regulation. Understandings about AfL gained from these experiences were shared, as they arose, during small group and class deliberations. This process was repeated from week 8 to 12 with reference to the extended essay.

As already mentioned, as part of in-class activities, teachers were asked to engage in various brainstorms and to continually reflect on what they were doing and learning. To facilitate this reflection, all class members completed a brainstorm activity during the first class session where they reflected on five prompts and recorded their ideas:

- Assessment for learning is ….
- Who benefits and how
- The role of the teacher…
- The role of the student …
- Describe how AfL is reflected in your/a classroom or center program.

This activity provided a permanent record of teachers' initial understandings and, when repeated again during week 12, served as a point of comparison that teachers could utilize as they reflected on changes to their thinking and or beliefs. An opportunity to discuss changes to thinking, with peers, was also provided during this time to support teacher reflection. Finally, to draw their reflections together, teachers recorded their ideas under a series of headings as follows:

- After comparing my two sets of responses my initial reaction is ….
- Identify the responses that have changed most, HOW they have changed and WHY they have changed.
- What is the MOST significant thing that you as a learner have learned about AfL and WHAT has prompted this learning?
- Outline briefly WHAT classroom/center practices you have changed as a result of your learning in this course and explain HOW they have changed.

As part of the research project, copies of data generated by these activities were collected to retain a permanent record of teachers' thinking. In addition, individual interviews with 14 of the 21 teachers were carried out during weeks 10–12 and in the 2 weeks following the end of the course. Given our aim to support teacher learning about AfL, we wanted to tap into teachers' reactions to the course and how it was structured. Specifically, questions tapped into how course experiences had contributed to teachers' knowledge and understanding of AfL strategies, and the perceived usefulness of these experiences to teachers' own learning and to their professional practice. To ensure teachers felt comfortable to give honest and open responses to these questions, an independent, experienced interviewer with no direct involvement in the course conducted the interviews. During the time when the project took place (2013–2014), Eleanor was the sole lecturer in the course.

Teacher Professional Learning: An Expansion of Teachers' Content and Pedagogical Content Knowledge

Learning About the Roles and Responsibilities of Teachers and Students

At the start of the course, teachers conceived AfL as an assessment event that helped them plan programs. Primarily, AfL was seen as involving teachers in eliciting information from students through specific assessment tasks, the interpretation of this information, and then taking action in terms of planning and teaching. Consistent mention was made by teachers of "using data from a range of assessment activities" (T3).[2] Mostly, AfL was interpreted as an event that involved the use of an instrument or activity to elicit information regarding the current state of students' learning or achievement. The formal and planned use of a range of assessment tools such as "standardised tests" (T3), "PAT [progressive achievement tests] ... reading comprehension [tests]" (T4), and teacher devised "pre-tests" (T5), were ways in which such information was gathered. Informal opportunities such as "in-class activities, e.g., question cards" (T1) and student "[work] samples" (T5) were also noted as ways in which teachers collected data.

While all teachers recognized AfL was concerned with students' learning, emphasis was placed on the teacher's role. Teachers' use of assessment information to inform program planning and teaching was seen as the way in which learning was supported and furthered. As a result, teachers identified themselves as the primary beneficiaries of AfL, as "from the data we [teachers] can get clear indications of what the children know and what their next steps will be" (T5). This in turn meant teachers were in a position to more effectively "direct ... and differentiate ... teaching" (T1), with a view to "improv[ing] achievement outcomes" (T18). Overall, students were regarded as recipients of information—a key role of the teacher was to tell students about their strengths and weaknesses and their progress. In short, sharing informa-

---

[2]The pseudonym used for each teacher, for example T1, T2, T3 etc.

tion with students enabled them to know "where they are at, where to go next, and how to get there" (T2). Essentially, the teacher was seen as playing a mediating role between the assessment information and the students.

In contrast, after completing the course, teachers depicted AfL as an everyday practice with "students, teachers and peers seeking, reflecting upon and responding to information from discussion and interactions in order to achieve goals" (T7). The role of the teacher had changed from administering assessment tasks to "sitting beside learners" (T15) or "walking alongside" (T18) students, taking a close interest in what they say, do, and write. Teachers acknowledged that they needed to be in a position to "notice, recognize and respond to critical thinking, behaviours and actions" (T8) "in the moment," as they happened. Students were characterized as "insiders [who] take responsibility for their learning" (T10). As a result, a more expansive role for students was articulated—one where students were expected to "monitor [their] learning, … work towards goals, … ask questions, … listen to feedback, … refer to exemplars and compare where they are at, to where they are going" (T7). Engagement in these activities helped students "to self-monitor and regulate their … learning" (T4). Nurturing and encouraging a "genuine learning partnership" (T2) between teachers and learners was seen as an important element of AfL. Significantly, if this partnership was to be effective, the classroom had to be "a safe place where risk taking is encouraged" (T2) and where "students have time to explore their ideas and mistakes" (T10). In essence, teachers in the study indicated that if AfL was to work, class teachers needed to build a climate of trust and mutual respect so students could take greater responsibility for their learning.

Learning About the Unitary Nature of AfL to Support Learning

Initially, all but two of the teachers equated AfL with learning goals or intentions and success criteria. These two strategies were considered the hallmarks of an AfL classroom, with no mention made of other strategies. Teachers thought learning intentions (LI) and success criteria (SC) were important as they helped them to be "clear about what is taught" (T2) and also enabled students to "articulate what they are learning and why and what they need to do to be successful" (T14). In saying this, teachers recognized the need for students to know "where they are going" so they could focus on the task at hand and become successful learners. To this end, teachers believed they had a responsibility to "specify in student friendly terminology what the learning intentions are … how to meet the learning intention … share learning expectations" (T12).

At course completion, teachers expressed a broader and more complex view of AfL. It was no longer associated solely with LI and SC. Rather, it was seen as a complex collection of inter-related and inter-dependent strategies that work together to support and further learning. In addition to promoting student understanding about the goal(s) of learning and what constitutes expected understanding/performance, teachers made specific reference to the generation of feedback related to current and desired understanding/performance. Student engagement in peer feedback and self-monitoring and the taking of action to bring about desired understanding/performance were also mentioned throughout teachers' responses, either singly or in combination. In the words of T2:

> I think the biggest impact for me is the unitary nature of AfL … you have to have everything otherwise it isn't assessment for learning… you have to have reflection … set some goals … the feedback needs to relate to those goals, there needs to be a really solid relationship with kids, learning focused relationship … give children more credit.

Learning Through Both Vicarious and Personal Experience

All teachers made reference to the fact that access to a range of scholarly articles and empirical studies helped them gain mastery over the body of knowledge associated with AfL. Together, teachers felt that group discussion of the readings resulted in a "dialogue … at the level that I really engaged with" (T2) and "a continual building … of knowledge" (T14), culminating in the attainment of an informed and "far more theoretical understanding" (T3) of AfL. Despite some initial trepidation, teachers soon became familiar with the language of AfL:

> The jargon, I [didn't] understand this. I felt really threatened … and then …. just talking about that [the reading] actually allows you to understand it and unpack it, and then come to a place where you know [you] … understand what [you are] talking about. (T15)

Scholarly articles "clarified … understanding" (T12) of the philosophical and theoretical underpinnings of AfL, thus expanding teachers' content knowledge. Readings focused on classroom-based studies were also seen as useful as these expanded teachers' pedagogical content knowledge. In addition, teachers made reference to the ways in which readings about classroom-based studies stimulated reflection on practice:

> [When reading] you're sitting there going tick, yes, I've done that, or oh my God, I've never thought of that before or I don't do it properly. So just bringing everything together … and understanding why they [teachers in the reading] do it. (T15)

Teachers valued these studies because of the models they presented. T13, for instance, talked about how "each week there's something that strikes me from … the readings which I can immediately implement and trial, experiment with and see the outcome of that."

Notably, as the course proceeded, teachers said they became aware they were "actually living how AfL should be" (T15). They recognized they had become participants in an AfL environment infused with "trust and respect" where the lecturer "modeled the role she plays as the teacher and we're … learners in terms of developing a classroom with AfL at its heart" (T14). Teachers talked about how they felt the essence and spirit of AfL through class teaching–learning activities and the pedagogical environment that Eleanor created:

> She [Eleanor] walks the talk … [there was] espoused theory and theory in use – her theory in use was what she believes, everything that she does in front of the AfL class drips her values, beliefs and assumptions about assessment for learning, so we were left in no doubt about what effective practice is. (T2)

From the perspectives of the teachers, reading about and experiencing AfL worked in tandem to help them master new knowledge, and deepen and strengthen understandings:

> So I think actually working through the AfL processes ourselves helped to bring that understanding… she practices what we're learning about really so the principles that we are learning about in class are what we are actually practicing in the course … I think it makes it easier to understand what you are actually learning about because it's part and parcel of what you are doing in each class … rather than just being all theory, that you actually knew what it was all about because you were participating [in it]. (T12)

As teachers read about theory informing strategies such as goal setting, the use of exemplars, peer review, and feedback, and the implementation of these in practice, they could see Eleanor deliberately and concurrently integrating these strategies into course sessions, talking about her pedagogical decisions at appropriate times. As a consequence, the teachers felt they knew "what we were doing and why we were doing [it]" (T2). Teachers made particular mention of Eleanor's use of exemplars and peer review of works-in-progress during the time they were working on their course assignments. They appreciated the opportunities to analyze a range of exemplars from previous years, and to share their works-in-progress with the intention of gaining peer feedback. That "everyone was sharing and you got time to discuss … and to analyze your thoughts with somebody else" (T5) was seen as a positive learning experience. T14's comments revealed she was beginning to see the effect of distributed cognition on her learning:

> We have an opportunity to talk with … a lot of collaborative work … so that the knowledge of a group of four is greater than individuals – so we are learning from our counterparts and that kind of discussion and that's another way that helped [my learning].

Teachers' direct encounters with the strategies of AfL were considered to have an impact in terms of their personal learning. A number spoke about how they had become more aware of the ways in which strategies such as peer review and dialogic feedback helped them regulate their thinking and behavior:

> As a direct result of both peer review and dialogic feedback I gained skills in several self-regulating strategies – engaging more deeply with my learning, asking questions, taking risks, monitoring my own learning, generating feedback and making adjustments to my work. (T15)

Others talked about how feedback, in the form of reflective questions during group activities and discussion, triggered further engagement with ideas:

> Eleanor walked the talk … we were allowed to co-construct, we were allowed to talk, we did lots of talking, we were never spoken over the top of … she got around the groups …continual clarification … the best feedback I got were reflective questions that then prompted my own thinking. (T2)

Experiencing AfL precipitated teachers' reflection on their own practice. In some cases, aspects of practice were confirmed, in other cases a reading, lecturer modeling, and/or participation in an activity underscored areas for improvement. For example, T5 indicated "modeling … highlighted for me parts of my program I probably don't do well enough … so my next step with [students is] … reflective questions and getting them to discuss the learning." Another explained, I could "hear [my] own voice … going 'ok, I used to do that, don't do it, you can do better'" (T16). For others, experiences prompted reflection on "[how] you would structure a classroom so that learners were giving feedback to other people" (T14), and provoked the realization that "in the classroom [the teacher isn't] the only 'go to' person because your peers then become your 'go to' people" (T15).

In addition, T17 talked about how, during a class session, "reflecting on which elements of AfL were evident in my own classroom practice" provided critical insights. Reflection on these elements drew attention to the impact of course experiences on this teacher's ability to monitor what and how she was learning, and how this in turn was shaping her teaching practice:

> As a learner, I was monitoring what I was learning and was able to make some adjustments to my classroom practice that reflected my new understanding about the use of LI and SC and where they fit in as part of AfL. I now have more discussion with my students at the beginning of a unit about the broad goals and their suggestions about how we could go about attaining them, together – proved valuable as they were able to take more responsibility at the outset.

Teacher Professional Learning: Becoming More Efficacious About AfL

T16 explained how "living … the idea of [AfL], has made a huge difference because I understand the impact of it [on my own learning]." Notably, not only could teachers see the value of particular activities on their own learning, they could also see the value to their students. As T15 explained:

> I can see the value of [peer review and feedback for me] … but I can see that it would be the same with kids.

A similar sentiment was expressed by T6, in relation to the potential of exemplars to support student understanding of the goals of learning and expected standards of performance:

> Another tool I can use … exemplars, as a scaffold … something to try … I was using it this morning] with [my] class … I can see the value in it … [because Eleanor had] just put us through it. (T6)

For these teachers, "living how AfL should be" (T15), and reflecting on the value of these experiences, drew attention to activities that could be applied in their classroom and the value of these activities to their students. Recognizing the potential value of such activities became a source of motivation for teachers to implement AfL in its intended form. Teachers who were teaching full time spoke about how they were already 'tweaking' aspects of practice, while those on study leave[3] talked about how excited they were to be returning to the classroom when they would have an opportunity to put their new content and pedagogical content knowledge of AfL into practice. T7, for example, felt a responsibility to "get it right ... because I feel I have been doing [the students] a dis-service—I [can] not wait to get back to [the] classroom ... to implement AfL." Alongside this excitement was a recognition that implementation would be "the biggest challenge ... making sure all those components [of AfL] are part of your classroom."

Experiencing AfL "increase[d] [the] desire" of T13 "to trial, experiment and take risks and give it a go and see what happens." However, teachers were aware of the magnitude of the task and they acknowledged implementation was demanding and daunting:

> I am really nervous, a big step. (T1)

> AfL, realistically I think a lot of teachers would struggle with it ... it's quite hard to build that idea of creating self-regulating [learners] ... taking some risks and trying the strategies [of AfL] will need some thinking through. (T17)

Despite some trepidation and recognition of the complexities ahead, the end goal of implementation made it all worthwhile because "you're engaged and it has value" (T8). T16 explained further:

> I [have now] thought about this ... for a long time ... the more I practiced and developed the skills of AfL within myself being in the role of the learner, I concluded why would anyone settle for anything less.

As a result of their experiences, teachers felt "empowered and excited about the potential" (T15) of AfL to assist their students in becoming self-regulated learners—it had worked for them as learners, and they could see how its benefits in terms of learning and how it could work in their classrooms, with their students:

> I can see the benefits of getting kids to be self-regulating learners ... to inspire that love of learning – see themselves as a learner and want to be able to monitor themselves. (T5)

> [AfL] is creating life-long learners, this is giving kids autonomy to drive their own learning in the future…[it can have a big] impact on kid's learning. (T15)

---

[3]In NZ, there is a contestable fund available which teachers can apply for to enable them to get paid study leave to complete a tertiary qualification. If successful, teachers can be released from their teaching duties for up to 32 weeks of a school year. A small number of teachers in the project were on paid study leave to complete their degree.

Teacher Educators: Our Learning About Teacher Learning

Through capturing the voices of our teachers, we would argue that their engagement in an assessment course that was by nature experiential and collaborative was an effective and powerful professional learning experience. It fulfilled a professional learning brief by providing participants with multiple opportunities to absorb new information, expanding their content and pedagogical content knowledge. In turn, these expanded knowledge bases helped teachers identify ways in which they could assist their students to become more effective learners, which, as Timperley (2011) has argued, is a desired outcome of teacher professional learning. Teachers also told us that being actively engaged during the course challenged their existing beliefs about what practices are important in the enhancement of learning. Experiencing AfL from a learner's perspective, as well as observing the course lecturer who had taken on the role of an AfL teacher, was catalysts that activated teachers' examination of their beliefs about the roles and responsibilities of teachers and learners in learning and assessment and the apparent validity of these beliefs. Although not an end in itself, at course completion, teachers enunciated a more complete, comprehensive, and complex understanding of AfL than previously articulated. This understanding we consider critical if teachers are going to develop assessment-capable students within the context of classroom learning and assessment.

As teacher educators, we firmly believe that self-efficacy (Bandura 1977) plays a significant role in teachers' adoption of new practices or new ways of working. In regard to the current project, we are confident that, together, Bandura's two components of self-efficacy (an efficacy and outcome expectation) provided teachers with the motivation and commitment to engage in changes such as those required to implement AfL in the spirit of its intent. It would appear teachers' positive, yet challenging, coursework experiences highlighted for them the beneficial effects of particular AfL strategies in regard to the enhancement of *their* learning. Teachers ostensibly valued their engagement over time in authentic and substantial learning opportunities, which expanded their knowledge bases. In turn, an expansion of content and pedagogical content knowledge developed teachers' willingness to support student assessment capability. The underlying message conveyed by the teachers in this project was that the benefits accruing to them as learners became a strong motivational force to make changes to the ways in which they had previously worked with their students. For a number of teachers, a growing consciousness of the effects of particular AfL strategies on their personal learning became a spur to action.

We realize that more comprehensive knowledge of AfL has the potential to be disconcerting for teachers as they gain a fuller sense of the magnitude of the task of utilizing a range of inter-dependent strategies, which support active learning and learner self-regulation. However, what we learned in the current project was that although teachers acknowledged their novice status and as a result showed some trepidation in regard to the task ahead of them, this was tempered by a sense of excitement and enthusiasm. Awareness of the magnitude of the task was counterbalanced by teachers' beliefs regarding the positive impact of specific strategies on learning. While the teachers realistically voiced some self-doubt (Bandura 1977), this was moderated by a strong sense of optimism in regard to what new ways of working could achieve. As a result, the teachers revealed strong aspirations to accept the challenge of taking on the role of the AfL teacher.

Within the broader context of teacher learning, Loughran (2004) has argued teachers' professional practice can be enhanced through the observation of credible role models who exemplify "best" practice. Seemingly, teachers in the current project supported this contention. The vicarious experience of observing Eleanor in the role of the AfL teacher was influential in relation to their learning and their aspirations of becoming an effective AfL teacher. As such, Eleanor's championing and demonstration of specific AfL strategies and approaches were given credence because she was seen as a credible and trustworthy role model. Teachers considered her passionate, committed, confident, and competent, which in turn evoked in them similar emotions. Given her perceived status as "an exemplary practitioner,"[4] teachers paid attention to noteworthy facets of her practice such as working alongside learners and encouraging active participation through the creation of dialogic opportunities within a respectful and trusting environment. Such was Eleanor's impact, teachers sought to emulate observed practice. In essence, effective modeling of the AfL teacher's role combined with Eleanor's ability to make "her pedagogical reasoning for practice clear, explicit and understandable" (Korthagen et al. 2006, p. 1036) provided teachers with a compelling argument for change as well as a concomitant vision for AfL practice.

A Final Note and Looking to the Future

From our perspective, the two complementary approaches utilized to deliver the course helped us to fulfill the aim of contributing to teachers' assessment literacy and capability. Teachers in the project acknowledged the usefulness of the conventional aspects of the course to their learning. Readings along with various in-class activities seemed to be particularly useful in regard to the development of teachers' content and pedagogical content knowledge. However, in the main, we attribute teachers' openness to new ideas and willingness to experiment with particular AfL strategies to the experiential approach used within the course. Experiential learning has been described as learning through reflection on doing (Kolb 1984) and is considered a potent way in which new knowledge, understandings, and attitudes can be created (Boud 1994). By listening to the teachers' voices, we came to realize that they ascribed considerable value to the opportunities created for them to learn by "doing and reflecting on that doing." We feel that together, these two components

---

[4] In 2015, Eleanor was the recipient of a national Sustained Excellence in Teaching Award from the Ako Aotearoa Academy of Tertiary Teaching. This award recognized Eleanor's ability to facilitate high levels of student engagement, and ownership of learning, as well as her ability to create a pedagogical environment that builds confidence and trust.

had a significant impact in relation to deepening teachers' knowledge bases as well as uncovering and challenging their beliefs. We would argue the provision of meaningful and substantive learning experiences that mirrored those expected of students in classrooms supported both teacher reflection-in-action and reflection-on-action (Schon 1983). Teachers valued the opportunity to analyze their reactions to, and feelings about their engagement in activities such as peer review and the self-monitoring of performance. On further reflection, teachers were able to take cognizance of the consequences of their actions, at the same time gaining new perspectives on both students' and teachers' roles in AfL. As a result, we believe teachers lived experiences provided them with a convincing case for change along with a vision for future possibilities—hence, our advocacy of an experiential approach to foster and facilitate teacher learning about AfL, and, in turn, what it means to be self-regulatory and thus assessment capable.

References

Bandura, A. (1977). Self-efficacy: Toward a unifying theory of behavioral change. *Psychological Review, 84*(2), 191–215. https://doi.org/10.1037/0033-295X.84.2.191.

Bandura, A. (1981). Self-referent thought: A developmental analysis of self-efficacy. In J. Flavell & L. Ross (Eds.), *Social cognitive development: Frontiers and possible futures* (pp. 200–239). New York: Cambridge University Press.

Black, P. (2015). Formative assessment: An optimistic but incomplete vision. *Assessment in Education: Principles, Policy and Practice, 22*(1), 161–177. http://dx.doi.org/10.1080/0969594X.2014.999643.

Booth, B., Dixon, H., & Hill, M. F. (2016). Assessment capability for New Zealand teachers and students: Challenging but possible. *SET Research Information for Teachers, 2,* 28–35.

Boud, D. (1994). Conceptualising learning from experience: Developing a model for facilitation. In M. Hyams, J, Armstrong, & E. Anderson (Eds.), *35th Adult Education Research Conference Proceedings* (pp. 49–54). Knoxville: College of Education, University of Tennessee.

Cowie, B., Moreland, J., & Otrel-Cass, K. (2013). *Expanding notions of assessment for learning: Inside science and technology primary classrooms*. Rotterdam: Sense Publishers.

Dixon, H. (2011). The influence of teachers' efficacy beliefs on their uptake and implementation of new ideas and practices. *Assessment Matters, 3,* 71–92.

Dixon, H., Hawe, E., & Parr, J. (2011). Enacting assessment for learning: The beliefs/practice nexus. *Assessment in Education, Principles, Policy and Practice, 18*(4), 365–379. https://doi.org/10.1080/0969594X.2010.526587.

Elliott, J. (1998). *The curriculum experiment: Meeting the challenge of social change*. Buckingham: Open University Press.

Gamlem, S. V., & Smith, K. (2013). Student perceptions of classroom feedback. *Assessment in Education: Principles, Policy & Practice, 20*(2), 150–169. http://dx.doi.org/10.1080/0969594X.2012.749212.

Hawe, E., & Dixon, H. (2014). Building students' evaluative and productive expertise in the writing classroom. *Assessing Writing, 19,* 66–79. https://doi.org/10.1016/j.asw.2013.11.004.

Hayward, L. (2015). Assessment is learning: The preposition vanishes. *Assessment in Education: Principles, Policy and Practice, 22*(1), 27–43. https://doi.org/10.1080/0969594X.2014.984656.

Hopfenbeck, T. N., Florez Petour, M. T., & Tolo, A. (2015). Balancing tensions in educational policy reforms: Large-scale implementation of assessment for learning in Norway. *Assessment in Education: Principles, Policy and Practice, 22*(1), 40–66. https://doi.org/10.1080/0969594X.2014.996524.

Kolb, D. A. (1984). *Experiential learning: Experience as the source of learning and development.* Englewood Cliffs, NJ: Prentice Hall.

Korthagen, F., Loughran, J., & Russell, T. (2006). Developing fundamental principles for teacher education programs and practices. *Teaching and Teacher Education, 22,* 1020–1041. https://doi.org/10.1016/j.tate.2006.04.022.

Loughran, J. (2004). *International handbook of self-study of teaching and teacher education practices.* Boston: Kluwer Academic.

Marshall, B. (2004). Goals or horizons—the conundrum of progression in English: Or a possible way of understanding formative assessment in English. *The Curriculum Journal, 15*(2), 101–113. https://doi.org/10.1080/0958517042000226784.

Ministry of Education. (2011). *Position paper: Assessment [Schooling sector].* Wellington: Learning Media.

Sadler, D. R. (1989). Formative assessment and the design of instructional systems. *Instructional Science, 18*(2), 119–144.

Schon, D. (1983). *The reflective practitioner: How professionals think in action.* New York: Basic Books.

Swaffield, S. (2011). Getting to the heart of authentic assessment for learning. *Assessment in Education: Principles, Policy and Practice, 18*(4), 433–449. http://dx.doi.org/10.1080/0969594X.2011.582838.

Tierney, R. (2006). Changing practices: Influences on classroom assessment. *Assessment in Education: Principles, Policy and Practice, 13*(3), 239–264. https://doi.org/10.1080/09695940601035387.

Timperley, H. S. (2011). Knowledge and the leadership of learning. *Leadership and Policy in Schools, 10*(2), 145–170. https://doi.org/10.1080/15700763.2011.557519.

Yung, B. H. (2001). Examiner, policeman or students' companion: Teachers' perceptions of their role in an assessment reform. *Educational Review, 53*(3), 251–260. https://doi.org/10.1080/00131910120085856.

Yung, B. H. (2002). Same assessment, different practice: Professional consciousness as a determinant of teachers' practice in a school based assessment scheme. *Assessment in Education: Principles, Policy and Practice, 9*(1), 97–117. http://dx.doi.org/10.1080/09695940220119210.

Chapter 5
Teachers' Understanding, Implementing and Reflecting upon Classroom Assessment in Primary and Junior High Schools of China

Decheng Zhao, Bo Yan, Liwei Tang and Yao Zhou

Abstract Good teachers should not only be experts in teaching, but also develop a deep understanding of classroom assessment. In order to explore how primary and junior high school teachers in China understand, implement, and reflect upon classroom assessment, as well as to discover the strengths and weaknesses in teachers' professional development, interviews were conducted with 18 teachers from primary and junior high schools in urban areas, counties, and rural areas of Beijing. Nonparticipatory observations of their classes were also conducted. The findings suggest that since the implementation of the New Curriculum in 2001, there has been a positive change in teachers' understanding and practice of classroom assessment. Teachers have accepted and taken the initiative in putting into effect the concept of developmental assessment, emphasizing the developmental function of classroom assessment. However, there are still some issues requiring urgent attention, such as: teachers don't reflect sufficiently on their assessment practice and lack the knowledge concerning meta-assessment; although teachers place high value on summative assessment, few of them provide in-class tests or feedback for students; teachers haven't mastered the necessary skills of assessment, not knowing how to assess students' pluralistic development accurately and effectively. Therefore, in the future, primary and junior high schools need to strengthen teacher-training projects and improve teaching and research activities so as to effectively improve teachers' evaluative qualities and professional development.

Keywords Classroom assessment · Chinese teachers · Teacher professional development · Teaching to the evaluation

D. Zhao (✉) · B. Yan · Y. Zhou
Faculty of Education, Beijing Normal University, Beijing, China
e-mail: zhaodecheng@bnu.edu.cn

L. Tang
Education Science College, Inner Mongolia Normal University, Hohhot, China

© Springer Nature Singapore Pte Ltd. 2018
H. Jiang and M. F. Hill (eds.), *Teacher Learning with Classroom Assessment*,
https://doi.org/10.1007/978-981-10-9053-0_5

Introduction

Classroom assessment is a dynamic analytical process, conducted by teachers during teaching, regarding a student's learning performance (Popham 2008; Davis and Neitzel 2011; Zhao et al. 2016). Only through constant monitoring and assessment can teachers analyze students' learning progress, diagnose the extent to which students have achieved the expected objectives, and therefore make their instruction better targeted, more appealing, and more effective in promoting student development. In this sense, even though teachers are very experienced, it will be very difficult for them to become true expert teachers should they not know how to assess accurately and effectively. Teachers should be experts both in teaching and classroom assessment (Zhao 2016b). In the model of teacher abilities raised by the International Board of Standards for Training, Performance and Instruction (IBSTPI), together with professional foundations, planning and preparation, instructional methods and strategies, and management, assessment and evaluation are considered essential professional abilities for teachers (Klein et al. 2004).

In China, the Ministry of Education (MOE) has launched basic education curriculum reform in 38 national pilot areas since 2001. Since 2005, the reform has been implemented nationwide. It is a comprehensive curriculum reform, attempting to construct a new basic education curriculum system in line with quality-oriented education requirements through reforming the curriculum's function, structure, content, and implementation methods (MOE 2001). Specifically, in regard to assessment, teachers in primary and junior high schools need to minimize screening and deepen the developmental function of assessment, realizing assessment's role in improving students' development and teachers' teaching. The core requirements are as follows (Dong and Zhao 2003; Zhao and Xu 2002): (1) change the practice of attaching too much importance to screening and ranking students, giving full play to the function of developmental assessment to facilitate teaching and learning; (2) diversify assessment content by emphasizing and evaluating other skills and qualities other than "knowledge and skills," especially critical thinking, creative, cooperative, and practical abilities; (3) stress students' roles in the assessment process, change the one-way assessment done by teachers, and make classroom assessment an interactive collaboration between teachers, students, and their parents; (4) rectify the practice of taking grading and examinations as the only means of assessment, and actively explore new assessment methods including performance assessment and portfolio assessment, ensuring the effectiveness and reliability of assessment; (5) focus not only on results but also more on the process of development and changes, combining summative and formative assessment.

The New Curriculum calls for new classroom assessment. The new assessment concepts have posed new challenges to teachers in primary and junior high schools. Will these teachers be able to meet the challenges? How do they understand, implement, and reflect upon classroom assessment? After a 15-year implementation of the curriculum reform, conducting research on this issue can evaluate not only the progress of the curriculum reform in China but also the growth of teachers in their teaching. Also, the research analyzes the strength and weakness of teachers' understanding and implementation of classroom assessment, which will help provide decision-making bases for better facilitating teachers' professional development.

Theoretical Framework

Effective assessment needs systematic design. Based on Stufflebeam (1974), the following questions provide systematic design: (1) What is the assessment? (2) What is the aim of the assessment? (3) What is the focus of the assessment? (4) What information does the assessment require? (5) Whom does the assessment serve? (6) Who should be involved in the assessment? (7) How should the assessment be implemented? (8) By what criteria should the assessment be judged? When designing classroom assessment, teachers need to consider and answer the questions above. Clear-cut and appropriate answers to these questions naturally form a high-quality assessment design. The assessment design procedures advanced by Linn and Gronlund (2003), Wiggins (2005), and others, are also intended to answer these questions, which are basically consistent with the opinion above.

In practice, classroom assessment occurs in every step of teaching, and teaching is inseparable from testing and assessment. Based on the point-in-time and function of the assessment, Bloom (1971) divided assessment in teaching into formative assessment and summative assessment, and later on added diagnostic assessment (Bloom et al. 1981). This assessment classification has been widely accepted and used, especially formative assessment and summative assessment. Many researchers (such as Black 2013; Randel et al. 2016; Simpson-Beck 2011) have discussed classroom assessment under this framework.

Diagnostic assessment is conducted before a teaching activity to ascertain the student's prior knowledge, current situation, strengths, weaknesses, and reasons for the above. For specific teaching activities, when designing the instruction for a unit, or even for class, teachers need to value diagnostic assessment to properly analyze a student's academic situation. Diagnostic assessment is an integral and indispensable part of teaching. The famed psychologist Ausubel (1968) wrote in the preface of his text on educational psychology: "If I had to reduce all of the educational psychology to just one principle, I would say this: The most important single factor influencing learning is what the learner already knows. Ascertain this and teach him (sic) accordingly" (p. 18). Diagnostic assessments reveal a student's needs and experience, and it is only through that revelation that we can ensure teaching is well-targeted, appealing, and effective (Zhao 2016b).

Formative assessment, also known as process assessment, refers to a range of assessments conducted by the teacher during the teaching process to judge students' learning progress and needs. These assessments are immediate and occur dynamically throughout the teaching process, aimed at discovering problems in the teaching process and providing timely feedback, adjustments, and solutions to pursue the optimal efficiency and effect. Formative assessment focuses on the process, serving as a critical measure that can modify teaching as well as improve students' development (Black and Wiliam 2010). Bangert-Drowns et al. (1991) conducted a meta-analysis on 29 related quasi-experimental studies and found that whether or not classroom tests had been conducted had a substantial impact on students' academic achievements. The frequency of formative classroom tests was found to be significantly associated with the level of improvement in students' performance. The more formative tests were done in a semester, the more students achieved academically. Hausknecht et al. (2007) conducted a meta-analysis on 107 related quasi-experimental studies and found similar results. Effective formative tests can promote the fulfillment of teaching objectives and an increase of teaching efficiency.

Summative assessment evaluates students' learning after a teaching project or program is finished. It focuses on the final outcome and is ex post facto testing; therefore, the results are compared with the objectives outlined before the instruction. Once the instruction for class, a unit, or a semester is finished, the teacher will assess the extent to which students have achieved teaching objectives. The differences between summative and formative assessments are relative. A test taken at the end of a unit is considered as summative assessment for the unit, while this test is formative assessment when the context of the entire semester is taken into account. In this article, we take one period of class as a unit of analysis and explore how teachers implemented classroom assessment. Hence, summative assessment is operationally defined as the assessment conducted at the end of class to assess students' performance. Formative assessment, therefore, refers to the assessment done during the teaching process for class, and diagnostic assessment is the assessment conducted before the instruction for class.

In China, developmental assessment is another frequently mentioned concept. It is close to formative assessment in meaning, but the two are different. In the past, for a long period, teachers usually regarded assessment as a means to screen and rank students, connecting the result with reward or punishment, but they ignored the function of assessment to facilitate teaching and learning. With the deepening of the New Curriculum in China, people began to replace traditional assessment with developmental assessment, and highlight the developmental functions of assessment to improve teachers' teaching and students' learning. Hence, developmental assessment mainly refers to formative assessment and diagnostic assessment, but summative assessment can also be developmental sometimes.

About the above concept models combined with China's current educational practices, this research focuses on the following questions:

Research Question 1: How do teachers in primary and junior high schools understand classroom assessment? What do they consider to be good classroom assessment?

Research Question 2: How do teachers in primary and junior high schools implement classroom assessment? Do they carry out the idea of developmental assessment in their teaching? How do they implement diagnostic, formative, and summative assessments? Do they integrate assessment well into teaching?

Research Question 3: How do teachers in primary and junior high schools reflect upon classroom assessment? How have teachers improved and what still confuses them about their practices of classroom assessment?

Method

We collected data in the real context of schools and classrooms through interviews and observations. An inductive method was then used to construct coding analysis and form interpretative understanding.

Interviews

Participants

One primary and one junior high school in each of the three types of areas in Beijing: urban, county, and rural, were selected. In each junior high school, one 8th grade Chinese teacher, one math teacher, and one foreign language teacher were chosen. In each primary school, one 5th grade Chinese teacher, one math teacher, and one foreign language teacher were chosen. Thus, in total there were 18 teachers: two male teachers and 16 female teachers. They are experienced teachers with intermediate academic titles. To protect the participants' privacy, their identities were based upon their location (urban, county, or rural), school type (junior high school or primary school), and teaching subject (Chinese, mathematics, or English). For example, if a teacher was labeled as "Urb_J_C," "Urb" represented the city; "J" represented junior high school; and "C" represented Chinese. Hence, she/he was a teacher of Chinese in junior high school in the city.

Instrument

The following interview questions were asked of each participant: (1) How do you understand classroom assessment? (2) What do you consider to be good classroom assessment? How do you ensure assessment improves teaching and learning effectively? (3) How do you and your colleagues implement classroom assessment in your teaching? (4) Looking back at your work experience in recent years, what are your progress and reflections regarding classroom assessment?

Data Collection

Two researchers worked as a team, conducting separate interviews with all 18 participants. Each interview lasted 30–45 min. To ensure the integrity of the data, a follow-up interview by telephone was conducted with some interviewed teachers. The interviews were recorded with the permission of the interviewees. After the interviews, the two researchers worked together and analyzed the data.

Observations

Subjects

The same as those in the interviews.

Instrument

During classroom observations, researchers mainly focused on the following aspects: whether or not the teachers conducted classroom assessment; how the teachers organized and implemented diagnostic, formative, and summative assessments; whether or not the teachers integrated the assessments well into their teaching. Figure 5.1 is the classroom observation form.

Data Collection

Two researchers working as a group observed one normal lesson, under the circumstances of the teachers being notified one day in advance. No recording or video was taken to relieve some of the stress placed on the teachers. The researchers filled out the observation form while they watched the lesson, and then collected relevant materials such as the students' learning plan, the teacher's lesson plan, the in-class quiz, and after-class work for analysis.

Overall Information					
Participant No.		Grade		Subject	
Teaching Content		Observer		Date	
Diagnostic Assessment					
No diagnostic assessment ☐ Performed diagnostic assessment ☐ If done, time of assessment: Before class ☐ During class ☐ Implementation method: Written ☐ Oral ☐ If written, feedback was given: To all the students ☐ To some students ☐ No feed-back☐					
Formative Assessment					
Numbers of questions asked: ( ) Numbers of evaluative questions: ( ) Numbers of paper-and-pencil tests: ( ) Duration of each test: ( ) minutes Numbers of cooperative tasks: ( ) Duration of each task: ( ) minutes					
Summative Assessment					
No summative assessment ☐ Performed summative assessment ☐ If done, time of assessment: In class ☐ After class ☐ If completed in class, feedback was given: On-class assessment and feedback ☐ Partial on-class assessment and feedback ☐ No on-class assessment and feedback ☐					
Other					

Fig. 5.1 Classroom observation form

Main Findings

The Teachers' Understanding of Classroom Assessment

The Teachers Were Aware of the Significance of Classroom Assessment in Teaching, but Some Still Had an Unclear Understanding of the Concept of Classroom Assessment

During the interviews, when the teachers were asked about what they knew and how they perceived classroom assessment, many talked about the function of the assessments and emphasized their significance, pointing out classroom assessment has a wide range of functions and meanings for teaching. The researchers divided the functions of classroom assessment into seven categories: navigation, monitoring, diagnosis, supervision, motivation, feedback, and improvement. The two researchers coded the interviewees' responses respectively and then discussed inconsistencies found in their coding together. The results were shown in Table 5.1.

Table 5.1 Teachers' understanding of the functions of classroom assessment

Function	Connotation	Teachers	Frequency
Navigation	Guiding students about what to learn and how to learn	9	25
Monitoring	Monitoring students' academic progress, evaluating the extent to which students have achieved the objectives	9	22
Diagnosis	Diagnosing students' strengths and weaknesses in their learning processes	14	29
Supervision	Urging students on to learn to achieve objectives and make progress	6	9
Motivation	Encouraging students to pursue progress constantly	13	30
Feedback	Allowing teachers to determine their teaching performance and students to know their learning performance	10	12
Improvement	Clarifying the direction and methods for teachers to improve	16	29

The analysis revealed that diagnosis (14, 29),[1] feedback (10, 12), motivation (13, 30), and improvement (16, 29) functions of classroom assessment were all mentioned by more than half of the interviewed teachers, and the cumulative frequencies were also relatively high. These results showed that teachers placed more emphasis on the developmental function of classroom assessment, and teachers thought that classroom assessment played a crucial role in improving their instruction. If a teacher wants to improve her/his quality of teaching, classroom assessment must be implemented. One junior high school teacher of English in the city (Urb_J_E) stated that classroom assessment has a diagnostic function: "I normally give a small test after the students learn something new. That way I can see exactly what they've learned, and this helps me understand what the students have grasped and what they have not." Another primary school teacher of Chinese in the city (Urb_P_C) stressed the motivation function of classroom assessment: "[When giving feedback], we always write something encouraging students at the end of the evaluation form, for example, he has made progress; what his classmates can learn from him; we hope that he will continue to the good work and do even better next time." More teachers emphasized the importance of the improvement function of classroom assessment, expressing that once they get all the information of the assessment, teachers could modify their instruction to be better targeted and more tailored to the individual needs of students. "At the end of each unit [teaching], we will give students a unit quiz, which summarizes the unit teaching, provides a reference for the teaching of next unit and helps clarify instructional intentions and determine the next lesson plan" (Urb_J_C). "Once I know what objectives a student has mastered and what he/she hasn't, I can

---

[1]The figures in parentheses indicate how many teachers mentioned a particular function, and how many times they mentioned it.

be aware of each student's performance. Once the parents are also aware, we both can provide the right instruction according to the student's aptitude" (Cou_J_C).

When asked to explain their own understanding of the concept of classroom assessment, most respondents used the sentence pattern "classroom assessment is…" to express their opinions. Below are some of the typical responses.

> The classroom assessment that I know of is school work and testing (Rur_P_E).

> In my opinion, classroom assessment means paying attention to students' grades and also their responses in class. You can tell what they're learning from their eyes and facial expressions. To me, this is also the classroom assessment (Cou_J_M).

> Classroom assessment is a very important motivational tool. Our 5th graders aren't as invigorated as when they were 1st or 2nd graders, so you must encourage them. Only then will they be confident, energetic and interactive in class (Cou_J_C).

> The assessment first means paying attention to a student's progress. It can also be frequent communications between colleagues. We all discuss after class who is doing well in class and what issues need to be stressed. This is also a crucial type of classroom assessment (Rur_J_C).

> Formal classroom assessment may be the exams. However, I personally feel that assessment doesn't necessarily have to be in a fixed form. It can be informal as well; for example, the teacher's language, behaviors or body language in the teaching process can either be encouraging or correcting students. Assessment can be spontaneous, not necessarily in the settled forms (Cou_J_E).

These typical responses showed that most of the teachers had a relatively broad understanding of classroom assessment, based on their own personal experiences. They discussed their personal viewpoints with their actual teaching, but very few could either clearly define classroom assessment from a professional point of view or clarify the essential characteristics of classroom assessment, which is to describe a student's progress and determine the level at which students have reached their goals. This lack of understanding had a certain amount of influence on the teacher's teaching and reflections.

Teachers Lacked Relevant Knowledge of Meta-Assessment and Did not Put Enough Thought into What Good Assessment Is

The assessment also needs to be evaluated. The evaluation of assessment can be called meta-assessment (Kevin and Scott 2016; Hicks 2016). To make good classroom assessment, teachers must not only focus on the conceptual importance of the assessment but also have the proper technical knowledge and skills about assessment; that is, they need to know what makes good assessment and how to evaluate the effectiveness of assessment. Knowledge of meta-assessment can help teachers explain the quality of classroom assessment and find an effective way to improve it. In the interviews, researchers asked the teacher participants "What do you consider to be good classroom assessment?" In reference to Standards for Educational and Psychological Testing compiled by the American Educational Research Association (AERA), the American Psychological Association (APA), and the National Council

Table 5.2 Teachers' understanding of meta-assessment

Indices	Connotation	Teachers	Frequency
Content validity	The extent to which test items suitably reflect the content or behavior domain they are supposed to represent	15	23
Criterion-related validity	The correlation between a predictor test and a predicted test. The degree to which a test accurately predicts a subject's subsequent status on another test on the basis of test scores	6	9
Construct validity	The extent to which a test measures a theoretical construct and characteristic accurately, i.e., Do the results support or explain a theoretical hypothesis, terminology or construct? How well do the results explain it?	0	0
Stability reliability	Under the same conditions, administering the identical test to the same group of subjects on two different testing occasions and computing a correlation coefficient between test scores on the two occasions	0	0
Alternate-form reliability	Administering two equivalent forms of the same test to the same group of subjects and computing a correlation coefficient between test scores on the two forms	0	0
Internal consistency reliability	A test's items are functioning in a homogeneous fashion. The extent to which the items of a test can measure the same content or characteristics	0	0
Rater consistency reliability	Score consistency displayed by different raters who grade the same test	0	0
Difficulty	Difficulty level of test items	9	9
Discrimination	The extent to which a test item can differentiate test takers' levels, i.e., differentiation for an item	8	14
Fairness	Being impartial and avoiding bias	2	2

on Measurement in Education (NCME), and to other researchers' opinions such as Popham (2008), researchers divided the meta-assessment concepts into 10 separate indices: content validity, criterion-related validity, construct validity, stability reliability, alternate-form reliability, internal consistency reliability, rater consistency reliability, difficulty, discrimination, and fairness. The two researchers respectively coded the interviewees' responses and then dealt with inconsistencies found in their coding together. The results are displayed in Table 5.2.

Further analysis found: (1) As a whole, teachers' understanding of meta-assessment was limited to their own experience; they lacked a systematic and deep understanding of meta-assessment. Some teachers admitted that "Our [school] has a test analysis system, but I never understand those [data reports]" (Cou_J_C).

(2) Within the ten commonly used meta-assessment indices, no teachers brought up construct validity, stability reliability, alternate-form reliability, internal consistency reliability, or rater consistency reliability.

(3) The index brought up most by teachers was content validity, with 15 interviewees mentioning it 23 times. Teachers understood that an exam must cover all the content they expected to test, and that test items must be able to represent the range of content to be measured. However, in regard to estimating the content validity of a test, it was rare for teachers to mention educational concepts like test blueprints, two-way detailed catalog, or representativeness of the item sample. Most of them based their judgments on their own experience. Cou_J_C said, "Determining whether content validity is good or not is based upon experience. We teachers usually choose test items for daily testing, and these items come from what the students have learned in class. The main purpose is to see if the students have learned what has been taught, so we combine examples from class and content that was previously learned. That's about it. Items for monthly or midterm exams are decided by a group of teachers and researchers. They are very experienced and have a firm grasp on the testing content; once the items are released, you can see that they did fairly well. Final exams are standardized by the district, and that group of teachers and researchers is even more experienced and professional" (Cou_J_M).

(4) About half of the teachers considered difficulty and discrimination as the basis for determining test quality. "Difficulty (of the test items) must be suitable. Otherwise it could be detrimental to students' positivity" (Rur_S_M). "Basically we approve of the test items given by the upper administration. Once we see the test we can tell that its difficulty and discrimination are suitable" (Rur_P_C).

(5) Teachers did not pay enough attention to fairness. Only two interviewees discussed the fairness issue. One primary school math teacher in rural Beijing (Rur_J_M) pointed out that "most of the test items require memorization, which is beneficial to female students but not to male students. We should make higher-level tests which can properly discern a student's complex thinking competencies." Another teacher of Chinese from a primary school in urban Beijing (Urb_P_C) also stated, "As a Chinese teacher in a primary school, I've discovered that most male students do not perform well at this stage in their education. However, once they are in junior high school, their grades will immediately improve which makes me think that the exams at this level are not properly assessing students' academic levels."

Teachers' Classroom Assessment Practices

Teachers' Self-reporting on Implementing the Newly Reformed Idea in Their Teaching

In the interviews, researchers asked the teachers how they implemented classroom assessment in their teaching, and they shared their experiences. Researchers found that the teachers accepted the idea of assessment reform that came along with the New Curriculum, and that they actively applied the new ideas in their teaching. The researchers divided the reformed assessment idea used by teachers into five different categories: (1) minimizing screening students, and giving more play to the developmental function of assessment; (2) diversifying assessment content; (3) diversifying assessment subjects; (4) actively exploring new assessment methods including performance assessment and portfolio assessment; and (5) combining formative and summative assessments. The two researchers then coded and analyzed the data, and the results are shown in Table 5.3.

Further analysis found: (1) In practice, teachers commonly focused on the developmental function of classroom assessment and used the assessment to improve their teaching. One primary school Chinese teacher in a county (Cou_P_C) compared the situation before and after the New Curriculum: "Before the curriculum reform, we paid more attention to grades and ranking, which was both tiresome and difficult for students and teachers. When I first started teaching, all of the students were ranked based on their grades. We worked from 6:30 in the morning and would not be leaving till 8:00 p.m. We were always giving more lessons even after school because we didn't want to have one student with a grade below 90. Now it's all different. We've minimized the ranking, and assessment is more diagnostic in nature as we let each student discover their own strengths and weaknesses. Each student has their own strong and weak areas, and every student has the chance to improve and be successful. Students are more relaxed, so are the teachers." An English teacher in a junior high school in urban Beijing (Urb_J_E) stated, "Our school is really emphasizing assessment research, and many of the teaching and research activities are about how

Table 5.3 Assessment reform idea used in teaching

	Teachers	Frequency
Minimizing screening students, and focusing more on diagnosis, motivation and development functions	17	27
Diversifying assessment content	12	17
Encouraging multi-subject participation in the assessment, with particular emphasis on students' self-assessment	6	8
Not only implementing traditional standardized tests, but also adopting new methods of assessment	12	12
Combining formative and summative assessments	14	18

to make the assessments. A good assessment can help discover students' problems in learning, analyze teachers' teaching efficiency, and improve teaching quality."

(2) Teachers attached importance to formative assessment and combined formative assessment with summative assessment. Fourteen teachers emphasized formative assessment in their interviews. "Our school places great importance on formative assessment. We have records of daily or weekly assessments that we do with students. We evaluate them on all different types of performances including attendance, classroom participation, and cooperation as well as communication. Through this way, we can detect what students are doing well and what they need to improve, and made adjustments accordingly in a timely way" (Urb_J_M). "We really emphasize encouraging our students in class. Once a student answers a question, we make sure to provide prompt assessment and feedback, most of which are motivational. This can help students feel a sense of accomplishment" (Urb_J_C).

(3) Teachers started to focus on involving students and their parents in assessment. Although only six teachers mentioned the emphasis on students' self-assessment and multi-subject participation, it can be inferred from all teachers' responses that teachers' assessment practices have something in common. For example, a Chinese teacher from an urban primary school mentioned in the interview that "our assessments not only include teacher participation but also abide by the Comprehensive Assessment Handbook given by the education committee. Students must perform their own self-reflection and self-assessment, and their parents will also assess their child's academic performance." Multi-subject participation in assessment has already become a uniform requirement of education committees. Some teachers valued peer assessment in their teaching: "Assessments in my class aren't always given by the teacher. Often times I won't say anything, and I'll just let the students assess amongst themselves. For example, they assess whether the recitation was good or if the subject was covered well. I let students make their own assessments" (Urb_P_C).

Most Teachers Integrated Assessment into Their Instruction; However, There Was Still Room for Improvement

In addition to interviews, the researchers also conducted a nonparticipatory observation of 18 different lessons. The observers found that most teachers emphasized classroom assessment. They also integrated it into their teaching. Specifics were as follows:

(1) Defining key and difficult points in teaching and teaching styles on the basis of the results found from diagnostic assessment.

Among the 18 teachers, 14 implemented diagnostic assessment. Two among those had the students complete the assessment before class; six had students first complete a paper-and-pencil test in class; six teachers conducted the assessment by means of oral questions and answers in class. Teacher Urb_J_M did a written diagnostic assessment. She mostly had the students work on quadratic equations. Once the bell announced the start of class, she had the students individually take a small test comprised of three questions. Students were required to solve three quadratic equations under fixed conditions. She kept patrolling to monitor students' process and progress in solving the equations. She then graded each question immediately after the student finished. After 5 min, she already had an idea of how much students were able to answer, how many students solved all three equations independently, and where the students were struggling. She then divided her class of 21 students into four groups, and the students discussed the answers with their group members. Once everyone understood, the teacher began to teach more difficult content.

Teacher Rur_P_C used oral questions and answers to conduct her diagnostic assessment. Her lesson was about a scientific article, "The Strange Amber." Once class started, she first asked what the students had learned when previewing the article. Students responded that they had learned some knowledge about science and understood the general idea of the article. Then she gave a short oral vocabulary test. She asked students questions individually regarding the meaning of certain words to see if they could use them correctly. She then asked students if there was anything that they wished to discuss with the rest of the class. Based on the questions raised, she lastly summarized the two key points of the lesson and began the class. Teacher Rur_P_C's diagnostic assessment had certain randomness, but she was able to understand the students' basic knowledge, confusions, and interests, which helped make her teaching better targeted.

(2) Placing more emphasis on student participation and formative assessment in class.

Most teachers were aware of the need to change their lecture-oriented teaching style and stressed student–teacher interactions in class. Fourteen out of the 18 teachers initiated small group activities in class with varied tasks: solving problems collaboratively, helping each other, making posters, or role-playing. Teachers paid attention to students' performance and provided timely feedback throughout the class. Additionally, a small in-class quiz was conducted by over half of the teachers (10 teachers), of whom two teachers provided two quizzes, and two others provided three quizzes. The duration of time for each quiz varied from 3 to 10 min. Teachers used these tests to find out the students' learning progress and problems in a timely manner.

(3) Paying attention to summative assessment, but seldom providing in-class tests and feedback.

Most teachers emphasized summative assessment after classroom teaching. Among the 18 teachers participating in this research, 16 assigned after-class work which was considered a type of summative assessment to judge teaching effectiveness. What is worth noting is that very few teachers allocated time in class to give the test and provide timely feedback for the students. Only seven among the 18 teachers allocated time for in-class tests, but no teachers provided enough time for most students to finish all test items. Moreover, only two teachers gave feedback when patrolling. Overall, though teachers were aware of the importance of summative assessment and allocated in-class tests or after-class assignments, teachers were unable to make objective and effective judgments on how well students had learned.

Teachers' Growth and Reflections

Teachers grew and made new discoveries; meanwhile, they experienced confusion and reflected on their teaching. Eighteen teachers reported in the interviews the progress they had made in recent years. To different extents, their progress was demonstrated in their understanding and practices of classroom assessment. Many teachers stated that since the New Curriculum, both educational administrative departments, of all levels, and schools had placed emphasis on related teacher training. Through the training, teachers accepted the developmental idea of classroom assessment from the ideological perspective; and from the practical perspective, they minimized screening students and reinforced formative assessment, encouraging students to keep on making progress. Meanwhile, teachers also faced some confusion in practice. The analysis of the interview data showed that teachers' major confusions and reflections were demonstrated in the following ways.

There Was Less Screening and Ranking Students. However Teachers Did not Give up This Practice Completely

Teachers clearly felt that since the implementation of the New Curriculum, policy makers, researchers, and educators had worked hard in minimizing screening as well as ranking, and in creating a relaxed and pleasant learning environment for students. In recent years, Beijing has placed great importance on reducing students' burden regarding their learning. Both senior high school and college entrance examinations have been reformed through simplifying tests and reducing tricky items, which has greatly relieved the pressure felt by teachers and students. However, not every teacher has responded so positively to these changes. Many of the teachers interviewed expressed that examinations today still focused on testing knowledge and not abilities, and that evaluation of teachers to a certain extent was still based on student achievements in examinations. Therefore, teachers did not have enough courage to change their teaching styles. Teacher Rur_S_M stated, "Examinations are how we test final learning results, so we must always keep that in mind. No matter what happens with the reforms, in the end, students' grades still determine their successes or failures. Since that's the way it is, the foundation clearly hasn't changed; in the end, we still value grades above all." A primary school English teacher of 19 years in rural Beijing (Rur_P_E) explained, "It always comes back to the grades. If the grades are good, then everything is fine, but if the grades aren't satisfactory, then nothing good comes of it. The school is requiring us to change our teaching styles, but I've already been a teacher all of these years, it's really difficult for me to adapt to those requirements. The old methods are still useful. To be honest, I still use the old ways of teaching most of the time. On the one hand I don't have the time or energy to work on the new requirements, and on the other hand, these old methods still prove useful. Students can use the time to do a great number of exercises, which is, in fact, efficient and can help students raise their grades."

Emphasis Was Laid on Students' Pluralistic Development, but Assessment Techniques Still Lagged Behind

The New Curriculum stresses pluralistic development for students and cultivation of students' core literacy. Teachers all accepted the reform idea and explored it in practice. "Currently we focus on conducting a wide range of assessments for students; we pay great attention to their all-round development, including their abilities to solve practical problems, learn new things, cooperate, communicate, listen, and how to behave well" (Cou_P_M). However, many teachers were still confused about how to assess these abilities and qualities. Some teachers wished to quantify the results of each aspect of the learning outcome, which would make assessment much easier. "We all have pluralistic teaching objectives; however we're not sure how to conduct a quantitative evaluation on some aspects of learning outcomes, including process and methods, as well as affective aspects, attitude, and values. It would be great if we could quantify each into a specific score, but the system itself is very complicated. It's not easy to make such evaluation" (Rur_P_E). Other teachers were perplexed by open-ended test items. "Researchers are saying that international exams often have open-ended items. There isn't one right or wrong answer for these items, which is good. But how do you grade? How do you determine the standard? How do you overcome subjective scoring? Also, the proposition of open-ended items itself is difficult too" (Cou_P_C). Some teachers hoped to obtain more concrete and specialized support in assessment techniques. "The New Curriculum standard emphasizes creativity and cultivation of space perception, but sometimes it's difficult to measure these abilities through testing. So how do we handle that?" (Rur_P_M). "Currently it's all about core literacy, but assessing things like communicative ability and critical thinking skills is quite difficult. We lack related experience because we used to stress the assessment of knowledge and skills. If experts could provide us more direct guidance and show us how to evaluate the core literacy, that would be very helpful" (Urb_P_E).

Teachers Wanted to Do More Research on Classroom Assessment, but They Didn't Have Enough Time or Energy

Many teachers had already realized that classroom assessment was the key to furthering teaching reform and this became a bottleneck in a teacher's professional development. Teachers were hopeful that they would not only learn how to teach, in their teaching and research activities, but also how to assess. But many teachers felt that they did not have the time or energy for it. Teacher Urb_P_E stated,

"Our school currently places much emphasis on researching assessment. A special research group has been established for it, and the director of the group gathers up teaching and research groups of all disciplines to discuss assessment issues. However, the teachers are very busy with their daily teaching load, so often this research must happen in their own time after work." Teacher Rur_P_C worried about lacking the energy for assessment: "Some teachers are very meticulous; they provide each student with a progress portfolio. I don't quite understand how to do that. I think they just put in all the student's work, the teacher's assessments, and notes on the student's good performance. They then give it to the student's parents during the teacher-parent meeting. The parents are always excited to see it. As soon as they open it, they can see how their child is performing at school, and they can see that the teacher is responsible and very involved in their children's learning. But there are only one or two teachers who actually do this. We primary school teachers are exhausted. I am in charge of classes with more than 30 or 40 children in each class, then how could I find the time or energy to do all of that? To be honest, preparing lessons and correcting assignments are tiring enough!"

Discussion

Changes Happened to Teachers: The Result of Various Policy Efforts

This research revealed that teachers had already been aware of the value of classroom assessment, and had made explorations in practice. Teachers' changes were mainly reflected in the following aspects: focusing on the diagnosis, feedback, motivation, and improvement functions of classroom assessment; emphasizing the developmental nature of assessment; strengthening diagnostic assessment before instruction; teaching on the basis of learning; making teaching better targeted; stressing formative assessment during instruction; and motivating students to actively participate in classroom interaction. In comparison to the situation before implementing the New Curriculum, teachers have changed greatly, and progress has been evident.

These changes are the result of various policy efforts. First, this round of curriculum reform was systematic; it not only emphasized changes in curriculum concepts, content, structure, and implementation but also stressed changes in assessment methods. Since the launch of the New Curriculum, classroom assessment has received unprecedented attention from the compilation of textbooks to instructional implementation, and from teacher training to teaching and research activities. Educators hope to diagnose better, motivate, and improve students' development through classroom assessment, and to explore some successful experience through practice. Second, there has been a great deal of attention placed on reducing burdens on students as relevant governmental documents have all clearly specified the scope of classroom assessment. In 2013, the Beijing Municipal Commission of Education and the

Educational Inspection Office of the People's Government of Beijing Municipality jointly issued the *Statement on Reducing the Academic Burdens Placed on Primary and Junior High School Students*, which required primary and junior high schools to strictly regulate exams and assessments, and to control all testing methods, subjects, difficulty, and frequency at the level of compulsory education. According to the Statement, primary and junior high schools were not allowed to arbitrarily arrange common examinations for students of different grades, and especially not allowed to rank students based on their grades. In this way, screening and selecting processes were to be minimized, and more of the developmental function of assessment was to be highlighted.

Besides this, there have been substantial reforms to both senior high school and college entrance examinations. The trend of new topic assignment has led teacher development. In recent years, senior high school and college entrance examinations in Beijing Municipality have not only lowered the difficulty for exam items but also reduced the number of tricky questions. The integration of real-life problems into the exam topics has been emphasized to test students' analytical and problem-solving abilities needed in real-life situations. These policies have strongly guided teachers in diversifying assessment content and updating assessment methods (Zhao 2016a).

Admittedly, teachers are not going to change overnight, and this type of transformation takes time. In the research, some teachers complained that current teacher evaluation was still based on grades and that teachers, to a certain extent, still need to teach with the sole purpose of ensuring the students get high scores. Thus, the changes in teaching styles have not been thorough, and there is still a lot of room for improvement in classroom assessment content and methodology. The major issues that Chinese educators must research and solve include how to, from a policy standpoint, alleviate pressure placed on teachers, and how to push for propositional reforms so that assessment can focus more on the complex abilities of students and compel teachers to transform their teaching and assessment behaviors.

Insufficient Teacher Development: Lack of Assessment Knowledge and Skills

This research also discovered that as teachers were actively making changes, there were still many problems that required urgent attention: some teachers were unclear of the classroom assessment concept, failing to grasp the essence of classroom assessment; some lacked the knowledge of meta-assessment, being unclear about what makes good classroom assessment; few teachers implemented in-class assessments and feedback. These problems are closely related to the fact that teachers lack the necessary assessment knowledge and skills. The evidence shows that both in preservice and in-service training for teachers, not enough emphasis has been placed on classroom assessment and that teachers have not received adequate, systematic training (DeLuca and Klinger 2010; Goslin 1967). Additionally, many teachers simply do not possess the knowledge or skills needed to perform classroom assessment (Bonner and Chen 2009; Brookhart 2001; Campbell 2013). In practice, teachers can only learn through "trial and error" and have to implement classroom assessment on the basis of their own experience (Zhao 2013).

To truly realize the positive effect of classroom assessment, teachers must continue to improve assessment quality not only by changing their attitudes towards it but also by gaining the basic knowledge and core skills needed to implement it. Based on the findings of this research, along with suggestions from other researchers, we believe that primary and junior high school teachers in China must improve assessment quality in the following areas: (1) Make an operational definition of teaching objectives. Assessment is a tool for measuring the extent to which teaching objectives have been accomplished. To implement classroom assessment successfully and analyze students' progress, teaching objectives must first be clarified. Teachers can only choose or design the proper assessment plan when teaching objectives are taken from the abstract to the concrete, where the statement of teaching objectives becomes more operational. It is only then that an assessment will have strong grounds. (2) Employ new assessment methods. Current teaching objectives for primary and junior high school teachers are no longer confined to traditional knowledge and skills, so teachers must focus more on the diversified development of their students. How to evaluate comprehensive practical abilities, critical thinking skills, inquiry abilities, and other core qualities of students will be teachers' new research subjects. This requires teachers to use portfolio assessment, performance assessment, and other new assessment methods, so they can properly measure a student's core qualities and complex abilities in real-life situations. (3) Conduct meta-assessment on the assessment. Educational evaluation needs to be critically judged. Only when teachers stress meta-assessment, will the assessment quality be guaranteed. Then the assessment will be able to truly serve, to teach and eventually improve teaching. Teachers must master the basic skills needed to perform meta-assessment, and they must judge all kinds of tests and assessments they use in teaching to analyze their validity, reliability, and fairness. Once the meta-assessment is conducted, any issue in the assessment can be found promptly and the assessment can be improved.

All these changes bring new challenges for teachers in primary and junior high schools today. The training for both preservice student teachers in normal education and in-service teachers in continuing education must be strengthened to develop their classroom assessment skills. Only when teachers have high-quality assessment competencies and have mastered the key skills needed for assessment, will they be able to successfully design and implement classroom assessment. Then they will be able to fully integrate assessment into their teaching, making assessment and teaching mutually beneficial so as to greatly improve their teaching efficiency.

Teachers' Learning and Growth: Taking Teaching and Research Activities as a Breakthrough

To make an improvement in teachers' assessment competencies, teacher training must be strengthened. However, training itself is not enough. The role of teaching and research activities in promoting teachers' assessment competencies needs to be given full play. In China, school-based teaching and research activity is the most common form of professional development activity for teachers. A school creates teaching and research groups based on grade levels and disciplines, and each group usually comprises five to 30 people. The main focus of these groups is to enter the classroom and to research problems in teaching; specifically, teaching and research content covers clarifying instructional pace, key and difficult instruction points, and discussing instructional design, quizzes, and exams. What is worth noticing is that for a long period of time, most teaching and research groups focused on how to improve teaching and learning (Lu and Shen 2010; Yang 2012); their main activities included collective preparation of teaching plans, lesson observation, as well as lesson discussion. Moreover, the teaching and research groups conducted relatively weak research and discussion on how to perform assessments. In the future, primary and junior high schools need to use teaching and research activities as a breakthrough and to strengthen assessment research. The core of these activities must switch from researching how to teach, to how to assess. In this way, teachers can master the necessary skills required for assessments and effectively promote students' learning.

Some people worry that this change will fuel the practice of "teaching to the evaluation." However, as a matter of fact, teaching to the evaluation is itself not necessarily good or bad. Whether it is good or bad all depends on the learning outcomes indicated by the evaluation and the specific strategies outlined in teaching to the evaluation (Bond 2008; Popham 2001). If the learning outcomes are confined only to isolated knowledge and skills, if teachers use real test items in high-stakes tests to train students, and teach only to make students able to answer test items, then the effects are clearly negative. However, if the learning outcomes are centered upon promoting the cultivation of students' core literacy and are aimed at achieving their overall and sustainable development, and if the teacher teaches in order to realize curriculum objectives, then this is a positive change that should be advocated. Currently, the New Curriculum implemented in China emphasizes the all-round development of students and the links between the curriculum content, the student's life, and modern society, advocating the change of teaching and learning methods. Under the guidance of the New Curriculum, diversification is being seen in teaching objectives in primary and junior high schools. In this context, if teachers, in their teaching and research activities, delve into how to evaluate a student's progress in reaching their learning objectives and also promote the implementation of these objectives, then this could lead to great improvements in teaching.

Fortunately, this study has found that there are already primary and junior high schools (such as Urb_J_E's urban junior high school) that focus on classroom assessment in their teaching and research activities. If more schools recognize the importance of it, attach more emphasis on "how to assess" in their teaching and research activities, and enable teachers to focus more on classroom assessment, to better design and implement classroom assessment, the positive functions of assessment will grow to their full potential. After all, assessment acts like a conductor's baton. Wherever it points, teaching and learning will follow. What to assess determines what teachers teach and what students learn. Likewise, how to assess determines how teachers teach and how students learn. Assessment will only become the driving force in the teaching reform when both schools and teachers devote themselves to assessment research. Then teaching will be truly improved.

References

Ausubel, D. P. (1968). *Educational psychology: A cognitive view*. London: Holt, Reinhart, & Winston.

Bangert-Drowns, R. L., Kulik, J. A., & Kulik, C. C. (1991). Effects of frequent classroom testing. *The Journal of Educational Research, 85*(2), 89–99.

Black, P. (2013). Formative and summative aspects of assessment: Theoretical and research foundations in the context of pedagogy. In J. H. McMillan (Ed.), *Sage handbook of research on classroom assessment* (pp. 167–178). Thousand Oaks, CA: Sage.

Black, P., & Wiliam, D. (2010). Inside the black box: Raising standards through classroom assessment. *Phi Delta Kappan, 92*(1), 81–90.

Bloom, B. S. (1971). *Handbook on the formative and summative evaluation of student learning*. New York: McGraw-Hill.

Bloom, B. S., Madaus, G. F., & Hastings, J. T. (1981). *Evaluation to improve learning*. New York: McGraw-Hill.

Bond, L. (2008). Teaching to the test: Coaching or corruption. *The New Educator, 4*(6), 216–223.

Bonner, S. M., & Chen, P. P. (2009). Teacher candidates' perceptions about grading and constructivist teaching. *Educational Assessment, 14*(2), 57–77.

Brookhart, S. M. (2001). *The "standards" and classroom assessment research*. Paper presented at the annual meeting of the American Association of Colleges for Teacher Education, Dallas, TX. https://eric.ed.gov/?id=ED451189. Accessed March 17, 2017.

Campbell, C. (2013). Research on teacher competency in classroom assessment. In J. H. McMillan (Ed.), *Sage handbook of research on classroom assessment* (pp. 71–84). Thousand Oaks, CA: Sage.

Davis, D. S., & Neitzel, C. (2011). A self-regulated learning perspective on middle grades classroom assessment. *The Journal of Educational Research, 104*(3), 202–215.

DeLuca, C., & Klinger, D. A. (2010). Assessment literacy development: Identifying gaps in teacher candidates' learning. *Assessment in Education: Principles, Policy & Practice, 17*(4), 419–438.

Dong, Q., & Zhao, D. C. (2003). Fazhan xing jiaoyu pingjia de lilun yu shijian [Theory and practice of developmental education evaluation]. *Zhongguo Jiaoyu Xuekan [Journal of Chinese Society of Education], 8,* 18–21.

Goslin, D. A. (1967). *Teachers and testing*. New York: Russell Sage Foundation.

Hausknecht, J. P., Halpert, J. A., Di Paolo, N. T., & Gerrard, M. O. (2007). Retesting in selection: A meta-analysis of coaching and practice effects for tests of cognitive ability. *Journal of Applied Psychology, 92*(2), 373–385.

Hicks, G. J. (2016). *A meta-assessment of the outcomes assessment practices of accredited radiography educational programs*. ProQuest Dissertations Publishing, 2016. 10254476.

Kevin, S., & Scott, B. (2016). Meta-assessment: Assessing the learning outcomes assessment program. *Innovative Higher Education, 41*(4), 287–301.

Klein, J. M., Spector, J. M., Grabowski, B., & de la Teja, I. (2004). *Instructor competencies: Standards for face-to-face, online, and blended settings.* Greenwich, CT: Information Age.

Linn, R. L., & Gronlund, N. E. (2003). *Jiaoxue zhong de ceyan yu pingjia [Measurement and assessment in teaching]* (8th ed.). Beijing: China Light Industry Press.

Lu, N. G., & Shen, W. (2010). Zhongguo jiaoyanyuan zhineng de lishi zhuanbian [The historical evolution of the function of the teaching and research staff in China]. *Quanqiu Jiaoyu Zhanwang [Global Education], 276*(7), 66–70.

Ministry of Education, the People's Republic of China. (2001). *Jichu jiaoyu kecheng gaige gangyao [The outline of curriculum reform of basic education].* http://www.moe.edu.cn/publicfiles/business/htmlfiles/moe/moe_309/200412/4672.html. Accessed May 24, 2016.

Popham, W. J. (2001). Teaching to the test? *Educational Leadership, 58*(6), 16–20.

Popham, W. J. (2008). *Classroom assessment: What teachers need to know* (5th ed.). Boston: Pearson Education.

Randel, B., Apthorp, H., Beesley, A. D., Clark, T. F., & Wang, X. (2016). Impacts of professional development in classroom assessment on teacher and student outcomes. *The Journal of Educational Research, 109*(5), 491–502.

Simpson-Beck, V. (2011). Assessing classroom assessment techniques. *Active Learning in Higher Education, 12*(2), 125–132.

Stufflebeam, D. L. (1974). *Meta-evaluation.* Kalamazoo: Evaluation Center, College of Education, Western Michigan University.

Wiggins, G. (2005). *Jiaoyu xing pingjia [Educative assessment: Designing assessments to inform and improve student performance].* Beijing: China Light Industry Press.

Yang, B. J. (2012, July 9). School-based teaching research: What teachers need to research. *China Education Newspaper, 7.*

Zhao, D. C. (2013). Performance assessment: History, practice, and future. *Curriculum, Teaching Material, and Method, 33*(2), 97–103.

Zhao, D. C. (2016a). Biaoxian xing pingjia yingyong zhong de wenti [Problems in the application of performance assessment: Analysis based on 2015 senior high school entrance examination and college entrance examination]. *Kecheng jiaocai jiaofa [Curriculum, Teaching Material, and Method], 36*(1), 53–59.

Zhao, D. C. (2016b). *Cujin jiaoxue de ceyan yu pingjia [Using assessment to improve teaching and learning].* Shanghai: East China Normal University Press.

Zhao, D. C., & Xu, F. (2002). Dangqian pingjia gaige zhong ying zhuyi de wenti [Problems should be paid attention to in current evaluation reform]. *Yuwen Jianshe [Language Planning], 2,* 42–43.

Zhao, X., Heuvel-Panhuizen, M. V., & Veldhuis, M. (2016). Teachers' use of classroom assessment techniques in primary mathematics education: An explorative study with six Chinese teachers. *International Journal of STEM Education, 3*(1), 1–18.

Chapter 6
Teacher Learning of Portfolio Assessment Practices: Testimonies of Two Writing Teachers

Ricky Lam

Abstract Teacher learning is a slippery, complex, and multileveled concept. Scholars argue that how the concept can be theoretically and epistemologically defined remains inconclusive. Some studies support the benefits of initial teacher education training in writing assessment, whereas others advocate teacher-initiated and collaborative school-based projects. Despite empirical evidence, we have little knowledge of how individual EFL writing teachers learn and develop new classroom assessment practices such as portfolio assessment of writing. Drawing upon teacher interviews, classroom observations and narrative frames, the study investigated two teachers' perspectives of how teacher learning had an impact on the trial of portfolio assessment and what school-related contextual factors influenced the teachers' experiences when attempting a portfolio approach. Findings reveal that if the teachers failed to encounter and resolve issues arising from the tryout, they were less likely to successfully master the underlying rationale and skills of a tried and tested assessment practice. Three school-related contextual factors appeared to facilitate and inhibit the implementation of portfolio assessment. They included the teacher evaluation system, school cultures, and opportunities for collaboration. The chapter ends with pedagogical implications, discussing which form of teacher learning is most appropriate for promulgating wider application of portfolio assessment in the Hong Kong context.

Keywords Assessment innovation · Portfolio assessment · Teacher education programmes · Teacher learning

R. Lam (✉)
Hong Kong Baptist University, Hong Kong, China
e-mail: rickylam@hkbu.edu.hk

© Springer Nature Singapore Pte Ltd. 2018
H. Jiang and M. F. Hill (eds.), *Teacher Learning with Classroom Assessment*,
https://doi.org/10.1007/978-981-10-9053-0_6

Introduction

Since Black and Wiliam's (1998) meta-analysis was published to validate how classroom assessment can support productive learning, there has been a global phenomenon of using assessment for its learning-oriented function on top of its summative and evaluative roles. Around the world, different versions of curriculum and assessment reforms are under way as a sociocultural response to a paradigm shift from assessment for accountability towards assessment for learning (Wiliam 2011). Despite a burgeoning body of research investigating the impact of classroom assessment practices, such as portfolio assessment, on student learning (Hamp-Lyons 2007), we, thus far, still have very little knowledge about how teachers strategically learn to implement these classroom assessment practices and what school-related factors could shape their innovative practices.

Teacher learning is conventionally defined as mastery of subject-specific knowledge and skills, which govern what teachers think and do when carrying out change in their pedagogical and assessment practices (Wilson and Berne 1999). The concept is also labeled as professional learning in most teacher education and professional development literature. Teacher learning opportunities take a plethora of forms including short-term workshops/seminars, action research, teacher education programs and qualifications, reflective practices, and university-school collaborations. In this chapter, we use the term—teacher learning—to refer to ongoing engagement with professional development opportunities, particularly those directly experienced by teachers in their own classroom contexts, namely on-the-job learning opportunities. Another key construct in this paper is classroom assessment, which is commonly defined as teacher-mediated, context-specific, and learning-enhancing assessment practices such as the use of writing portfolios wherein constructive feedback information is generated to improve teaching and learning (Davison and Leung 2009). While teachers can utilize a range of teacher learning events to enhance professionalism, it remains unclear the extent to which the process of teacher learning could bring about change and what contextual factors would affect their innovative assessment practices (cf. James and Pedder 2006).

From the classroom innovation literature, there has been no shortage of empirical research exploring how practitioners innovate their pedagogical and assessment practices as agents of change. However, most of these studies report less than satisfactory results and indicate that change was usually mediated by personal (teacher beliefs), school-related (school climate) and larger societal (education system) barriers. Take for example, Humphries and Burns' (2015) study in which entrenched teacher beliefs and lack of adequate understanding of the new instructional approach caused the failure of the introduction of a communicative language teaching pedagogy in an engineering university. Similarly, Earl and Timperley (2014) found that teacher conceptions of assessment play a crucial role in determining whether the implementation of assessment for learning as classroom assessment is successful or not. They argue that effective implementation of learning-oriented assessment practices requires a shift in conceptual understanding rather than just a change in practice at the surface level.

In Hong Kong, there are studies exploring how a teacher professional development program on written feedback impacted two in-service secondary-level teachers' assessment practices (Lee et al. 2016), and how two primary-level teachers implemented peer assessment as innovative assessment practices through university-school collaboration (Carless 2005). Despite these studies, not much has been done to examine how the process of teacher learning may impact the teachers' attempts to innovate their classroom assessment practices, for instance, through portfolio assessment. And not much has been done to explore what school-related contextual factors, in addition to teacher beliefs about assessment, possibly influence the wider implementation of portfolio assessment in local classroom settings. To fill the gaps, this study looked into the process of teacher learning in the implementation of change, and identified school-related contextual factors as experienced by secondary-level writing teachers in Hong Kong.

Framework

Process of Teacher Learning in Educational Change

The process of teacher learning has become a cornerstone in educational change since theorists revealed how teachers can transform their assessment practices from assessment of learning to assessment for learning or even assessment as learning, be it through preservice teacher education programs or engagement in collaborative action research projects (Hill 2011, 2016). In the educational assessment literature, teacher conceptions/beliefs of assessment take a lead role in the construct of teacher learning. For instance, the ways teachers assess their learners depend very much on what they believe to be the function of assessment (i.e., assessment of accountability) and how they were formerly assessed as students (Lee 2015). While researchers have argued that teachers' entrenched beliefs about assessment of learning are a major obstacle to introducing assessment for learning practices at the classroom level (Davison 2013; Earl and Timperley 2014), there are studies demonstrating that teacher education programs can change and shape preservice teachers' conceptions about the application of more learner-centric assessment approaches such as self- and peer assessment (e.g., Smith et al. 2014).

Despite the value of some teacher education programs, commentators contend that many teacher preparation and professional development programs may not be productive of teacher learning, especially when such programs adopt a model of knowledge transmission rather than a model of knowledge transfer which underscores teacher agency in the process of professional learning (Stevens 2004). To this end, scholars have long recommended a bottom-up, teacher-initiated, and collaborative professional learning model, where teachers can assume a more proactive role in facilitating the change process mediated by a community of practice (Hargreaves 2013; Hill 2016). In these learning communities, teachers are likely to be empowered by situated, sustained, dialogic, and professional interactions which could extend teacher pedagogical content knowledge such as the application of alternative assessment practices. Through active participation in teacher learning, classroom teachers could further enhance their conceptual understanding towards the essence and rationale of assessment for learning principles (Marshall and Drummond 2006; Xu and Liu 2009). As argued by Hyland and Wong (2013), without developing a clear and in-depth understanding of change, any curricular and/or assessment innovations are doomed to failure. Besides enriching teacher conceptual understanding of change, more has to be done to investigate how teacher learning plays a role in affecting teachers' classroom assessment practices. This study aimed to find out how the process of teacher learning influences what and when teachers attempt innovative classroom assessment practices.

Factors that Shape Classroom Assessment Innovation

To initiate classroom assessment innovation, three levels of contextual factors determine how successful such implementations may be. These are the micro-level (personal level), meso-level (school-related level), and macro-level (societal level) (Carless 2005; Jang 2014). The micro-level refers to personal factors mediated by the immediate classroom environment, encompassing its key players and their interrelationships such as teachers (conceptions and beliefs), students (perceptions and motivation), teacher-student interaction, and physical classroom settings, for example. The meso-level is concerned with factors that are usually outside the confines of the classroom itself, including but not limited to school-related matters—school policy, school culture/climate, and support from senior management. The meso-level factors could, at times, go beyond school-related level and include parents' demands. The macro-level encompasses the educational system, educational governance and policy, and cultural norms. An example in the assessment context could be an exam-oriented culture (for details, refer to Fulmer et al. 2015, pp. 476–77).

Among these three levels of contextual factors that govern how teachers plan, develop, and innovate their assessment practices, there have been ongoing research studies exploring micro-level factors including various teacher conceptions of alternative assessment (Tan 2013) and impacts of assessment training (Koh 2011), and macro-level factors entailing national reforms on raising accountability (Klenowski 2012). Despite this evidence, Fulmer et al. (2015) and Fives and Buehl (2012) contend that compared to micro-level and macro-level factors, there has been a dearth of scholarship exploring how meso-level (school-related level) contextual factors affect teacher assessment practices. Undoubtedly, meso-level contextual factors serve to determine whether they facilitate or inhibit teacher learning, because frontline teachers, particularly in East Asian settings, are likely to comply with top-down decisions made by the senior management and are therefore less inclined to innovate their classroom assessment methods in comparison with their Western counterparts (Benson 2010; Tong 2010). Additionally, teacher learning does not happen in a vacuum but is socio-contextually mediated by school ethos, school climate, tenets of sponsoring bodies and probably expectations from parents and the public. With this in mind, it is imperative to explore how meso-level contextual factors specifically influence teacher assessment practices when teachers attempt to try out alternative forms of classroom assessment, such as portfolio assessment.

Writing Assessment Practices in Hong Kong

In Hong Kong, school-based writing assessment generally refers to timed and impromptu essay testing in the end-of-term examination, usually taking place twice in one academic year. Throughout an average school term, senior secondary-level students (Grades 10–12) are required to write eight to ten full-length essays of 400 words, together with other short writing tasks including newspaper clippings, integrated language skill tasks, and weekly journals. These full-length and short writing tasks are considered mini-summative assessments rather than opportunities for formative assessment since process writing is typically not encouraged. Peer assessment remains uncommon, and student-teacher conferences are almost nonexistent because of teachers' heavy workloads (Lee 2011). Even after the implementation of the New Senior Secondary Curriculum in 2009 where classroom-based writing assessment approaches such as portfolio assessment were promulgated, teachers remained reserved and skeptical about trying out alternative classroom assessment owing to their entrenched beliefs, limited knowledge and skills, and other school-related constraints such as appraisal systems (Lee 2016; Qian 2014; Tong 2011).

In the past decade, through university-school collaboration, teachers have been encouraged to innovate their writing assessment practices at the classroom level, including the application of the process writing approach (Hamp-Lyons 2007), innovative written feedback practices (Lee et al. 2016), and portfolio assessment, underscoring reflection and revision (Lam 2013). Despite these professional development efforts, scholars have identified that due to a lack of in-depth conceptual understanding of change (personal level) and the prevalence of a larger exam-oriented culture (societal level), the participating teachers typically fail to sustain these innovations and find it cumbersome to try out the intended innovative assessment practices in their work contexts (Carless 2005; Dixon et al. 2011). Thus far, we have limited knowledge about how teachers are influenced by the meso-level contextual (school-related level) factors when innovating with portfolio assessment. These factors include school culture, teacher autonomy, school policy, and leadership styles. Based upon the above theoretical framework, this chapter addresses the following two research questions:

1. How did the process of teacher learning influence the teachers' attempts to innovate with portfolio assessment in their work contexts?
2. What meso-level contextual factors influenced the teachers' implementation of portfolio assessment?

The Study

Context of the Study

The current study derived from a larger study which investigated how eight Hong Kong secondary-level English teachers innovated and developed context-specific portfolio assessment models in their writing classrooms. The original project aimed to identify how the teachers adapted and tried out various versions of portfolio assessment programs to fit their specific work contexts, including accommodating learner preferences, classroom environments, school cultures, teacher knowledge, and conceptions of writing assessment. Seven secondary-level schools were involved in the larger project. These schools were of different types: government schools (funded and administered by the Hong Kong Government); aided schools (fully funded by the Education Bureau and managed by individual sponsoring bodies); and Direct Subsidy Scheme schools (partially funded by the Education Bureau and managed by individual sponsoring bodies) with autonomy to select the medium of instruction and curriculum development. The students' academic levels in these seven schools varied, ranging from top-performing to underperforming students. The eight teacher informants adopted diverse classroom-based assessment strategies in order to upgrade their writing instructional practices. Based upon the data analysis of the larger study, the eight teachers are thematically grouped into three broad categories, namely (a) proactive innovators (most committed change agents); (b) enthusiastic followers (committed change agents); and (c) compliant executors (moderately to less committed change agents).

In this chapter, the data from two top-performing schools, labeled as Band 1, which admit the top 20–30% of Grade 7 students (aged 11–12) in the territory, were included. School A[1] is a traditional government school and School B[2] is a Direct Subsidy Scheme school; students in these two types of schools generally have solid academic foundations and are very proficient in both spoken and written English. Both schools use English as the medium of instruction except for Chinese-related subjects, but School A follows the curriculum as prescribed by the Education Bureau and School B adopts a school-based curriculum designed by the teachers themselves. In School A, teachers primarily use commercial textbooks and follow their curriculum whereas in School B, teachers develop their own teaching and learning materials.

---

[1] The government school in Hong Kong is fully subsidized by the Hong Kong Special Administrative Region Government and supervised by the Education Bureau, the centralized quasi-government agency responsible for planning, developing, and evaluating wider educational policies in Hong Kong. Students admitted to the government schools have to join the Secondary School Places Allocation Scheme.

[2] The Direct Subsidy Scheme school in Hong Kong is partially funded by the Hong Kong Special Administrative Region Government and supervised by the Education Bureau. However, the direct subsidy scheme schools have autonomy to recruit students, formulate the curriculum content, and decide the medium of instruction, etc.

Portfolio Assessment

Portfolio assessment refers to an alternative pedagogical and assessment approach which encourages students to reflect upon their writing development over time. The portfolio assessment approach can be flexibly incorporated into writing curricula, emphasizing learner agency in the acts of composing, revising and reflecting. Since the 2000s, portfolio assessment has become popular in the second language writing context (Hamp-Lyons 2007). In 2009, portfolio assessment was promulgated in the New Senior Secondary Curriculum as a larger part of assessment for learning curriculum reform. However, its wider application remains very restricted as a result of a range of teacher, school-related, and sociocultural factors. Furthermore, teachers tend to consider the implementation of portfolio assessment a controversial "reform" initiative rather than a valuable educational practice which supports learning of writing (Lam 2016). In the context of this chapter, portfolio assessment is defined as a classroom assessment innovation although this assessment practice has been on the curricular reform agenda in Hong Kong for almost a decade.

Participants

Two teachers participated: Willy from School A and Winifred from School B. Both names are pseudonyms. The two participants were identified based on three criteria: enthusiasm about assessment innovation, possession of pertinent teacher training, and work experience in the profession. Besides, they were selected because both received the same teacher education training and worked in the mainstream local secondary-level schools. Informed consents were sought before the study. Willy had 4 years of teaching experience whereas Winifred had 6. They graduated from the two Hong Kong government-funded universities with a bachelor's degree in English language education and English studies. At the time of the study, Willy was applying for tenure as an education officer (a permanent civil servant post) in School A. Willy was also pursuing a part-time 2-year Master of Arts in English language teaching program at a local university and was taking up a new leadership role in the counseling and extra-curriculum teams. Since Willy was enthusiastic to improve his assessment practices, he volunteered to join the current project on portfolio assessment. Winifred was the associate panel head in the English Department of School B. She agreed to join the project as she had implemented a similar language program emphasizing learner reflection, parallel to the theoretical principles of portfolio assessment. Derived from the larger study, Willy was classified as a "compliant executor", who was a moderately committed change agent, whereas Winifred was classified as a "proactive innovator" who was a most committed change agent even before participating in the study. The selection of these two informants intends to showcase the extent to which teacher agency is contextually mediated by the process of teacher learning when teachers attempt classroom-based assessment such as portfolio assessment of writing.

Data Collection

In the study, qualitative data were collected through (1) individual teacher interviews, (2) classroom observations, and (3) narrative frames. The teacher semi-structured interviews were conducted three times throughout the 1-year project duration. Each interview lasted around 30–35 min. The interview protocol comprised questions regarding teacher perceptions about the process of teacher learning such as its forms, effectiveness, and sustainability; how teacher learning assisted the process of change; and school-related factors that facilitate or impede the implementation of portfolio assessment. For classroom observations, Willy's Grade 11 writing class was observed once, whereas Winifred's Grade 9 class was observed twice. The observation form sought general information about the lesson, learning objectives, class procedures, observers' reflection, and significant critical incidents. Field notes were kept while the two teachers were being observed. Narrative frames, and scaffolded writing tasks, were adopted as one research tool to help Willy and Winifred recollect their past and present aspirations regarding their lived teaching experience as English language teachers, the roles they play in teaching writing and the ways they initiate the change process. The narratives were collected near the end of the project.

Data Analysis

Teacher interview data, field notes, and narratives were transcribed by the research assistant and then analyzed by me three times to identify appropriate codes and themes to address the two research questions. These emerging data were verified against the data from individual classroom observation scenarios to find out how the process of teacher learning and school-related factors influenced the decisions made by the two informants when they innovated their classroom assessment practices using the portfolio approach. To further enhance the validity of this analysis, I attempted to triangulate the processed data with current assessment literature to confirm whether my interpretation of the data sets was trustworthy.

Findings

In this section, the abbreviation *ID* denotes interview data; *Ob* observation data; *FN* researcher's field notes; and *TN* the teachers' narratives. The findings are reported in response to the two research questions, namely, what influenced each teacher's learning in their attempt to implement portfolio assessment, and, second, how the school-level (meso-level) factors influenced their learning regarding this form of classroom assessment practice.

Sources of Influence in Classroom Assessment Learning

Formal Learning Versus On-The-Job Learning

Asked what they understood of the idea of teacher learning, Winifred and Willy described teacher learning as one form of professional development. Winifred interpreted teacher learning as one-off workshops, and seminars and Willy felt that teacher learning equated to academic study programs (ID). Despite this divergence, Winifred and Willy agreed that teacher learning played a key role in facilitating the setup of classroom assessment innovation. Willy said, "Without prior understanding and knowledge, it is challenging to initiate portfolio assessment or other innovative practices" (ID). While believing teacher learning typically refers to formal and structured academic programs including credit-bearing coursework or certified face-to-face/online workshops, Winifred stated that teacher learning could happen daily in her work context, especially through solving pedagogical and/or assessment-related problems (TN).

In the literature, the initiation of teacher learning could be placed in a continuum, with one side being the bottom-up approach (teacher-initiated change) and the other being the top-down approach (change initiated by others; Harlen 2010). Prior to the trial of portfolio assessment, Willy reported that he recalled the rationale of portfolio assessment learned in a course entitled Language Assessment in his undergraduate study. He had read a few published journal articles about self-assessment and formulated how to incorporate the element of self-reflection in the writing curriculum (FN). Initially, Willy planned to conduct a small-scale action research project to measure how portfolio assessment had an impact on student writing performance. The idea originated from a course he was attending in his master's program. Because of his work commitments, he relinquished this plan (TN).

Despite his efforts and knowledge base, Willy consulted me to look for possible alternatives to implementing writing portfolios. In one meeting, I advised Willy to use self-reflection forms which assisted students to reflect upon their writing after they completed their full-length essays. Willy told me that he once adopted process writing. He then explained to me that he required students to write paragraphs in stages rather than expecting them to revise the compositions substantially. When I observed the writing class, students did not put their drafts in the portfolios (FN). In the lesson, Willy simply taught the students how to fill in the reflection form by pointing out the strengths and weaknesses of a sample written work. In the post-observation interview, Willy reported that he learned about this by following one journal article he had read for his MA program (ID). After the reflection task, Willy asked students to swap their work and comment on the quality of self-reflection, followed by student oral presentations of their critiques (Ob). It appears that Willy's conception of teacher learning is primarily derived from his former teacher education training (bachelor's degree) and current academic program (master's degree). When facing the complexities of enacting an assessment innovation, Willy simply counted on his formal educational training rather than insights gained from hands-on practice, since he rarely had opportunities to seek professional advice from his colleagues who were used to following commercial textbooks.

Unlike Willy, Winifred valued sustained professional dialogue with colleagues such as sharing good practices on how to incorporate reflection in portfolio assessment (FN). Being one of the associate panel heads of the department, she regarded mentoring new colleagues as one form of teacher learning as she said, "When I discuss with new colleagues on how to encourage students to reflect upon their writing in the portfolio process, we can generate lots of thoughtful and constructive ideas (ID)." In her portfolio lesson, Winifred invited students to reflect upon what they learnt in the previous unit called "Our Home—Hong Kong," what they learnt well (places, language, and skills), what they did not learn so well, and what advice they would like to make on improving the unit, in the form of mind maps. The students were divided into groups to address the above four questions. After the task, the students passed their mind maps to another group for comments and elaboration. These group mind maps served as input for individual student's mind maps when they were asked to construct their own as the assignment (Ob). The lesson was interactive and dynamic, and all the students were on task (FN). In the post-observation interview, Winifred told me that she learned how to facilitate students' metacognitive skills by consulting senior colleagues and reflecting upon her practices using the trial and error method. Although Winifred did not mention what she learned from her teacher education program, she pointed out that she preferred trying out various assessment methods to see how these methods impacted student learning (ID). To Winifred, teacher learning is primarily derived from the site of lived pedagogical experiences and what works in her class after repeated practices (Gleeson and Davison 2016). In other words, when it came to deciding which classroom assessment practices were adopted, Willy primarily counted on formal learning events (e.g., teacher training programs) and my input, whereas Winifred preferred having on-the-job learning opportunities. One point worth noting here is that although Willy gained the pedagogical knowledge on innovating portfolio assessment from me, he received no peer support from the senior colleagues in his school.

Knowledge Transmission Versus Knowledge Transfer

When asked whether teacher learning contributes to the development of professional knowledge, Willy and Winifred had different opinions.

Willy believed that teacher learning would bring about enhanced professionalism, namely how to apply the portfolio approach in the writing classroom. However, he noted that whether portfolio assessment could effectively promote student learning of writing through self-reflection was an issue, because learner agency and metacognitive skills, which are the key features of portfolio assessment, were rarely taught in the local English curriculum (ID, FN; Lee 2016). In the classroom observation, I found that Willy's students were not particularly proficient in self-reflecting upon their writing performances although they were considered more able students. Winifred remained skeptical regarding the effectiveness of alternative assessments, mainly as a result of empirical research and formal professional learning events. She said, "Teachers could refer to the current literature and see which assessment approach works for their classroom situations. Yet they should try out these approaches and modify them to accommodate their students' needs" (ID). In his narrative frame, Willy emphasized the significance of teacher education programs (recognized academic qualifications including B.Ed. and M.A.) which constantly shaped his professional identity and equipped him with up-to-date pedagogical and assessment knowledge. Willy considered that he preferred following those tried and tested methods as suggested by scholars in published research as this input was trustworthy (FN). Conversely, Winifred felt that the usefulness of teacher learning relied very much on whether teachers could transfer the knowledge learned from theories provided in staff development seminars to authentic classroom assessment practices (TN).

When asked how he implemented portfolio assessment other than the observed lesson, Willy reported that he required students to do self- and peer assessment after they completed their drafts. When asked whether there was any follow-up to self- and peer assessment, Willy said no; he simply asked students to correct the errors as suggested by peers (ID). During the lesson observation, one of Willy's students admitted that she did not like the idea of peer assessment as her classmate was weak in English and unable to mark her work accurately (Ob). Also, after the observed portfolio lesson, Willy revealed that his students did not like reflecting upon their drafts as it was somewhat boring (ID). Willy's students expressed concerns that the peer assessment task and reflection activity were monotonous (FN). Willy did not modify or make these two tasks more interactive but uncritically followed what he learned from the published journal articles and my suggestions. Willy's case is an example of direct knowledge transmission from teacher learning, although he had adopted a simplified version of portfolio assessment in practice for achieving a quick-fix approach to change (cf. Earl and Timperley 2014).

Winifred incorporated the elements of "end-of-unit" and "end-of-year" reflection into the school-based curriculum. These reflective components, encouraging students to review their writing development, overall language learning and content of each teaching unit, became the framework of the portfolio assessment system in Winifred's school (ID, FN). As shown in her narrative frame, Winifred felt strongly that she and her colleagues should not use the same format of self- and peer assessment or similar reflection tasks repeatedly. Otherwise, students would get bored easily. From time to time, Winifred and her colleagues had regular co-planning meetings to discuss, review, and develop pedagogical/assessment ideas which kept the whole team up-to-date with vibrant ideas (TN). She further recommended that helping students to think aloud about what they had learned and incorporating this metacognitive thinking process into writing tasks, say reflection on learning experience, would be more effective than conventionally decontextualized writing tasks (ID). Near the end of the semester, she asked her students to reflect upon what unit content (the last unit of work) should be added or deleted in a discussion task. Students then offered suggestions, shared their ideas, drew mind maps, and recorded the ideas to prepare for their year-end reflection tasks to be kept in the portfolios (FN). Winifred's case illustrates an instance of knowledge transfer since she has innovated portfolio assessment with a critical eye, which could be classified as the empowerer's assessment practices in Dixon et al.'s (2011) study.

In sum, Willy implemented the portfolio assessment method by following what the literature suggested and what he had learned from the teacher education program. On this note, Willy had strong faith in authoritative input from scholars and published research, probably because of their credentials. It appears to me that Willy's work context might deny him access to a collegial situation that might lead to a more bottom-up approach to change, resulting in the adoption of a knowledge transmission approach to teacher learning. Owing to Winifred's autonomous work context, she critically explored various assessment methods before deciding which one was appropriate for her students. Winifred considered that teacher learning best took place in one's immediate classroom environment, and one's professional knowledge should build upon ongoing experimentation with her practices rather than being directly transmitted from external sources. It can be said that in this study, Winifred adopted a knowledge transfer approach to teacher learning with a focus on collaborative inquiry.

Meso-Level Contextual Factors

Three pertinent themes were identified in relation to the second question regarding the meso-level factors impacting teacher learning. These were: the type of teacher evaluation system, the school culture, and opportunities for collaboration.

Teacher Evaluation System

Willy admitted that he was under contract and under tremendous pressure to apply for tenure in School A. To scale up his track record, he agreed to take up more administrative work including leadership roles in the uniform unit and counseling team (ID). Despite these additional non-teaching duties, Willy insisted that he would like to develop his professional knowledge of classroom assessment practices since he viewed himself as a language teacher rather than a school administrator (TN). During the trial of portfolio assessment, Willy emphasized that he encouraged students to perform self-reflection to acquire metacognitive composing skills and intended to separate the assessment and learning functions of writing portfolios (ID). Asked why he did not consider aligning teaching, learning, and assessment of writing through the portfolio program, he said that students were grade-conscious and might not like the idea of portfolio assessment (ID). Furthermore, Willy worried about receiving complaints from students and/or parents if the portfolio approach was graded or affected students' final examination results (FN). Willy described having low-bargaining power in his workplace owing to the teacher evaluation system, which had an impact on his career advancement. When Willy demonstrated how he taught students to perform self-reflection in the observed lesson, he invited the English panel head and principal to sit in for the purpose of teacher evaluation (Ob).

Winifred did not experience the same pressure of "keeping the job," as the teacher evaluation system in School B is different from that of School A. In School B, staff members' contracts are reviewed once every 3 years and each colleague is expected to submit an annual performance report to the school management for the purpose of appraisal (FN). School B, under the Direct Subsidy Scheme, has greater flexibility to hire and retain staff despite its high turnover in the past few years (ID). Asked about the impact of teacher appraisal, Winifred responded that she was happy with the system and asserted that she taught the same way with or without evaluation. She explained to me that after the introduction of the school-based curriculum, she and other colleagues had more motivation and autonomy to try out the interactive oral tasks, portfolio assessment and the inclusion of language arts component in the classroom (ID, FN). Like Willy, Winifred was on contract and shouldered heavy administrative responsibilities, but she did not concur that the teacher evaluation system would dictate her educational philosophy and instructional approaches (i.e., student-centeredness), given that it provided her with an opportunity to review what she had contributed, how well she had performed, and what could be done to enhance her pedagogical/assessment practices (TN).

School Culture

In the interview and narrative frame data, Willy reported that School A was relatively conservative despite the introduction of some the latest programs including Campus TV and morning reading lessons. He commented that the pedagogical approach in his school was primarily product-based and textbook-bound, emphasizing rote learning and repeated practices. When asked how school culture influenced the trial of portfolio assessment, Willy confessed that he had to keep it small and had implemented a watered-down version of the portfolio assessment model which merely featured learner reflection on single-draft composition, with no comprehensive review of writing development. Also, he did not involve other colleagues to innovate with portfolio assessment as they would regard this assessment practice as "extra work" or "something not practical" (ID). While the medium of instruction in School A is English, I discovered that students primarily used Cantonese for academic purposes, namely lectures, interactions with teachers, oral presentations and so forth (FN, Ob). It appears that despite Willy's readiness and enthusiasm, School A constrained his practice and remains a major stumbling block to the implementation of portfolio assessment.

In School B, Winifred had more autonomy to plan and develop the school-based curriculum as the school did not use any commercial textbooks. Winifred and colleagues codesigned all teaching and learning materials for each form level. Throughout the trial, the principal and panel head lent full support to Winifred's leadership and professional judgment when she introduced the idea of reflective components in the portfolio program (TN). Despite the initial challenges, including student reluctance to reflect, Winifred attempted to help students cultivate a habit of reflective thinking with the support of the consultant, who was a senior expatriate colleague taking charge of all curriculum matters in School B (ID, FN). He suggested diversifying the formats of end-of-unit reflection activities using oral tasks, role-play, mind-mapping, letter writing, and debates in order to facilitate uptake of key metacognitive skills, namely reviewing and monitoring (ID, Ob). Besides collegiality, the English-rich environment (a high percentage of native-speaking English teachers) and medium of instruction (integrative use of English outside classroom) had a role to play in supporting the full implementation of a portfolio-based approach, which characterized record keeping of assessments, prewriting scaffolding, a feedback-rich environment (self-, peer and teacher feedback), and frequent update of unit content (Ob, FN).

Opportunities for Collaboration

Willy's school joined a project entitled "Quality School Improvement Plan" where the university researchers gave advice to Willy and his colleagues on how to improve their pedagogical approaches and developed a set of instructional materials for the teachers to recycle in the forthcoming academic years (ID). However, Willy felt that his role was somewhat passive and that he was unable to get more involved in the project as he and his colleagues mainly followed the directives and advice from the project team rather than working out alternatives to improve teaching effectiveness together (FN). The opportunity to have external collaboration with the university proves to be a good start for teacher learning and professional development. However, according to Harlen's (2010) typology, Willy's collaboration with an external institution was only limited to Model C "trial and adjustment" which emphasizes teachers trying out classroom assessment materials/approaches designed by others and encourages teachers' exploration of the underlying principles of these classroom activities. For my portfolio assessment project, Willy said that it was again a joint venture with an outside researcher (the author), yet he had more "professional space" to think about the ways portfolio assessment practices could be integrated into the current English curriculum (ID). Although Willy had more autonomy to attempt innovative assessment practices in my project, he primarily counted on published research and prior knowledge he acquired in the teacher education programs. The knowledge transmission approach he adopted implies that his professional space could be somewhat restricted by the larger work environment, which led to classroom isolation, and the conservative school culture.

While Winifred's school has launched a range of school-based programs such as the literacy program and language arts program in the English Department, these innovative initiatives are from the English team and senior management rather than research projects with scholars or university researchers (TN). For instance, led by the panel head, Winifred and the panel members constructed relevant course packages for these school-based programs. Before printing, select panel members were assigned to peer review each other's teaching and learning materials. This kind of in-house editorial mechanism enriches the process of teacher learning as a community of practice. Asked how these school-based programs facilitated the trial of portfolio assessment, Winifred stated that despite the novelty of portfolio assessment, she and her team had an adequate consensus and had communicated with students, parents and senior management in launching new assessment programs, especially those emphasizing how to use assessment information to support learning (ID). Additionally, Winifred pointed out that the portfolio approach shared one of the characteristics of assessment for learning which was to enable learners to become independent in the learning process. Although not everyone in the English Department would possibly have understood the rationale of portfolio assessment nor bought into the idea of reflective practices, Winifred argued that with consistent efforts, mutual trust, and shared visions, she and her team could launch another welcoming assessment program that benefited students' eventual learning (ID). Looking over Winifred's student portfolios (despite not being a formal part of data collection), I noticed that three out of the four students were able to comment on their strengths, weaknesses, and areas of improvement in the end-of-year reflection pieces in great detail (FN). Winifred obviously had valuable opportunities to collaborate with her colleagues when innovating portfolio assessment practices.

Discussion

To summarize, Willy viewed the formal teacher education training and professional development events as the major avenues of teacher learning. Because of his lack of in-depth understanding, he was only able to introduce portfolio assessment as a set of technical procedures rather than getting to the bottom of its pedagogical rationale such as using self-reflection to align teaching and assessment of writing to further promote learning. The meso-level contextual factors that mediated Willy's assessment innovation were the teacher evaluation system (application for tenure), lack of support from School A due to conservatism, and lack of horizontal collaboration opportunities such as collective endeavors in launching portfolio assessment. In contrast, Winifred regarded teacher learning as sites of lived experiences and "trial and error" in enacting diverse instructional approaches. A collegial and English-rich school environment facilitated Winifred's trial of student reflection in the portfolio program. Continued support from the senior management and the whole-school approach further materialized the application of portfolio assessment as a viable classroom assessment. Based on the above results, two emerging issues—assessment training and school-level factors in teacher learning—are worthy of in-depth discussion.

Teacher Learning and Assessment Training

As revealed in the findings and in the teacher learning literature (Desimone et al. 2002; Opfer and Pedder 2011), teacher learning is a complex construct beyond the confines of formal assessment training as typically provided by initial teacher education programs and other professional development events. Instead, professional knowledge from teacher learning relies very much on how teachers internalize the theory-practice nexus and make knowledge transfer as part of professional learning. Structured assessment training only provides teachers with domain-specific input, but teachers should take every opportunity to trial, develop, and evaluate how these assessment ideas can work contextually in their classrooms. For instance, Willy has uncritically followed the practices of self-assessment and reflection in portfolio assessment without considering his students' preferences, institutional constraints, and tensions between the product and process approaches to assessment. Also, frightened of obtaining an unsatisfactory teacher evaluation and upsetting a relatively conservative school culture, Willy had to relinquish his "professional space" and emulate the portfolio assessment practices as suggested by me. Simply carrying out portfolio assessment practices as a set of techniques, Willy is unable to "unlearn" what he has learned from the professional learning events by comparing and contrasting the disconfirming evidence or problems arising from the portfolio trial (Gleeson and Davison 2016). Xu and Brown (2016) argue that to become assessment-literate, teachers need to engage in reflective practices and participate in community activities as Winifred does by performing school-based collaborative professional learning. With this in mind, assessment training should underscore individual reflective activities, e.g., reflection-in-action (Farrell 2016) together with active involvement in a community of practice. Although, in Hong Kong, not every school can afford to provide teachers with autonomy to develop professional knowledge collectively, teachers may form a critical mass, trying out portfolio assessment and sharing with colleagues the pros and cons of this alternative assessment approach. With convincing educational evidence, other stakeholders including parents, principals, students, and sponsoring bodies are likely to buy the idea of portfolio assessment in the long run.

Meso-Level Contextual Factors Relating to Assessment Innovation

As pointed out by Fulmer et al. (2015), there has been plentiful scholarship on the micro-level and macro-level contextual factors that influence teacher assessment beliefs and practices and the interrelationships of two levels. That said, there remains inadequate evidence to examine how the meso-level factors including school culture and teacher appraisal system have influenced teacher implementation of portfolio assessment. For example, both Willy and Winifred are open-minded, enthusiastic, and committed to trialing the portfolio assessment program as they volunteered to join the research project. However, because of systemic constraints like career advancement mechanisms, individual school cultures, and level of teacher autonomy, Willy and Winifred have reacted very differently when implementing a novel classroom assessment practice, despite their willingness and teacher education. It can be argued that Willy and Winifred may have divergent career orientations and motivational traits, with Willy aspiring to be substantiated as a civil servant and Winifred being in a middle management position (as one of the associate heads). From the findings, it is clear that the two teachers are intrinsically motivated to implement the innovation—portfolio assessment. Nonetheless, Willy has met with more meso-level constraints, including lack of school support (collaboration), conservatism, and high-stakes teacher evaluation systems, whereas Winifred has more autonomy to introduce the new assessment initiative with mutual trust and support from the senior management. Besides teacher conceptions of assessment and wider cultural norms, the meso-level contextual factors play a key role in explaining why the implementation of portfolio assessment always "comes and goes" because teachers have not received adequate support from their immediate work contexts (van Tartwijk et al. 2007). To this end, fostering a culture of school-based collaboration, providing professional space to facilitate change, and including innovation as part of teacher evaluation appear to be imperative if teachers and administrators wish to implement portfolio assessment successfully.

The findings further imply that despite certain institutional and work-related challenges, Willy and Winifred have learned about the issues attached to practicing portfolio assessment in EFL contexts (motivating students to self-reflect), learned how to make use of this innovative practice (enhanced understanding of the rationale behind portfolio assessment), and learned to adapt their teaching to improve students' learning (integrating portfolio assessment in the writing curriculum). While the impact of teacher learning from classroom assessment may not always be substantial, it is worthwhile to note that the two participants have sustained on-the-job learning opportunities to experiment with various portfolio assessment methods which could be said to improve teaching and learning of writing.

Conclusion

While the study reports on two teachers' implementation of portfolio assessment, it adds new knowledge to the educational assessment literature by illustrating how the process of teacher learning and certain meso-level contextual factors such as school culture could influence the likelihood of introducing an alternative classroom assessment practice. The results of the study are likely to enrich our understanding that teacher learning is a slippery concept and a complex process, which is beyond the provision of initial teacher education, short-lived professional development and participation in school-based collaborative projects among colleagues and/or with university researchers. In this study, the characteristics of portfolio assessment including self-assessment, learner reflection, continued monitoring and reviewing of composing processes (i.e., self-regulated learning) are all theoretically connected to assessment for learning practices, which require in-depth conceptual understanding and proficient mastery of skills to support positive student learning. While teachers' understanding can be enhanced through exposure to professional training, experience, and repeated practices, questions remain how these teachers can precisely learn to translate this prospective learning-oriented assessment into practice, especially in the EFL writing environment. It is hoped that with more teacher-initiated professional development endeavors backed by collegial school culture, teachers will be able to "unlearn" their current writing assessment practices and "relearn" how the unique facets of portfolio assessment such as metacognitive thinking and composing skills can be productively incorporated into the English curriculum to facilitate student learning of writing, in general, and to equip students with lifelong learning skills, in particular.

Acknowledgements The work described in this paper was fully supported by a grant from the Research Grants Council of the Hong Kong Special Administrative Region, China (HKBU 22400414).

References

Benson, P. (2010). Teacher education and teacher autonomy: Creating spaces for experimentation in secondary school English language teaching. *Language Teaching Research, 14*(3), 259–275.

Black, P., & Wiliam, D. (1998). Assessment and classroom learning. *Assessment in Education: Principles, Policy & Practice, 5*(1), 7–74.

Carless, D. (2005). Prospects for the implementation of assessment for learning. *Assessment in Education: Principles, Policy & Practice, 12*(1), 39–54.

Davison, D. (2013). Innovation in assessment: Common misconceptions and problems. In K. Hyland & L. L. Wong (Eds.), *Innovation and change in English language education* (pp. 263–275). Abingdon: Routledge.

Davison, C., & Leung, C. (2009). Current issues in English language teacher-based assessment. *TESOL Quarterly, 43*(3), 393–415.

Desimone, L. M., Porter, A. C., Garet, M. S., Yoon, K. S., & Birman, B. F. (2002). Effects of professional development on teachers' instruction: Results from a three-year longitudinal study. *Educational Evaluation and Policy Analysis, 24*(2), 81–112.

Dixon, H. R., Hawe, E., & Parr, J. (2011). Enacting assessment for learning: The beliefs practice nexus. *Assessment in Education: Principles, Policy & Practice, 18*(4), 365–379.

Earl, L. M., & Timperley, H. (2014). Challenging conceptions of assessment. In C. Wyatt-Smith, C. V. Klenowski, & P. Colbert (Eds.), *Designing assessment for quality learning: The enabling power of assessment* (Vol. 1, pp. 325–336). Dordrecht: Springer.

Farrell, T. S. (2016). *From trainee to teacher: Reflective practice for novice teachers*. London: Equinox.

Fives, H., & Buehl, M. M. (2012). Spring cleaning for the "messy" construct of teachers' beliefs: What are they? Which have been examined? What can they tell us? In K. R. Harris, S. Graham, & T. Urdan (Eds.), *APA educational psychology handbook: Individual differences and cultural and contextual factors* (Vol. 2, pp. 471–499). Washington: American Psychological Association.

Fulmer, G. W., Lee, I. C., & Tan, K. H. (2015). Multi-level model of contextual factors and teachers' assessment practices: An integrative review of research. *Assessment in Education: Principles, Policy & Practice, 22*(4), 475–494.

Gleeson, M., & Davison, C. (2016). A conflict between experience and professional learning: Subject teachers' beliefs about teaching English language learners. *RELC Journal, 47*(1), 43–57.

Hamp-Lyons, L. (2007). The impact of testing practices on teaching: Ideologies and alternatives. In J. Cummins & C. Davison (Eds.), *The international handbook of English language teaching* (Vol. 1, pp. 487–504). Norwell: Springer.

Hargreaves, E. (2013). Assessment for learning and teacher learning communities: UK teachers' experiences. *Teacher Education, 24*(3), 327–344.

Harlen, W. (2010). Professional learning to support teacher assessment. In J. Gardner, W. Harlen, L. Hayward, G. Stobart, & M. Montgomery (Eds.), *Developing teacher assessment* (pp. 100–129). New York: Open University Press.

Hill, M. F. (2011). 'Getting traction': Enablers and barriers to implementing assessment for learning in secondary schools. *Assessment in Education: Principles, Policy & Practice, 18*(4), 347–364.

Hill, M. F. (2016). Assessment for learning community: Learners, teachers and policymakers. In D. Wyse, L. Hayward, & J. Pandya (Eds.), *The Sage handbook of curriculum, pedagogy and assessment* (Vol. 2, pp. 772–789). London: Sage.

Humphries, S., & Burns, A. (2015). 'In reality it's almost impossible': CLT-oriented curriculum change. *ELT Journal, 69*(3), 239–248.

Hyland, K., & Wong, L. L. (2013). Introduction: Innovation and implementation of change. In K. Hyland & L. L. Wong (Eds.), *Innovation and change in English language education* (pp. 1–10). Abingdon: Routledge.

James, M., & Pedder, D. (2006). Beyond method: Assessment and learning practices and values. *The Curriculum Journal, 17*(2), 109–138.

Jang, E. E. (2014). *Focus on assessment: Research-led guide—Helping teachers understand, design, implement, and evaluate language assessment*. Oxford: Oxford University Press.

Klenowski, V. (2012). Raising the stakes: The challenges for teacher assessment. *Australian Educational Researcher, 39*(2), 173–192.

Koh, K. H. (2011). Improving teachers' assessment literacy through professional development. *Teaching Education, 22*(3), 255–276.

Lam, R. (2013). Two portfolio systems: EFL students' perceptions of writing ability, text improvement, and feedback. *Assessing Writing, 18*(2), 132–153.

Lam, R. (2016). Implementing assessment for learning in a Confucian context: The case of Hong Kong 2004–14. In D. Wyse, L. Hayward, & J. Pandya (Eds.), *The Sage handbook of curriculum, pedagogy and assessment* (Vol. 2, pp. 756–771). London: Sage.

Lee, I. (2011). Issues and challenges in teaching and learning EFL writing: The case of Hong Kong. In T. Cimasko & M. Reichelt (Eds.), *Foreign language writing instruction: Principles and practices* (pp. 118–137). Anderson, SC: Parlor Press.

Lee, I. (2015). Student teachers' changing beliefs on a pre-service teacher education course in Hong Kong. In T. Wright & M. Beaumont (Eds.), *Experiences of second language teacher education* (pp. 15–41). London: Palgrave Macmillan.

Lee, I. (2016). Teacher education on feedback in EFL writing: Issues, challenges, and future directions. *TESOL Quarterly, 50*(2), 518–527.

Lee, I., Mak, P., & Burns, A. (2016). EFL teachers' attempts at feedback innovation in the writing classroom. *Language Teaching Research, 20*(2), 248–269.

Marshall, B., & Drummond, M. J. (2006). How teachers engage with assessment for learning: Lessons from the classroom. *Research Papers in Education, 21*(2), 133–149.

Opfer, V. P., & Pedder, D. (2011). Conceptualizing teacher professional learning. *Review of Educational Research, 81*(3), 376–407.

Qian, D. D. (2014). School-based English language assessment as a high-stakes examination component in Hong Kong: Insights of frontline assessors. *Assessment in Education: Principles, Policy & Practice, 21*(3), 251–270.

Smith, L. F., Hill, M. F., Cowie, B., & Gilmore, A. (2014). Preparing teachers to use the enabling power of assessment. In C. Wyatt-Smith, V. Klenowski, & P. Colbert (Eds.), *Designing assessment for quality learning, the enabling power of assessment* (Vol. 1, pp. 303–323). Dordrecht: Springer.

Stevens, R. J. (2004). Why do educational innovations come and go? What do we know? What can we do? *Teaching and Teacher Education, 20,* 389–396.

Tan, K. H. (2013). Variation in teachers' conceptions of alternative assessment in Singapore primary schools. *Educational Research for Policy and Practice, 12*(1), 21–41.

Tong, S. Y. (2010). Lesson learned? School leadership and curriculum reform in Hong Kong. *Asia Pacific Journal of Education, 30*(2), 231–242.

Tong, S. Y. (2011). Assessing English language arts in Hong Kong secondary schools. *The Asia-Pacific Education Researcher, 20*(2), 389–396.

van Tartwijk, J., Driessen, E., van Der Vleuten, C., & Stokking, K. (2007). Factors influencing the successful introduction of portfolios. *Quality in Higher Education, 13*(1), 69–79.

Wiliam, D. (2011). What is assessment for learning? *Studies in Educational Evaluation, 37*(1), 3–14.

Wilson, S. M., & Berne, J. (1999). Teacher learning and the acquisition of professional knowledge: An examination of research on contemporary professional development. *Review of Research in Education, 24*(1), 173–209.

Xu, Y., & Brown, G. T. (2016). Teacher assessment literacy in practice: A reconceptualization. *Teaching and Teacher Education, 58,* 149–162.

Xu, Y., & Liu, Y. (2009). Teacher assessment knowledge and practice: A narrative inquiry of a Chinese college EFL teacher's experience. *TESOL Quarterly, 43*(3), 493–513.

Chapter 7
Integrating Assessment into Classroom Instruction to Create Zones of Development for Teachers and Learners: Some Perspectives from India

Tara Ratnam and Jacob Tharu

Abstract Public education in India, with its roots in the colonial system introduced in the nineteenth century, is marked by centralized state-level policy formulation that extends, significantly, to the substance of the school curriculum. The washback effect of an externally controlled examination system curtails teachers' flexibility in the everyday classroom curriculum transaction. Against this backdrop, a recent curriculum initiative was introduced, aimed at making assessment in schools more flexible. This initiative carries the potential to dislodge the summative examination system from its heavily dominant position by invoking an assessment component aligned closely with classroom instruction. The authors consider teachers' assessment practice at the classroom level as a vital, perhaps most important, source of their growth as professionals and as people. The factors influencing this space for teacher growth, at the formal curriculum policy and immediate supervisory levels, are analyzed in the case of one among numerous possible local settings in the enormously diverse landscape of schooling in India. The aim is to understand better how teachers engage with the challenges and opportunities relating to the assessment component of classroom practice, and what this might reveal about their growth and its impact on student learning.

Keywords Assessment reform · Classroom assessment · Leaner development · Sociocultural perspective · Teacher growth

T. Ratnam (✉) · J. Tharu
Independent Teacher Educator and Researcher, Mysore, India
e-mail: tararatnam@gmail.com

J. Tharu
e-mail: jimtharu@gmail.com

T. Ratnam · J. Tharu
Center for Evaluation, English and Foreign Languages University, Hyderabad, India

© Springer Nature Singapore Pte Ltd. 2018
H. Jiang and M. F. Hill (eds.), *Teacher Learning with Classroom Assessment*,
https://doi.org/10.1007/978-981-10-9053-0_7

119

Introduction

Public education in India, still in the mold of the colonial system introduced in the nineteenth century, is marked by centralized state-level policy formulation that extends, significantly, to the substance of the school curriculum. The syllabus, textbooks, and evaluation schemes for every grade level are prescribed by the many state education boards to one of which every school is affiliated. There is typically a tight calendar for completing the syllabus ("portions" is the popular expression). The board-controlled matriculation examination serves in practice as the model for all unit, mid-term, and annual tests conducted by schools. These factors curtail the teachers' flexibility in day-to-day curriculum transaction. Preparing students for pre-set tests dominate classroom instruction. Despite its obvious distorting effect on learning and teaching, this external examination system has proved to be remarkably tenacious, with decades of earnest and vigorous examination reform efforts (e.g., Government of India [GOI] 1966, 1986; Hunter 1882) reaping little positive effect. The urgency of reform remains.

Against this cheerless backdrop, a curriculum renewal exercise, initiated in 2005, carried the potential to dislodge the summative examination system from its heavily dominant position by invoking an assessment component aligned closely with classroom instruction. Its foundation is the National Curriculum Framework (NCF) 2005 (National Council for Educational Research and Training 2005). The proposed curriculum draws on ideas/ideals aligned with learner centeredness: reaffirming the value of each child and enabling all to experience dignity and the confidence to learn, valuing the experience and knowledge children bring to school, promoting all-round development of the child while welcoming diversity among learners as a resource. The inclusivity stressed in this approach reflects a deep commitment to universal elementary education (UEE). It marks a shift in perspective on knowledge and pedagogy: knowledge as discovered and not unfolding, and pedagogy as facilitation more than transmission. Such an exploratory pedagogy does not traverse a sequence of predefined milestones. It requires internal monitoring to maintain progress in the right direction. This internal monitoring, which amounts to assessment running hand-in-hand with teaching, was not recognized as relevant, let alone endorsed, in the earlier system that was based on the transmission of prepackaged knowledge and accountability-oriented summative evaluation. The new perspective brings openness to the possibilities of formative evaluation introduced in Bloom et al. (1971; see also Andersson and Palm 2017; Black and William 1998; Stobart 2009; Wylie and Lyon 2012). The familiar term *formative evaluation*—long a mere slogan—is now being carried into practice in Indian education.

The essential principles of the NCF reform were adopted with variations by all the state education boards. The NCF 2005 discussion relating to this new position on assessment that integrates it into teaching, wisely noted the need for further exploration and thinking through before its implementation as a systemic change. However, the state boards, in need of a package of practical evaluation procedures that could be mandated, bypassed this stage of seeking clarity and came up with variants of a detailed scheme labeled Continuous and Comprehensive Evaluation (CCE) prepared initially by the Central Board of Secondary Education (CBSE) in 2009. In Karnataka State, where this study was located, a revised curriculum and a CCE manual were mandated in 2012. CCE is essentially a set of procedures for teachers to follow faithfully. They are to assess learners *continuously* by observing learners' performance on various classroom activities, and *comprehensively* covering co-scholastic areas in addition to subject-related knowledge. At the same time, conventional tests at regular intervals remain in place. In the current CCE package, *formative assessments* (FA) is a descriptive label covering observation-based assessment of students as they engage in learning activities, and *summative assessment* (SA) refers to the mid-term and year-end formal examinations. The uneasy coupling of FA with SA has given rise to contradictions at the classroom level and these have been the focus of several investigations (e.g., Srinivasan 2015). The present study notes these problems. However, its primary focus is on teacher practice and learning in the setting represented by CCE.

A Perspective on Teacher Learning Possibilities in the New Approach to Classroom Assessment

CCE as a policy mandate includes, as we have pointed out, a component of continuous and comprehensive evaluation in the classroom alongside teaching, and a component of formal summative tests. The primary focus of this study was on teacher learning as they engaged in continuous (ongoing) classroom assessment integrated with teaching, in a potentially formative role. We use CCE (in lower case) to indicate this process that allows teachers some autonomy. The spirit of CCE presumes an active and responsive role from learners as contributors, from their cultural and experiential location to the co-construction of the knowledge they gain. Learning is based on what students do in collaboration with teachers and peers and not on what they can recall and reproduce after the lesson. Seen in this light, purposeful CCE can have meaning only within a pedagogy that is "dialogic" (e.g., Lima and von Duyke 2016) in nature. It cannot be conceptualized within a behaviorist, knowledge transmission, teacher-centered pedagogy. In India, the strong tradition of teacher-centered practices typically takes the form of the teacher explaining the matter in the prescribed lesson, giving notes that are answers to likely test items, and getting students to memorize them through repeated rehearsals before tests of such knowledge are administered.

As mentioned earlier, a shift in the focus of assessment from the product to the process of learning echoes and reinforces a parallel shift of role for the teacher from being a "source of knowledge to being a facilitator" (National Council for Educational Research and Training [NCERT] 2005, p. 109). It implies new dimensions of learning for the teacher as such exploratory pedagogy leads to contingencies arising from the emergent and unstructured interaction inside the classroom with and among students, and also those arising in the institutional context of teachers' work. The teacher's focus has to change from giving knowledge to promoting students' understanding through provocations that "ontologically" engage them in inquiry and make them justify the perspective they choose from among alternative responses (Matusov 2011). This involves not only generating but also interpreting and responding to student feedback, typically received in a dynamic and disorganized manner. The teacher, in her new role, has to learn to "listen", "observe" and understand students' meaning making, that is, the potential for development or what Vygotsky (1978) calls "maturing functions". This emergent information viewed diagnostically spurs teacher reflection on creating new zones of development to extend students' thinking further along the path of learning. Familiar teaching skills delivered during training by external agents (experts) are not adequate to meet the new challenge created by this interdependence of assessment and teaching. It calls for the development of teachers' own agentive power to deal with uncertainties of an open-ended dialogue taking place in real time.

Besides, it is important to note that teachers' work is socially situated in the "contested classroom space" (Craig 2009) where a complex mix of desires and imperatives exerts pulls in different directions creating tensions for the teacher to negotiate. Therefore, teachers' agency extends beyond what they teach (the subject matter) to the people they are. The teacher, in this view, is not an "implementer of other people's knowledge" (Cochran-Smith and Lytle 1999, p. 16), but a "curriculum maker" (Clandinin and Connelly 1992). He/she can generate knowledge that contributes to his/her personal and professional theory of teaching and learning as he/she negotiates the work within the resources and constraints of his/her context. In short, teacher learning, in this new pedagogy, involves teachers developing a culture of inquiry (Kincheloe 2003), to thoughtfully review what they observe in class. Such a culture of inquiry includes their own culturally embedded practice, and the beliefs and assumptions underlying it, and explores ways in which they can better facilitate student learning.

Questions of the Study

Our study seeks to understand teachers in the process of interpreting and engaging with the "forces of change" (Fullan 1993, p. vii) ushered in by the CCE policy:

1. How do teachers negotiate the new demands placed on their daily classroom practice within the cultural and institutional context of their work?
2. To what extent does CCE help them see, experience, and inhabit the classroom in new ways and, therefore, foster their growth and students' learning?

Theoretical Orientation

We use a Vygotskian sociocultural perspective while responding to the questions above, because it helps us unpack the contradictions and challenges inherent in the social setting in which teachers' work is situated. The situated nature of thinking advanced by a sociocultural perspective helps us see that thinking is not merely a psychological process taking place in the mind of the individual in isolation. Individuals are connected to the social fabric of life and their thinking is mediated by the surrounding cultural world (Vygotsky 1978). Therefore, the cultural context in which a teacher's work is nested becomes significant in the construction of his/her self as a teacher. This view of teacher learning, as a process mediated by the cultural mores of his/her workplace, places cognition in the realm of culture and offers a framework to capture the dialectical interplay between institutional mandates and cultural expectations, on the one hand, and teacher orientations, on the other. It is in this dialectical interaction that teachers' responses (including teacher learning) to the new demands of classroom assessment placed on them, take shape.

Sample Selection and Setting

Schools in India fall into two parallel organizational sectors: the government and the private. We chose the state-run government school category for our study because this is where mass education is delivered. Our interest was linked to the fact that it served the children from marginalized segments that lacked the financial resources and cultural capital that provide alternative means of gaining school knowledge. We also believe that assessment in support of teaching and learning (understood here as CCE) is potentially an important lever for raising quality. Insights into teachers' engagement with this resource and their professional growth aided by it could be a significant contribution flowing from the study.

Our study was located in the primary school system in Karnataka state. The Karnataka state is divided into four educational divisions, each covering six to nine districts. We decided on Mysuru district as it is large and offers wide variations in the urban and rural schools that come under it. Such variety can yield rich data. Our sample consisted of 16 schools, both urban and rural. We call each school a context (C) in keeping with the study's focus on schools as developing contexts in which teachers' work is embedded. The schools varied in size from 21 to 120 students for the lower primary schools (Grades 1–5), and from 51 to 510 students for the upper primary schools (Grades 1–7). One school had no building of its own, and used a community hall; two had separate buildings about 400 meters apart. Five schools had only two rooms for five classes and the office space, and children sat on the floor in clusters. In other schools where a few benches were available, some children sat on them and others on the floor. Thus, there was no typical classroom size and general layout.

The deployment of teachers (from the general pool) to a school is to maintain an overall teacher–pupil ratio of 1:30 or 1:40 depending on the total strength being below or above 120. The number of classes is not considered. Teachers may be required to teach any subject whether or not they have the relevant subject or method's training.

Another aspect of the classroom setting was the highly diverse home backgrounds of the children: linguistic, ethnic, caste identity, socio-economic status, cultural conventions, values, and especially attitudes to and expectations from formal schooling. Children with special needs have to be admitted to the government school. But the schools as a whole are not designed to "include" such children. This description highlights the ways in which the schools in the sample vary and points to the gap between them as a whole and the hidden assumptions of a normal school in the standard curriculum.

Participants and Sources of Data

Fifty-seven teachers (T1–T57) from 16 school contexts (C1–C16) who completed all the procedures, including questionnaires, interviews and class observations, participated in the study. The teachers were interviewed both before and after classroom observations. The academic support for teachers is provided by the District Institute of Education and Training (DIET). The DIET teachers are the main resource persons (DRPs) who receive training at the state level, along with chosen block resource persons (BRPs) and cluster resource persons (CRPs). They, in turn, train four master resource persons (MRPS) from each block. The MRPs, in turn, cascade the training further down to the teachers under the supervision of DRPs. The school head teacher (HT) and teachers are at the bottom rung of the hierarchy of the education system. The DIET principal, 4 DRPs, 1 BRP, 5 CRPs, and HTs of all schools also participated in the study.

The sources of data are teacher questionnaires (T-qn), interviews (T-int), and class observations (Cl ob); interviews with the DIET principal, DRPs, BRP, CRPs, HTs, and teachers; documents including the literature pertaining to school administration and training, official circulars, various records maintained in schools and by teachers, student profiles (portfolios), and textbooks; cluster-level interaction meetings and teacher training; and, field notes (FN) with impressions of what was being observed in the classroom, staffroom and about the general ecology of the school contexts. All the interviews with teachers and other RPs were semi-structured and conducted loosely, much like the flow of a casual conversation. Besides these interviews, we have had ongoing conversations with teachers, HTs and other RPs, both face-to-face and over the phone.

Generally, the school year commences in the last week of May and closes in the second week of April, with a mid-term break of 17 days in October. The first month of school is set aside for the bridge course, and the last month before the summative examination is reserved for revision. The class observation was carried out in the second half of the academic year 2015–16 and the first part of 2016–17. It was in three stages to capture the different phases of teaching: (1) the bridge course, (2) teaching the class syllabus, and (3) revision. In all, 104 lessons of 40 min each were observed covering the various subjects[1] taught and in various seasons—bridge course (18 lessons), syllabus teaching (66 lessons), and revision (20 lessons).

---

[1] Kannada (regional language), Hindi, Urdu, English, social studies, science, and mathematics.

The language of the transaction in schools is the regional language, Kannada. All the interviews and class observations were recorded and transcribed and translated into English from Kannada. Many of the transactions in the English classes were also in Kannada as the teachers' proficiency in English was low.

Permission for the field study was obtained from the concerned authorities in both the Block Education Office and the DIET. This put an obligation on the teachers to comply. The teachers' initial response was guarded and evasive, much in line with the way they would react to officials who came to inspect them. We had to break the barrier of power created by teachers' gaze and earn our credibility by building relationships of reciprocity and trust where teachers felt confident to voice real concerns without the need to put on an act.

Data Analysis

In our ethnographically oriented study, the main focus was on teachers' lived experiences within the dynamics resulting from the opposition between normative standards and procedures set by the institution, on the one hand, and ground realities, on the other. We have undertaken both "phenotypic" (descriptive) and "genotypic" (explanatory) analysis (Lewin 1935 in Vygotsky 1978, 62). The phenotypic analysis, using data from teacher questionnaires, class observations and post-class conversations, helped us see the fit between teachers' espoused epistemological beliefs and practice, while the genotypic analysis helped trace the roots of the observed phenomenon and its future orientation. For the latter, we drew on all the sources of data to lay bare how teachers' agency interacted with cultural contextual factors to mediate their thinking and action in particular ways. The data analysis showed teachers' common cultural perceptions and, within the framework of these cultural realities, how individual learning paths developed in response to external demands and internal dispositions. The developing perceptions of teachers are seen on a continuum formed by the two orientations to teaching: (1) learning and assessment discussed earlier, viz, monologic transmission where assessment is used for evaluative judgment of students, on the one hand, and (2) formative use of assessment in a dialogic meaning-making process, on the other (Fig. 7.1).

The categories identified regarding teachers' learning or developing perceptions have emerged through a reflexive iterative process based on both relevant literature and "visiting and revisiting the data and connecting them with emerging insights" (Srivastava and Hopwood 2009, 77). Keeping in mind issues of validity such as the representative nature of the findings and the ethical aspect of the intersubjective undertaking, we took several measures to promote the credibility and dependability of our findings (Guba and Lincoln 1989), by triangulating diverse sources of data and multiple and developing meanings of participants.

Findings

The CCE training manuals and the trainers tell teachers that they should not explain or use the lesson to transmit knowledge, but facilitate students' construction of knowledge as they engage in group activities. The model for facilitation given to teachers consists of 5 Es: engage, explore, express/explain, expand, and evaluate. Evaluation involves ongoing and sensitive observation of learners through all other stages, integrating assessment with teaching, as teachers first *engage* students in learning using a priming activity, and through problem-posing activities have students *explore* and *express/explain* the meaning they have constructed and finally *expand* their learning by linking learning to their life. The books have some activities to engage students thoughtfully in learning and project work, to encourage independent learning.

Since the introduction of the new approach to teaching and assessment in Karnataka, there is an acknowledgment that teachers need a lot of support to understand and put it into practice. A manual (Department of Public Education, Government of Karnataka 2013) and several supplements have been brought out with details of principles and practice of CCE within the new curriculum. Besides, teachers have been given several rounds of training. In a year, a teacher receives about 18 days of training that includes six 1-day cluster-level monthly interaction meetings. The training consists mainly of lectures and demonstrations by RPs, videos of "best" practices, reading, group discussion, and presentations, followed by clarifying feedback by RPs. RPs also visit schools and observe teachers' classes and provide feedback.

Phenotypic Analysis of Teachers' Practice

We began our analysis with teachers' thinking and practice using data from teacher questionnaires (T-qn), class observations (Cl ob) and post-class conversations with teachers. The categories, constructed and triangulated with the findings from DIET

Fig. 7.1 Teacher's development trajectory

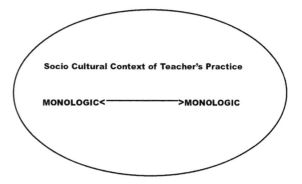

studies and documents, helped locate contradictions between teachers' espoused beliefs and their practice.

What Teachers Say

Following the new approaches to teaching and assessment, all the teachers said that earlier they used to "explain" the whole lesson while students listened (T-qn13). Now they were only "facilitators," guiding children as they constructed their knowledge. Teachers were unanimous in their claim that activity methods promoted learning; everyone participated and enjoyed the activities. They felt that students understood and remembered what they learnt by doing. They also pointed out that evaluation was now not just written examinations, but also included oral discussions and participation in activities. All the teachers said that they assessed students continuously in class by observing how they participated in activities and group discussions, and responded to questions in class (T-qn 12). They also said that they used this form of classroom assessment to check and reinforce learning and to give grades. Most teachers (48) claimed that they "build in activity as an integral part of teaching" (T-qn 10c). However, questioned when they did activities in class, the majority of teachers (41) ticked the option, "for lessons which are suited to activity" (T-qn 9a). Twelve of them said, "one activity per lesson" (T-qn 9b) and five, "when I have to record grades" (T-qn 9c). The inconsistencies in teachers' responses seemed to point to a mix of what teachers thought they were expected to do and what they did. This became apparent in the genotypic analysis.

The overall picture emerging from an analysis of T-qn was that teachers seemed to be answering based largely on what they understood as a desirable practice. This was not only consistent with the findings of the studies conducted by the DIET (e.g., DIET 2015) regarding teachers' views and implementation of the new teaching and CCE, but also with the teacher self-evaluations reflected in the performance index (PINDIX) form given to them by the department. The PINDIX analysis showed teachers' performance on the index to be beyond the expected level. The next section compares this "espoused model" with their "enacted model" of teaching and assessment (Ernest 1989).

What Teachers Do: How Teachers Practice Classroom Assessment

As mentioned earlier, cce hinges on the nature of interaction in the classroom. When interacting with students, and in the interaction among students, the teacher has an opportunity to both generate and provide feedback by identifying students' learning and deciding on the nature of support and challenge that will create new zones of development in the learner. Therefore, effective means of assistance to learning presupposes a participatory space in the classroom dialogue (with inherent assessment) to which students contribute with their subjective perceptions of knowledge on the way to developing a new understanding as has been pointed out. Our analysis is based on three broad approaches employed by teachers that the data helped us identify: (a) *staying with tradition*, (b) *constructing new practice through an old lens* and (c) *reconstructing practice with new understanding*. In synthesizing these categories, the focus has been on the extent to which classroom interactions took the form of dialogic meaning making, integrating assessment into the teaching-learning process, as opposed to being monologic and teacher dominated using assessment to check if the *given* was learned (see Fig. 7.1). Limited by chapter length, we provide one or two examples to illustrate the nature of each approach but further examples are available should readers be interested.

Staying with Tradition Eleven teachers were found to be strictly text-bound and believed that students needed direct teaching. Typically, they passed the content of the lesson through stretches of explanation punctuated by questions to check comprehension. In most cases, questions were either answered by the same two to three students or by the teacher himself/herself. The main concern of all language teachers was to enable students to read and write. Reading instruction consisted largely of making students read aloud, which gave teachers the opportunity to locate mistakes and correct them, while writing involved copying, either from the text or the blackboard. The math teachers usually made students work out problems on the blackboard and provided several rounds of explanation as they corrected the students, illustrated here:

(T37 was helping students identify by sight whether a number was divisible by 2)

1. T37: Shashi, is this [number 290] divisible by 2?
2. Shashi: No.
3. T37: What's in the unit place?
4. Shashi: Zero.
5. T37: (explains) 0, 2, 4, 6, and 8 are composite numbers. If they are in the unit place, what should you say? It is divisible by 2.

Teachers provided individual attention to students after the whole class explanation. However, the operational frame of classroom assessment and feedback was product oriented. It involved noting incorrect answers and providing corrective feedback. Students were made to repeat the *correct* answers, after the teachers, with no opportunity for them to think and construct their understanding. The post-class interviews with teachers showed that the new discourse about students being self-regulated learners was not convincing for these teachers: "They say students can learn on their own. How is that possible? How can they know what division is and how to do sums without first explaining it to them? Even then they make many mistakes and we have to keep on correcting…." These teachers felt CCE was a wasteful experiment cutting into their teaching time.

Constructing New Practice Through an Old Lens A majority of teachers (36/57) described their practice using the new discourse of CCE and its suggested pedagogical model, the 5 Es. Teachers started their class with a rhyme or story to "engage" the students. Then they posed a question or conducted an activity to assess students' previous knowledge that they called the "explore" stage. Under "express/explanation", teachers explained the lesson they had planned to teach for the day. They said that they integrated assessment into teaching by posing questions after teaching each subsection of the lesson. By way of linking learning to life ("expand"), teachers set some project work.

Only two teachers (T27 and T36) were able to speak English spontaneously. T56, for instance, said, "I don't know English very well. I manage the lessons with the help of words and flash cards and students respond. When students don't understand, I repeat in Kannada." The following excerpts from T56's 6th grade English class exemplify what happened more generally in a language class. They show how teachers' "new practice" tilted toward tradition.

(Kannada used in class is italicized)

1. T56: I give you flash cards, spelling read. *Read out the spelling and then the word* (points to one student) your card read.
2. SS1: c-l-a-s-h.
3. T56: Clash. Say it!
4. SS1: Clash.
5. T56: Next, you (pointed to another student)
6. SS2: T-a-b-e-l
7. T56: *Is that right?*
8. SS:(chorus) No
9. SS2: t-a-b-l-e (Other students take turns to read from their cards.)
10. T56: Mention any sportsman you know.
11. SS3: Virat Kholi.
12. T56: Which game is he famous for?
13. SS3: Cricket.
14. T56: Any other sportsman?
15. SS4: Blade runner.
16. T56: Sit down. Now I show some pictures. (Held up a chart with pictures of sportspersons and explained who they were. Finally pointed to one SS). Who is this? You must know him. He is India's pride.
17. SS5: Chess.
18. T56: Now we learn about a sportsman. He is Carl Pistorius. (Read the lesson first and then made students read aloud with her help. She explained the lesson in Kannada posing questions in between in English). Tell the name of the sportsman.
19. SS7: Oscar.
20. T56: Not only Oscar. You must say full name: Oscar Leonard Carl Pistorius. (Made students repeat the full name) When he was born? *In which year was he born?* (After the oral question/answer session, T56 divided the class into seven groups of 5–6 students each and distributed cards with a list of words to each group). Read and then write the opposite words (repeated instruction in Kannada. T56 went to each group making them read the words and checking if they knew the opposites and helped them with the ones they didn't know).

21. T56: *Now I give you project work. You must make a list of sportsmen and what they play. You will find it in the newspapers. Did you understand?* (Repeats instruction.)

About her class, T56 said:

I did the spelling and word reading activity to *engage* the students with what they already knew. Then I made them *explore* by showing the chart. They found out about the pictures. I also taught LSRW: made them listen when I read, and they also read after that. Then in the *explain* stage, I explained the lesson and gave group activity where they had to write opposite words. I also made them *go beyond the textbook* by asking them to list names of other sportsmen.

For these teachers too, like the traditional teachers mentioned earlier, classroom assessment under CCE was largely synonymous with continuous noticing and correcting:

I was listening to how students were answering and giving feedback. In the first activity, that boy said t-a-b-e-l and I corrected him. I also corrected while students read, answered my questions. I was observing them during group activity. Although I had done the opposites earlier, they were making mistakes and I helped them. (T56)

Like T56, teachers' descriptions of their practice had all the desirable dialogic ingredients of the new approach to teaching and assessment. However, their classroom practice showed them still firmly anchored in traditional monologic practice. While teachers endorsed in theory that the primary focus of assessment was to understand how to have students think and express themselves, the classroom interaction was primarily teacher generated. The learner's independent voice was hardly audible, because the space to explore and make sense on their terms was hijacked by teacher explanation. Even the activities used by the teacher in the initial and concluding stages of the class (1 and 20) were well structured with no open space for students to make their unique contribution. This showed a gap between teachers' desire to take advantage of the opportunities for engaging in CCE that the activity-based lessons made available and their actual practice of using assessment simply for providing corrective feedback. There were several other instances where activities provided a livelier space for student voices to break the teacher's monologue, as the following example shows, despite the teacher's stance.

T3, who was doing a unit called "Avoid Plastics" with Grade 7 students, had set a group activity. The students had to circle the objects they would choose from an array of mixed plastic and eco-friendly utility items. This was followed by a presentation session where students from different groups justified the choices they had made while the other groups commented. In one of the groups, there was a difference of opinion with two students opting for plastic plates, and the rest, a banana leaf, for serving food:

1. T3: (to the two students) Why did you choose plastic?
2. SS1: *because the gravy flows out of the leaf and becomes a mess. Plastic plates contain it neatly.*
3. SS: (chorus) No, no.

4. SS2: When you put hot food in plastic plate, the chemicals in the plate mixing with food. That [is] bad for health.
5. SS3: In both advantages and disadvantage
6. T3: So, which one you will choose?
7. SS3: Leaf.
8. SS1: Plastic.
9. T3: But it is bad for health.
10. SS1: *Nothing will happen if we use good* quality plastic.
11. T3: (after *explaining at length the harmful effects of plastic partly using Kannada and partly English*) So, we should not use plastic.
12. SS1: Yes.

The teacher mediation led the students to the teacher-defined (curriculum-designed) endpoint (11), and took away the indeterminacy of an open dialogue where there was also some scope for spontaneous interaction as students justified what they said (2,4,10). In a conversation with this teacher after class, she explained that she used real-time assessment for diagnosis and remediation: "Rajendra [SS1] had a wrong concept about plastic. His friends told him. I also told him. Then he accepted it. … The wrong concept is corrected…." This approach, however, shuts out the possibility of Rajendra's perspective becoming part of a classroom dialogue calling forth a possible rethink by all participants involved and beyond having to comply with the 'correction' offered by the teacher.

Reconstructing New Practice with New Understanding The potential for genuine student participation and dialogue, with classroom assessment and evaluation forming an integral part of listening to and responding to others in the spontaneous teacher–student and student–student interaction of the classroom, was seen in a few lessons (13/104). After teaching her Grade VII students a unit on energy in physics, T42 set a debate on the proposition, "We cannot do without electricity." T42 divided the class into two groups. Group A was to argue for the motion and Group B against it.

1. T42: (initiated the debate) We can't live without electricity because, from the time we get up in the morning, we need electricity for mixer, light and so on. (To Group A.) Now you continue.
2. SS1 (A): We use electricity for cooking, to run the mixer and grinder. Without electricity we can't survive, we need fan and fridge.
3. T42: Now Group A has made a point. Let Group B respond.
4. SS2 (B): You say you can't live without a fridge. We can keep water in an earthen pot. We can do without a fan, if we stop cutting trees. Then we will have plenty of fresh air.
5. SS3 (B): Electricity is dangerous. It can give shock.
6. SS4 (B): Why should you cook using gas or electricity? We can build a mud oven and use firewood to cook. If you use electricity, you have to pay for current. There are many people living without electricity—Ask Manasa or Priya, how they manage.
7. T42: Now the other group, you speak.

8.   SS5 (A): During summer, we can't do without fan.
9.   SS6 (A): When we use a mixer, our work is made easy and fast. If we use firewood, there's a lot of smoke.
10. SS3 (B): In our house, we use gas. It burst and my brother was hurt. It took a long time for him to recover. Electricity also can cause danger like that. Firewood is healthy. In the olden days people used firewood and were strong.
11. SS7 (A): Maybe it is healthy to cook with firewood. But you have to cut trees and we are destroying our surrounding....

(The argument continued and at one point the teacher intervened).

12. T42: Now let's vote. In the debate one group had to argue for "yes" and another "no". But when you vote, you give your subjective opinion.

(The debate did not stop even after the vote. Students kept challenging each other with fresh questions.)

13. SS8: I have my grandmother at home. If she wants to take something in the night, she needs electric light. How can she manage without it?
14. SS9: My parents are not at home when I go back and I have to cook. I find electricity convenient. Then we also need light to do homework.

The students, involved both cognitively and affectively in voicing their diverse points of view, were open to connecting with others' responses. Their perceptive responses to one another, which wove the debate, would not have been possible without evaluation being an integral part of these responses. Each student reached new understanding by approaching the other's point of view from his/her evaluative stance. Students pushed each other to more complex levels of thinking about the issue without the need to converge toward agreement. The teacher contributed significantly to promoting developing perceptions of the participants in this dialogic meaning-making process without seeking to close it with a predefined (her) conclusion. Allowing the students to vote (12) freely signaled that her opinion in the debate (1) was only one of the voices in the dialogue.

The phenotypic analysis of what teachers *say* and *do* indicated that a majority of teachers used the new jargon to describe their practice, picked up while working within a common cultural framework of curriculum prescription, mandates, expectations, and training. However, the same was not reflected or only partially reflected in their practice. There seemed to be a gap between their claim which had all the elements of what was socially desirable and expected of them such as inclusivity, on the one hand, and their practice, which was convergent and not sensitive to diversity as a resource for learning, on the other. The basic principle of giving initiative to students to think and express themselves from their cultural location, in a genuine dialogue of difference which is the crux of formative assessment and the spirit of CCE, was largely missing in the classroom transactions. Even the teachers, who displayed many features of learner-centered practice and formative use of data from assessment during the teaching phase, regressed markedly towards didactic practice during the time set aside for the bridge course and revision, encouraging rote learning. We questioned why the teachers inclined towards tradition despite the instructional interventions that incorporated teaching materials with several meaning-focused activities and extensive teacher training. To look for possible explanations of this puzzle we undertook the genotypic analysis. Here we examined the institutional context of teachers' work and their deep-rooted beliefs. It is in this dialectic between culture and cognition, as mentioned earlier, that teachers' response to new expectations needs to be seen.

Genotypic Analysis of Teachers' Practice: Why Teachers Enact CCE Poorly

As mentioned earlier, the evaluative component of the curriculum has strikingly new elements, the most prominent one being the emphasis on observation by the teacher for all performances of students as they engage in activities during the lesson. However, contradictions in the conceptualization of student assessment as accommodating diverse learning pathways in monitoring progress has reduced its function to diagnosis and remediation. This is very obvious, especially in the data from observation of the bridge course and revision, which showed teachers teaching "toward yesterday's development" (Vygotsky 1978, p. 89) using drill and practice. The express purpose of the bridge course, for instance, was remedial: to identify students who had not mastered the given list of grade-appropriate competencies (actually, knowledge) through a pre-test, to remedy the deficiencies in learning, and measure progress with a post-test at the end of the bridge course.

However, CCE combines the record of during term FA and end-of-term SA; the report card for students, generated six times a year, contains the statement of learners' achievement obtained from 4 FAs and 2 SAs. The FA too is reduced to a quantified summative (static) picture. With no discussion about a complementary relationship and the possibility of compensation to yield a balanced holistic picture of the learner, the dominance of conventional achievement test scores as the index of successful learning remains unchanged in public perception. This long-standing tradition of recording and reporting test-based information to satisfy external authorities appeared to leach CCE of its dynamic potential, making teachers largely lapse into teaching to the test. The potential for FA as a process to improve learning thus became a series of discrete assessments, that is, instances of continuous summative assessments. There are several emerging reasons why this might be the case. We explore these next.

Teacher Overload The government schools do not run like clockwork, despite the laid-out schedule. The following describes the scene on the first day of the researcher's field visit:

> The HM was collecting records from all the teachers about the implementation of ERWC (Early Reading and Writing with Comprehension) program which she had to submit at a meeting in the Block Education Office later in the afternoon. One of the teachers (T39) was compiling the information. Another teacher (T40) was collecting students' ration cards and unique identities and filling out their scholarship forms. I entered T38's class for observation.

> She was telling me about her plan, "I started the topic 'reproduction' in the last class and I am continuing that." By then a girl came to tell her that the HM wanted her. Before leaving, she asked the students to read the lesson and prepare five questions on what she had taught. She told me that she had some other work in the afternoon and would be away on training for a week from tomorrow. So she suggested that I observe her class after her return from the training. Of the four classes I had planned to observe today I managed two, one in the morning (T37) and one in the afternoon (T40).

This experience of seeing classes being disrupted was not just in one school on a particular day. It seemed endemic to the system (see also Vasavi 2015). As well as the routine monitoring and maintenance of detailed records of school-based meals, health and nutrition interventions, teachers shared the burden of non-teaching work with the HT. A large part of this was cumbersome paperwork, records and other data for use at higher administrative levels. These higher authority-required tasks got priority over the teachers' primary responsibility of teaching. This problem was voiced by all the teachers: "If we are allowed to work in the classroom uninterrupted, there is so much more we can do, such as conducting regular activities to improve children" (T43). Teachers' academic work was no less daunting:

> This method [the new approach to teaching and assessment] is good because we have to reach the weakest child also. But we need time. We start the actual teaching after 25th June [after the bridge course]. In July, August we have so much portions to complete, plus all the office work, preparing students for school and interschool programs. In September, we have to conduct the first semester oral and written exams. The syllabus is new. CCE is new. We find it difficult to adjust to everything at one go. We have to learn new content as we have to teach different subjects. I was doing science, and now I have to do math and social studies. Because it is central syllabus, the standard is high. We have to go deep into the subject. It is very difficult. Then we have to combine classes because we don't have one teacher per class. (A teacher at Block-level training, 18-12-2015)

Problems with Training: Overambitious Plan CCE came across to teachers as an extra load, because of the way it was communicated to them with very unrealistic expectations. The mandate on recording every student's performance continuously, using a checklist of criteria against the competencies taught using activities in the classroom, overwhelmed teachers.[2] For teachers used to text and tradition, ideas such as 'integrating activity into teaching,' 'competency-based teaching,' 'checklists', and 'criteria' were difficult to make sense of. The impracticality of this was voiced by teachers:

> We have to handle all the eight periods in a day and take 10–15 classes because we teach multi-grade classes. We also handle two or three different subjects. For every class, we have to prepare activities, choose tools and techniques for CCE, prepare criteria and document every child's progress. Where is the time to prepare all this every day? (T25)

However, the system's concern with accountability made record keeping the main focus of change. In the debate over recording students' real-time performance in class, the substantive aspect of CCE, such as creating and extending new zones for promoting learning, seemed to have become side lined.

---

[2]These difficulties faced by teachers in the Indian context echo the experiences of teachers elsewhere (e.g., Brown 2003; Chen 2015).

Lack of Conceptual Clarity at all Levels The formative nature of assessment implied by CCE has not been made clear to the teachers. They were confounded by the conflicting messages in the training manuals and also the training regarding the purpose of CCE. As mentioned earlier, despite exhorting the prospective aspect of assessment, which is to gain an understanding of where students are going and how they can be helped to move forward in their diverse trajectories, what gets stressed in the manuals for record keeping, is the retrospective remedial purpose of assessment. Therefore, most teachers had a very facile understanding of the purpose of continuous assessment (CCE): "Earlier also we used to check if students have learned what we teach by asking questions in class. Now we have to record it" (T23).

The training seems to have failed to help teachers understand the pedagogic value of diversity. While all the teachers said that students respond in different ways to the stimuli in class, the difference in student response was associated with deficiency: "I don't say wrong. I want to be positive. So, we accept whatever students say and then correct them" (T19). For teachers, struggling as they were to get all students to a common curricular end-point, anything that did not approximate to the privileged schooled discourse seemed deficient. The latter formed the criteria of success in the year-end examination and teachers' performance was judged based on student performance. At the same time, teachers were not unappreciative of the non-scholastic competencies the culturally diverse students displayed:

> A student who can't read or write fixed my scooter when it didn't start. Different children are good in different ways. We haven't been able to recognize and value this in our education system. Now we have CCE. If a child is good at drawing or singing, we can give marks for that, not just for his ability to read and write. But this is only for FA. What about SA and SSLC [matriculation] examination? We have to teach them to write correct answers. SSLC certificate is very important for a job. (T12)

This tension for the teachers can also be seen as the larger contradiction in the system mentioned earlier, between a vision that values culturally situated processes and a curriculum that prescribes uniform, decontextualized knowledge. This contradiction made it difficult for teachers to imagine students' diversity as having any intrinsic pedagogic advantage beyond being a token for motivating students and leading them towards learning the given. However, diversity is not a default situation. Visible differences can be a trigger for dialogue and the learning promoted by it. Training hasn't sensitized teachers to the pedagogical possibility of seeing diversity as an opening to the genuine discussion in classroom activities.

One of the more discerning DRPs admitted, "We are not doing anything with the diverse backgrounds, culture and knowledge students bring to class. We just tell the teachers to encourage all students to talk about their experience, but beyond that, nothing. We are not trained for it." This reflects the inadequacies of the cascading input–output model of training: The DRPs tell the MRPs what they are told at the state-level training given to them. They, in turn, tell the teachers what they know within the limits of their understanding, and teachers implement what is possible within the constraints of their social situation. The RPs keep doing more of the same in the training sessions scheduled for teachers, year after year, and teachers are training fatigued. All seem to lack the support to make them think outside the box by holding their practice to scrutiny. The assumption that every teacher has to simply adopt the best practice relayed to them fails to acknowledge teachers as persons with goals, values, interests, and beliefs, with the ability to reflect and respond to ideas in a way that is "internally persuasive" for them (Bakhtin and Holquist 1981). By imposing what teachers must know and do, the training attempts to change teachers by replacing their held beliefs and values, in effect disempowering them.

Teacher Learning from Practicing CCE and Its Impact on Teaching and Students' Learning

A focus on the individual dispositions and actions of teachers by the RPs, and the many survey studies undertaken by DIET, tend to give a deficit view of teachers by pointing to teacher attitude as the main obstacle to their learning and change in practice—"Teachers have problems, but they are not insurmountable if the teacher has the initiative and interest in her growth. Some are good" (a DRP). However, our view, stemming from a sociocultural perspective, goes beyond these stereotypical categories of "good" and "bad" teachers. It has enabled us to illuminate the cultural frame in teachers' practice and the thinking that is implicit in this culture, which is traditionally transmissive in nature. Our interpretation has led us to a developmental view of the gap between teachers' espoused theory of teaching and their actual practice, with the introduction of the new pedagogy aligned with the spirit of CCE. Freeman (1991) speaks of teachers' thought and action as two kinds of action. This distinction is crucial for our findings to explain why what teachers *say* and *do* is not parallel. Our findings show that teachers' thought and actions are dialectically merged. In this dialectic process, thought and action feed into one another. For instance, in the debate that T42 conducted, the authentic questions that students raised and responded to made their conceptual horizons more visible and this became the basis for a more dialogically interactive classroom. After class, T42 shared her developing insights from her experience, "We constrain their [students'] learning by intervening too much. We must leave them free and then they find themselves." At the same time, she also believed, like the others, that direct teaching was necessary while teaching science or math concepts, "Different subjects and activities need different kinds of teaching support. We can't always do such activities. It takes too much time and we have other lessons to complete." Such insights gained from a reflection on practice, in turn, add to teachers' repertoire of conscious acts. However, her teaching during the revision showed regression in response to the demands of high stakes examinations. This showed that despite individual intention and ability, teachers' practice was constrained by a lack of correspondence between the goals, values, beliefs, social relationships and the expectations held by different constituencies in the institutional context of teachers' work.

Like T42, the data showed several other examples of teachers at various intermediary stages of new understanding and practice. This seemed to be an indicator of the 'non-negotiable imposition' of the new curriculum becoming internally persuasive for teachers over time (Matusov 2015). Teachers' experience seems to have reached a threshold level (Vygotsky et al. 1987) where through an appropriate mix of situated support and challenge, they could be helped to develop their perceptions and practice (Ratnam 2016). The researcher experienced the beneficial impact of such support on teachers in a few contexts (C1–4, C14–16) where she slipped from observer role into the role of a participant observer, providing "metacognitive support" (Rogoff 1990) to teachers in organizing group activities strategically, with a focus on purposes and values. This created occasions for mutual engagement where teachers' routine responses, colliding with researchers' perspectives, came up for scrutiny, as the following excerpt from an after-class conversation with the teachers (C4) illustrates:

> T20: We don't involve so much like you did to analyze what's going on in the groups [during activity] or when they [students] make the presentation. We simply give them the chance to say what they want to say, so it becomes a little mechanical. But in today's class I noticed, students became more conscious of what they were saying, not just saying, what they knew. They were thinking about what others were saying and responded to that. There was continuity in the interaction.

> T19: Yes and we are now slowly opening our eyes to see how to make students understand and react to what others say and not simply sit and listen.

Thus, the findings show that even while enacting the expected components of CCE in its token form, teachers seem to be becoming more consciously aware of the implications of CCE for their practice. This new self-managed learning observed among teachers as they responded to the demands of ongoing classroom assessment (CCE) as part of CCE was qualitatively different from the incremental change in a predetermined direction upheld and expected by the top-down training provided to them. An explanation of this quite unexpected finding is sought in the dynamics of classroom lesson space framed by the continuous and comprehensive orientation to assessment (CCE) and material (textbook) resources.

The CCE-linked ongoing classroom assessment based on observation of varied performances importantly makes children-as-persons visible to the teacher in a manner that off-line evaluation of test-elicited answer scripts does not, and cannot. The teachers now feel that they have a renewed understanding of their students, as many said, "We know our children better now." Although the teachers' practice is largely routinized in response to mandates, paradoxically, the imperative to conduct group activities has displaced the didactic teacher talk, at least partly, allowing some room for spontaneous reactions and responses from students. The teacher is now, at least in recurring spells, in a social relationship of partner, a listener with her students—one that is supportive of dialogue (as in the example of the debate conducted by T42). The indeterminacy of the spontaneous dialogue (as opposed to predetermined and rehearsed answers), made possible now through group activities, poses a new challenge to the teacher. The teacher, in the role of participant observer in this classroom dialogue, is slowly developing the disposition to live with uncertainties by letting go of the stable image of the teacher as the *knower* (e.g., T42). Emerging classroom dialogue draws on the active investment of both teachers and students in listening to and responding to the other as mindful people engaged in the evaluation. It is this teacher/learner investment that is the essence of genuine understanding and learning (for both teachers and learners), virtually impossible under rote practices. Thus, CCE seems to have opened a window on formative classroom assessment practice, fostering spontaneous and situational learning in both teachers and students.

Conclusion

A description of teachers' assessment practice in a particular cultural setting in India reveals a preponderance of directives, both in the curriculum policy represented by CCE and also the training given to teachers. Many day-to-day instructional acts of teachers are the mere implementation of demanded methodology such as the five E's, without assessment being an inherent part of these teaching-learning processes as envisioned in the NCF 2005. Besides these workaday routines, teacher learning is set in very demotivating conditions of work: swamped by the irksome procedure of voluminous record keeping, time lost on non-academic chores, and having to cope with impossible demands such as handling multi-grade classes without adequate provision for it. The desire to be free, do more and serve better has not been extinguished.

Our sociocultural analysis of teachers' practice has helped us see a forward movement in teacher learning beneath what seemed like a static picture of teachers implementing CCE conventionally. This learning seems to be largely the result of the disequilibrium created by the new demands placed on teachers.. What is to be noted here is that this process of meaning making and developing perceptions were not stimulated by any strategic thinking at the system level that avowedly targeted teachers' lived experience, values, and beliefs as a critical factor in the wholesome curricular transaction and the training-support programs (which were therefore largely ineffectual). Instead, they were shaped in the classroom dynamics that emerged as teachers carried out the new assessment routines within the bounds of their institutional contexts. However, from this threshold level to reach new levels of learning that would enable teachers to develop the ability to identify students' learning needs and modify teaching and learning accordingly and, through this, sustain a systemic change in the desired direction, teachers need interactions with purveyors of alternative ideas. Teacher education can play this role, not by objectifying teachers as passive receivers of skills and knowledge transmitted to them, but by initiating a process of enculturation which is anchored in teachers' classroom experience so that it facilitates their 'subjective involvement' (Rey 2017) with alternative forms of action.

References

Andersson, C., & Palm, T. (2017). The impact of formative assessment on student achievement: A study of the effects of changes to classroom practice after a comprehensive professional development programme. *Learning and Instruction, 49,* 92–102. https://doi.org/10.1016/j.learninstruc.2016.12.006.

Bakhtin, M. M., & Holquist, M. (Eds.). (1981). *The dialogic imagination: Four essays by M. M. Bakhtin* (C. Emerson & M. Holquist, Trans.). Austin: Texas University Press.

Black, P., & William, D. (1998). *Inside the black box: Raising standards through classroom assessment.* London: King's College.

Bloom, B. S., Hastings, J. T., & Madaus, G. F. (1971). *Handbook of formative and summative evaluation of student learning.* New York: McGraw-Hill.

Brown, G. T. (2003). *Teachers' instructional conceptions: Assessment's relationship to learning, teaching and curriculum, and teacher efficacy.* Paper presented at AARE/NZARE, Auckland, New Zealand.

Chen, J. (2015). Formative assessment as a vehicle for changing classroom practice in a specific cultural context. *Cultural Studies of Science Education, 1*–10. https://doi.org/10.1007/s11422-014-9599-7.

Clandinin, D. J., & Connelly, F. M. (1992). Teacher as curriculum maker. In P. Jackson (Ed.), *Handbook of curriculum* (pp. 363–461). New York: Macmillan.

Cochran-Smith, M., & Lytle, S. (1999). Relationships of knowledge and practice: Teacher learning in community. *Review of Research in Education, 24,* 249–360.

Craig, C. (2009). The contested classroom space: A decade of lived educational policy in Texas schools. *American Educational Research Journal, 46*(4), 1034–1059.

Department of Public Education, Government of Karnataka. (2013). *Sadhana.* Bengaluru, India: DSERT.

District Institute of Education and Training. (2015). *NCF/CCE/RTE-2009 Concerns and Problems.* Mysuru, India: DIET.

Ernest, P. (1989). The impact of beliefs on teaching of mathematics. In P. Ernest (Ed.), *Mathematics teaching: The state of the art* (pp. 249–254). London: Falmer Press.

Freeman, D. (1991). *Language teacher education, emerging discourse, and change in classroom practice.* In Plenary address given at the First International Conference on Teacher Education in Second Language Teaching, City Polytechnic of Hong Kong, Hong Kong.

Fullan, M. (1993). *Change forces.* London: Falmer Press.

Government of India. (1966). *Report of the Education Commission (1964–66) Education and National Development.* New Delhi: Ministry of Education.

Government of India. (1986). *National policy on education.* New Delhi: MHRD Department of Education.

Guba, E., & Lincoln, Y. (1989). *Fourth generation evaluation.* Thousand Oaks: Sage.

Hunter, W. (1882). *Report of the Indian Education Commission.* Retrieved from http://archive.org/details/ReportOfTheIndianEducationCommission.

Kincheloe, J. L. (2003). *Teachers as researchers: Qualitative enquiry as a path to empowerment* (2nd ed.). New York: Routledge Falmer.

Lewin, K. (1935). *A dynamic theory of personality (D.K. Adams & K.E. Zener, Trans.).* New York: McGraw-Hill.

Lima, A., & von Duyke, K. (2016). Reflections on a dialogic pedagogy inspired by the writings of Bakhtin: An account of the experience of two professors working together in the classroom. *Dialogic Pedagogy: An International Online Journal, 4.* http://dpj.pitt.edu, https://doi.org/10.5195/dpj.2016.159.

Matusov, E. (2011). Authorial teaching and learning. In E. J. White & M. Peters (Eds.), *Bakhtinian pedagogy: Opportunities and challenges for research, policy and practice in education across the globe* (pp. 21–46). New York: Lang.

Matusov, E. (2015). Legitimacy of non-negotiable imposition in diverse approaches to education. *Dialogic Pedagogy: An Online International Journal, 3*(2015), 1–38. https://doi.org/10.5195/dpj. 2015.110.

National Council for Educational Research and Training. (2005). *National Curriculum Framework (NCF) 2005*. New Delhi: Author.

Ratnam, T. (2016). Mediation of culture and context in educating a teacher educator to become a researcher: A self-study. In J. Kitchen, D. Tidwell, & L. Fitzgerald (Eds.), *Self-study and diversity II: Inclusive teacher education for a diverse world* (pp. 95–120). Rotterdam: Sense Publishers.

Rey, F. G. (2017). *Play and ludic situations: Their relevance to overcome learning difficulties*. Paper presented at the 5th International Society for Cultural historical Activity Research (ISCAR) Congress, Quebec, Canada.

Rogoff, B. (1990). *Apprenticeship in thinking*. Oxford: Oxford University Press.

Srinivasan, M. V. (2015). Centralized evaluation practices: An ethnographic account of CCE in a government residential school in India. *Contemporary Education Dialogue, 12*(1), 59–86.

Srivastava, P., & Hopwood, N. (2009). A practical iterative framework for qualitative data analysis. *International Journal of Qualitative Methods, 8*(1), 76–84.

Stobart, G. (2009). *Keeping formative assessment creative*. Paper presented at IAEA 35th Annual Conference, Brisbane.

Vasavi, A. R. (2015). Culture and life of government elementary schools. *Economic and Political Weekly, 50*(33), 39–50.

Vygotsky, L. S. (1978). *Mind in society: The development of higher psychological processes*. Cambridge: Harvard University Press.

Vygotsky, L. S., Rieber, R. W., & Carton, A. S. (Eds.). (1987). *The collected works of L. S. Vygotsky. Vol. 1. Thinking and speech* (N. Minick, Trans.). New York: Plenum Press.

Wylie, E. C., & Lyon, C. (2012, April). *Quality instruction and quality formative assessment: The same or different?* Paper presented at the annual meeting of the American Educational Research Association (AERA), Vancouver, Canada.

Chapter 8
Teacher Learning from Classroom Assessment in Japan: Responsive and Emergent Classroom Assessment in Lesson Study

Terumasa Ishii

Abstract This chapter discusses teachers' classroom assessment as embedded in the Japanese traditional whole-class teaching that revolves around class-level activity. The ideas of "teaching that builds on stumbles" and "stimulation" can provide clues for future assessment research when examined from the perspectives of "assessment for learning". If we strive to have assessment embedded in teaching and learning, formative assessment needs to be framed: (1) not only as a closed reflective process but also as an open emergent process; and (2) not only as a visual and rational process whereby the teacher subject sees the student objects and tries to visualize their learning process but also as a sensual and aesthetic process whereby the teacher naturally develops a sensitivity in the responsive relationship between teacher and students. Thus, there is a need to redefine the concept of formative assessment as "responsive and emergent assessment".

Keywords Assessment for learning · Classroom assessment · Lesson study Responsive and emergent assessment

Introduction

This chapter discusses teachers' classroom assessment as embedded in the Japanese traditional teaching style.

In Europe and the US, the debate about educational measurement and assessment has historically moved from outside the classroom to inside it, and from relying on testing specialists to teachers and even students (Black and Wiliam 1998; Bloom et al. 1971; Brookhart 2007; Tanaka 2008; Wiliam 2011; McMillan 2013). The edu-

T. Ishii (✉)
Kyoto University, Kyoto, Japan
e-mail: ishii.terumasa.3w@kyoto-u.ac.jp

© Springer Nature Singapore Pte Ltd. 2018   141
H. Jiang and M. F. Hill (eds.), *Teacher Learning with Classroom Assessment*,
https://doi.org/10.1007/978-981-10-9053-0_8

Table 8.1 Feature of assessment *of, for,* and *as* Learning

Approach	Purpose	Reference points	Key assessor
Assessment *of* learning	Judgments about placement, promotion, credentials, etc.	Other students	Teacher
Assessment *for* learning	Information for teachers' instructional decisions	External standards or expectations	Teacher
Assessment *as* learning	Self-monitoring and self-correction or adjustment	Personal goals and external standards	Student

(Earl 2013, p. 31)

cational measurement movement aimed to make education scientific and objective. Tyler (1949) proposed the concept of "educational evaluation" as a way to improve educational activities following educational goals; his proposal served as a corrective to the measurement movement's stance of not specifying the aim of measurement. Bloom et al. (1971) proposed "formative assessment" as a way to revise and improve the trajectory of ongoing educational practice, rather than only evaluating after the fact and for grading purposes. In recent years, under the heading of "assessment for learning" formative assessment has been integrated into the everyday mutual interactions of teaching and learning in the classroom. Moreover, under the heading of "assessment as learning", research on learner metacognition, self-regulated learning, and educational assessment are abundant and connected, opening up for further exploration of how teachers and students can understand assessment data and improve learning (see Table 8.1).

In contrast to these developments in assessment research in Europe and the US, test specialists and others in Japan have not necessarily accumulated enough measurement and assessment research, yet this does not mean that assessment has not been conducted in Japan. Rather, Japanese teachers, especially elementary school teachers, have worked to sincerely understand the children and to generate excellent teaching and learning through creative whole-class teaching that systematizes children's speech and thinking as well as facilitating deeper reflection through classroom discussion (Tanaka 2017). The act of assessment was embedded in the teacher's teaching process, in the creative dialogue between teacher and children. In recent years, the maturation of "lesson study", highlighted as a culture of teacher co-learning in Japan, is intimately connected with the craftsmanship of the teachers who have strived for creative whole-class teaching (Ishii 2017).

That is to say, lesson study in Japan has developed as a setting where teachers can observe and emulate each other's skills, where they can show and cultivate those skills, and where they debate practical philosophy and their profound beliefs as investigators, who seek after the truth. Behind lesson study lies the craftsmanship of Japanese teachers, who understand hourly lessons as a complete experience that is performed and carefully created like a drama.

These teachers' art of response, inherently fulfilling an evaluating function, has much in common with the ideas behind "classroom assessment" and "assessment for learning". This teacher responsiveness, which is supported by various tools that visualize children's thinking, has usually been discussed regarding teaching technique and cultural script of teaching (Tulis 2013; Arani et al. 2017). By examining this from the perspective of formative assessment, we should find suggestions that can add to the recent assessment scholarship, which aims toward an assessment that is embedded in classroom teaching and learning.

This chapter first introduces some cases that became the historical beginnings of the creative dialogue teaching style. By analyzing these cases, I extracted the fundamental idea of "teaching that builds on children's stumbles or mistakes" and discussed the clues provided toward future research on formative assessment. Based on this, I consider practical systems and tools that may help make possible creative dialogue in teaching and improve teachers' assessment competency in the teaching process.

The Relationship Between Classroom Assessments and Teacher Learning

I will first discuss the significance of looking at teachers' learning to investigate classroom assessment through a consideration of the history that led to the focus on the importance of classroom assessment.

In "standards-based reform" and "outcome-based reform", which create competition between schools based on the results of standardized tests, assessments function as a tool to rank and control children, teachers, and schools. The importance of classroom assessments was identified as part of grassroots initiatives to reconfigure assessments as a tool to improve schools and identify quality and fairness in education (Ishii 2011). For example, under the heading of "authentic assessment" (Archbald and Newmann 1988; Wiggins 1993), the new paradigm of assessment was proposed in the USA at the end of the 1980s as part of the criticism directed toward standardized testing, leading to the creation of new techniques and ways of thinking about assessments such as "performance assessments", "portfolios", and "rubrics". These were intended to make visible the authentic achievement fostered by teachers' creative teaching practices that were evident in each classroom and school.

One of the concepts in this new paradigm was that the teachers in the classroom were best placed to assess the authentic achievement or competence of students as they could understand the quality of the child's learning in the specific context in which they were placed. Classroom assessment is based on the teacher's daily practice and accompanying qualitative judgment. In assessment reform based on classroom assessment, it is more important to have faith in the teacher and allow his or her assessment capabilities to grow than it is to develop new assessment tools and technologies. Also, as will be discussed at length later in this chapter, responsiveness and reflective thinking in the practice process form the core of a teacher's abilities, and it is important in a teacher's learning for them to reflect on, and learn from, their experiences. Building a teacher's assessment capabilities through classroom-based assessments is the central theme of teachers' learning. It is crucial to note that lessons in Japan are not intended to be an application of technologies developed outside of the classroom, but should be a craft-like endeavor where the teacher creates activities with the child in the classroom. Creative whole-class teaching, which is now the ideal image of lessons in Japan, requires a teacher's assessment capabilities to be an art form. Starting with lesson study, the teacher's learning systems that make creative whole-class teaching possible contain the strategies and tools to enhance teachers' assessment capabilities.

In this way, an emphasis on classroom assessment will not exist without teacher learning, and the quality of classroom assessment holds the key to it. In the next section, I will discuss case studies that form the historical starting point of creative whole-class teaching based on responsive dialogue.

The Beginnings of Creative Whole-Class Teaching in Japan

A good number of Japanese teachers have pursued creative whole-class teaching as a way to realize learning on a class level, drawing out and facilitating cross-pollination of the thoughts of individual children. Through the exchange of various ideas and the stimulation that occur as they intermingle, the children can make discoveries and construct knowledge in ways that would not have been possible if studying individually. By implementing this method, teachers have sought to enable learners' growth and achievement, while also enriching the learning process. The teaching methods of Saitō (1958) and Tōi (1987), practitioners of the post-World War II era, are the epitome of this. In the following sections, I will introduce practical examples from the teaching of both of them, during the 1950s, and clarify their characteristics from the perspective of classroom formative assessment.

Case ①—Teaching that Investigates Children's Stumbles Through Cooperation

I will first introduce one 2nd grade elementary math class led by Sakiko Funato, a teacher at Shima Elementary School whose principal was Saitō (1958).

The students were learning 2-digit multiplication, and as Ms. Funato was walking around checking the students' calculations, she noticed that Sakae had calculated $90 \times 70 = 63,000$ and that other students had made similar mistakes. Since this was their first time doing 2-digit multiplication, Ms. Funato wanted them to learn

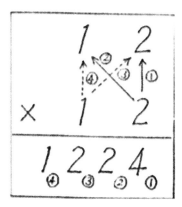

Fig. 8.1 Sakae's mistake (Saitō 1958, p. 236)

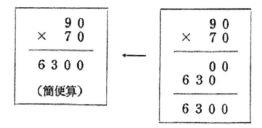

Fig. 8.2 Shortened calculation (Saitō 1958, p. 238)

it properly. She decided to show Sakae's mistake to the whole class and have them solve it together (see Fig. 8.1).

Ms. Funato asked Sakae to write and explain her calculation using the blackboard. Sakae wrote the calculation as shown in Fig. 8.1 (in the order of arrows ①–④ as shown in the figure). In response, some students said that it was wrong and the classroom atmosphere became lively. Ms. Funato told the students not to be harsh on Sakae for having made this mistake, but urged them to think about how this mistake happened based on the method shown on the blackboard, independently of Sakae. An active discussion followed, with exchanges such as, "Maybe Sakae followed the same pattern as for when we did 24 × 40?" and "No, that wouldn't give this answer" (Saitō 1958, p. 237). It became clear that even among the students who had reached the correct answer, there were several who had not understood the meaning behind the shortened calculation.

Ms. Funato retaught the students how to approach the shortened calculation process for 90 × 70, making a clear distinction between calculating 12 × 12 and 90 × 70 (see Fig. 8.2). In the end, it was clarified at what point Sakae's calculation had gone wrong and everyone, including both Sakae and many students who had been confident about their calculations, had gained a deeper understanding of 2-digit multiplication. Ms. Funato happily announced that this was a "Sakae-equation mistake," celebrating that Sakae, as well as the other students, had worked together to generate joint knowledge to avoid repeating this mistake.

In Ms. Funato's class, opportunities to look at mistakes together were regularly given to students. In the beginning, there were those who hesitated to show their mistakes to others, but by building joint knowledge in the form of "so-and-so-equation mistakes", an atmosphere conducive to openly sharing mistakes was created. Moreover, it was observed in later classes that students could cooperate by remembering what they had learned previously, pointing out that "that's a so-and-so-equation mistake".

In Ms. Funato's classroom, students did not only explain their calculations but were also given the opportunity to examine other students' calculations and imagine how that student reached his or her conclusion. Take the following problem: "Every student in Tadashi's class buys one pencil at a price of 3 yen and 50 sen each. How much did they pay if the number of students was 40?" Let us say Jirō writes his calculation ($40 \div 2 = 20$, $3 \times 40 = 120$, $120 + 20 = 140$) on the blackboard and another student explains it by saying, "The first 40 is for the number of students. He divided 40 by 2, because 50 sen is one-half of 1 yen so that if they each pay 1 yen, it's 40 yen. Because it's half that, he divided by 2, $40 \div 2 = 20$, meaning 20 yen" (Saitō 1958, p. 246). Ms. Funato then asked Jirō if he agreed with the explanation and he nodded happily.

When discussing Hisako's calculation ($50 \times 40 = 2000$, $3 \times 40 = 120$, $120 + 2000 = 2120$), one student remarked, "That's a bit odd," to which Ms. Funato replied, "If something's a bit odd, let's fix it together by thinking about Hisako's method" (Saitō 1958, pp. 252–253). At this point, one student pointed out the reason for Hisako's stumble, saying, "I think $50 \times 40 = 2000$ is about sen. And I think the unit for $3 \times 40 = 120$ is yen. But Hisako went wrong when she mixed them up by counting $120 + 2000 = 2120$" (p. 253). Going further, the mistake was corrected by providing an imaginative explanation that followed Hisako's thought process, explaining, "50 sen is 0.5 yen, so 50×40 should be $0.5 \times 40 = 20$, meaning 20 yen. And then we have $3 \times 40 = 120$, so that's 120 yen. Together it's $120 + 20 = 140$, meaning 140 yen" (p. 253). Here, we can see how the students discovered their stumbles by themselves, thought about why they had stumbled and learned their lessons jointly.

Case ②—Teaching that Stimulates Students' Thinking Through One Student's Stumble

Next, I will introduce a summary of the teaching of *The Burning of the Rice Field*, which was conducted among 5th grade elementary school students by Tōi at the end of the 1950s (Kawaji 2005; Tōi 1987).

The Burning of the Rice Field is a story in which a village headman named Gohee has a premonition that a tsunami will hit his village. To save the 400 villagers from the tsunami, he sets fire to the rice fields, which are awaiting the harvest, inducing the villagers to flee to the top of a hill to escape the fire, and saving their lives. In reading this work, Student A wrote in his notebook a reading that differed from the author's intent. The scene described how Gohee set fire to all of the rice fields, threw away his torch and gazed out at the coast. Student A wrote, "Gohee has burned all of the rice plants that had produced a bumper crop, and then is gazing out at the coast while probably thinking to himself that he has done a regrettable thing" (Tōi 1987, p. 135). Tōi had Student A present this reading during group in his class.

When he had done so, the other classmates unanimously muttered: "That's strange!" Accordingly, Tōi intentionally posed a question that supported Student A: "So Gohee set fire to the rice that had been harvested with such difficulty, and then probably thought that he did something regrettable, right?" (p. 136). When the teacher said this, the students said, "If it were us, we would probably think that we had done a regrettable thing, but we think that that is not the case with Gohee" (p. 136). In response, the teacher asked, "If so, what is the evidence for that?" (p. 136). With that question, the students eagerly set about finding the evidence.

When they had thought about it for a time, Student B called out, "Before Gohee set fire to the rice fields, he said "It is a waste, but I can save the lives of the entire village by doing this." If we read here, we can see that on the one hand, Gohee thinks that it is regrettable that he has set the fire. However, the word "but" is added after that, and that is saying the opposite. Here, he is weighing the value of the rice against the lives of the villagers. However, as a result of weighing these against each other, Gohee has been able to decisively state that 'the lives of the entire village can be saved by this'" (p. 137). This meaning of Gohee's decisive statement was a point that even Tōi had not noticed. In response to this discovery by the students, Tōi thanked Student A, saying, "Today we were able to engage in a wonderfully vigorous and valuable study; however, if we consider the reason why, it is because Student A shared that reading with us" (p. 139). In Tōi's practice, not only was the reason for the stumble cooperatively investigated but as the teacher actively demonstrated that even the stumble had a point to it, the students who were confident in their correct reading were stimulated, inducing cognitive disagreement, and triggering their thinking.

Formative Assessment Embedded in Japanese Creative Whole-Class Teaching

The teaching methods of Saitō's Shima Elementary School and Tōi are said to be the epitome of Japanese creative whole-class teaching. What they have in common is the idea of teaching that builds on stumbles. In other words, the child's stumble (an erroneous response or opinion that diverged from the correct response) was not treated negatively; rather, "elaboration" was launched with the stumble or "productive failure" as the starting point. This way of proceeding is meaningful not only for the child who has stumbled but also for other children who think that they know the correct answer. It is common that these children, even when they can express their answer clearly, cannot respond skillfully when pressed about the reasons for their idea. It is possible to achieve a deeper level of understanding by explaining one's ideas and citing one's evidence to a person who may have a different idea, or teaching a person who has yet to understand the point.

This is a kind of responsive teaching that builds on the teacher's perception of the actual conditions of student learning, creative teaching starting from learning assessment. By doing this, the learners' metacognition is fostered, and it becomes a form of teaching that extends teacher assessment to student self-assessment ability, the ability to discover one's stumbles and build on them in one's learning. This certainly resonates with recent ideas about assessment for learning and assessment as learning, and can be seen as attaching importance to "the meta-cognitive formative assessment that investigates children's stumbles through co-operation." Moreover, as seen in Tōi's practice, the stumbles that are uncovered in the formative assessment of the teaching process encourage metacognition through students' reflecting on their thought processes, but, on top of this, they also stimulate their thinking, serving as teaching material that incites cognitive disagreement—material that suddenly appears in the teaching process, which can be used impromptu. Learning-triggered formative assessment stimulates the entire class of students' thinking through one student's stumble. Formative assessment should be framed not only as restorative or developmental guidance aimed at goal achievement, or as something that spurs on learners' self-learning ability—a closed reflective process—but also as something that suggests new learning objectives, triggers students' thinking and subjective participation, and invigorates teaching—an open, emergent process.

Therefore, making it possible for stumbling to happen in lessons requires the creation of an open classroom environment, where students can express anything without fear of stumbling. Many teachers attempt to create a classroom culture that hinges on the belief that classrooms are places where mistakes happen and "you come to school because you can't study by yourself", by giving clear messages to their pupils that stumbling is allowed and that "not being able to do something" is alright. Moreover, the elementary school teacher Imaizumi (1998) explained the importance of the teacher reflecting on his or her views on mistakes to enrich them. Mistakes made by students are created by exaggerating one aspect of the matter. As long as even this one aspect of the matter is in some way connected to reality, then the mistake can be construed as essential to approaching the truth of the matter. If the teacher can genuinely adopt this way of thinking, then he or she will become more naturally attuned to what each student is saying. To create lessons where stumbling happens, it is important to form the students' learning and assessment values which see stumbling, an inability to do something or an assessment opportunity, as an opportunity for learning and growth.

In the next section, I summarize the Japanese view of teaching that forms the background of this teaching that builds on stumbles and values stimulation.

Teaching as a Drama and the Teacher's Art

Teaching as a Drama

There is a tendency when discussing teaching to encounter the extreme argument that anyone can handle teaching if he or she is familiar with the content to be taught, or when there is a manual. In contrast, some may claim that teaching depends on talent and personal charisma. It is certain at least that teaching demands skill and competence from teachers. Teaching is an occupation in which the tone of the teacher's voice, the way in which he or she makes eye contact, and his or her physical stance and posture all make a statement, and in which the personal maturity of the teacher is also consistently under scrutiny. However, it is possible for anyone to achieve such skilled competence by continuing to learn in a research-type fashion amidst one's daily practice, with a proper methodology. This practice is referred to as "teaching as the practice of a profession."

Teaching is a process in which teacher and students interact through the medium of "teaching materials", leading cultural content to be acquired and abilities to be gradually formed. That situation can be established by a deliberate approach based on the teacher's sense of purpose, within a curriculum and learning environment organized by educational intent. Mukōyama (1985), who led the Teacher's Organization of Skill Sharing, cited the following example: "Is it satisfactory for a doctor whose patient says "I have had a high fever for three days' just to express his sympathy by responding, 'That must be terrible'? Would you entrust your life to a doctor who said, about a commonplace disease, 'I do not understand the cause, and I do not know any method for treating it. In any event, I will try to do my best'?" (Mukōyama 1985, pp. 77–78). While citing this example, Mukōyama stated that the teacher's work lay precisely in making it possible for students to do what they could not previously do and that what was needed was not only love and thought but also concrete techniques that could change children's cognition and behavior.

However, what deserves attention here is that techniques in education cannot be implemented mechanically, like a factory, at the convenience of their creator. Every child has his or her personality, and children teach themselves ceaselessly, improving themselves by their desire and effort. Moreover, the occupation of teaching is a creative process in which students interact with each other in complicated ways, where learning often goes beyond the teacher's intentions and is deployed in a rhythm of tension and relaxation in the atmosphere ("teaching as drama"; Yoshimoto 1983). It is precisely because lessons in school are a creative, dramatic process that it is possible to realize comprehensive and meaningful teaching effects, including not only deeper understanding and creative thinking but also rich internal experience (see Fig. 8.3).

As shown in Fig. 8.3, a lesson is a process with a logical, rational structure directed toward a target achievement. However, while it may be possible to learn zweckrational aims when there are "easy-to-see outcomes" such as basic skills, "hard-to-see outcomes" such as thinking processes and dispositions are attained

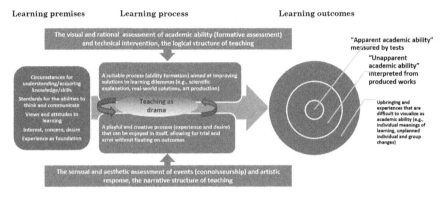

Fig. 8.3 The model of classroom learning and assessment process (Ishii 2012, p. 143)

only through the detours of accidental learning with trial and error, this does not fit within the target framework. Learners develop as humans in lessons through the inclusion of zweckrational structure and playful creativity of the experience. Japan's skilled teachers are thorough in their targets and planning. However, they leave these behind during the lesson process, when they follow the flow of the children's learning and place great emphasis on turning a stumble in a student's understanding of the academic content into an opportunity for learning. Many teachers plan their lessons with great hopes for what they can achieve through such lessons. The paradox that a teacher's targets for a lesson cannot be achieved by direct, efficient progression toward them, but by first beginning learning in a way that does not fit in with the teacher's set plan is now understood to be the essence of any lesson.

By understanding lessons as drama, teachers in Japan have come to appreciate the storytelling nature of learning in each hour-long lesson, and have come to conceptualize lessons with a beginning, middle (climax) and an end. For example, teachers gradually tease out the learners' motivation when they first present the teaching materials, followed by the climax in which they create a setting for the learners to struggle and compete with their differing opinions, finally ending in agreement, or, in cases where more discussion is desired, ending with a buildup of anticipation for the next lesson.

Practical Deliberation and Consideration as the Core of a Teacher's Competency

If we understand teaching as a creative occupation like drama, it becomes clear that it cannot be carried out simply by generalized individual techniques and the application of material or method X. In interactions in which the children, the teacher, and the subject matter are interwoven, the teacher makes a decision instantly. The teacher receives the individual reactions of the children, reconsiders and recombines his or her techniques to create something new in response, boldly changes the initial plan, or resets the objectives of teaching themselves. What we refer to as teaching technique can be characterized as an art of reception, where the teacher assesses the children's learning and responds.

The importance of such thoughtful judgments, deliberation, and careful consideration in the teacher's work has been emphasized in a variety of forms (Satō 2010; Shibata 1967; Yoshimoto 1983). For instance, Herbart (1806) proposed the concept of "tact of teaching"—the ability to respond as the occasion may demand in teaching, and Lampert (2001) conceptualized it as "dilemma management"—the work of a teacher making split-second decisions from time to time and continuing to make do in response to the innumerable dilemmas that arise in the process of teaching. In daily teaching, which appears plain and unconnected to drama at a glance, a teaching approach is established by the continuation of extemporaneous decisions. As noted by Herbart (1806), educational tact is the minimum requirement but at the same time the maximum requirement for teachers. What determines the level of a teacher's competency is the validity of his or her extemporaneous decisions and the extent of his or her forethought as played out in the teaching process.

We should be able to reappraise this kind of "pedagogical tact" from the perspective of classroom formative assessment. Saitō (1969) expressed the essence of a teacher's capacity for judgment in the classroom as "seeing". Seeing is not to consciously "see", but denotes what naturally enters the teacher's field of vision in the classroom, matching the teacher's level of experience and competency. It signifies his or her sensitivity to the reality of the children and the classroom, connoting the direction of his or her next action. Seeing has less to do with the visual and logical process that assumes a distance between subject and object and more to do with the sensual and aesthetic process that derives from the responsive relationship between subject and object (Fig. 8.3).

Fundamentally, the act of assessment, which should be consciously "seen" as the school's obligation, derives from when the teacher wants to grasp the learning circumstances of all students and devises methods for visualizing them. From this point, we can understand that processes like pedagogical tact and seeing contain elements that fundamentally were never included in the concept of formative assessment. Rather, they seem to have been conceptualized by phrases like "educational connoisseurship" (Eisner 1979) and "reflection in action" (Schön 1983).

To expand the concept of assessment to include sensual and aesthetic sensitivity by responsive relationships, is to reduce assessment theory to teaching theory or, conversely, to reinterpret teaching theory as assessment theory. This comes with the danger of obfuscating the unique meaning of the assessment act. Nonetheless, to embed formative assessment into classroom teaching and learning, we must be aware of both sides, the visual and rational process as well as the sensual and aesthetic process.

A Methodology for Increasing Teacher Competency and Implementing Responsive and Emergent Assessment

The Teacher's Path of Learning

How could a teacher's practical skills and judgment, which include competency for responsive and emergent classroom assessment, be polished? That process takes the form of "learning by doing", like the study of skills in sports and the performing arts (Korthagen 2001; Schön 1983). In other words, it is not a matter of studying theory outside the classroom and applying it in practice; rather, the teacher thinks reflectively over the course of practice and continues to self-regulate his or her practice to make it better, while accumulating discipline as a kind of practical knowledge. Therefore, to polish a teacher's abilities, the key point is how the entire process of design, implementation, and reflection for teaching is to be enhanced by increasing the opportunity for study by teachers themselves.

Also, such learning by teachers is carried out within multilayered joint relationships, in vertical, horizontal, and diagonal directions, among teachers of the same age (horizontal), between them and their senior colleagues (diagonal), and between them and administrative teachers (vertical). For example, the process of learning from expert senior colleagues and creatively imitating them as models is important for inexperienced teachers. "Imitating" as used here does not mean simply mimicking their actions superficially, but also thinking things like "What would Teacher So-and-So think about this?" in response to situations before their eyes, and sharing their vision of teaching as well as their ways of thinking and feeling with the experienced teachers (Ikuta 2011). The more thoroughly the experienced teachers' ways of facing up to problems and objects as practitioners are imitated and implemented, the more likely a younger teacher will be to achieve the confidence and grounding to begin to build his or her personal style and develop a new model which is different from the experienced model teachers.

The majority of the practical knowledge needed to support excellent decisions is hard to put into words that are logical and explicit. Instead, it is accumulated by practitioners individually and in collaboration with implicit sensory and unconscious knowledge rooted in memories of specific episodes and the feelings and meanings attached to them. This kind of practical knowledge is accumulated in communities of practice and learned on an ongoing basis through vicarious and direct experiences and the chance to apply one's intuitive judgment and see it mediated by real episodes and examples (Connelly and Clandinin 1988; Elbaz 1991; Shulman 1986). Crucial elements of this process are thinking in the manner of admired teachers every day, engaging in dialogue about teaching and students with one's colleagues, and reading and writing records of practice. However, to make this kind of practical knowledge not inherent in any specific context, and to be studied as a typical case with generalized versatility, it must be studied through a research cycle as shown in Fig. 8.4.

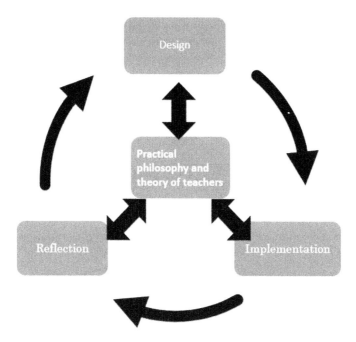

Fig. 8.4 Cycle of teacher's practical research (created by the author)

Figure 8.4 illustrates the cycle of a teacher's practical research: the steps of class development and implementation, design, implementation, and reflection. The direction in which the practical research cycle develops is guided by the philosophy of the teacher, including his or her ideal images of students, classes, and schools, and fundamental values. In addition, the validity of judgments made at each phase is governed by "theory in practice", consisting of tacit knowledge and explicit knowledge concerning curriculum content, students, class format, and classroom management methods built up by the teacher through theoretical learning and practical experience. At the same time, throughout the design–implementation–reflection cycle of educational activities, teacher philosophies, and theories are re-thought in practice. All phases of a lesson—design, implementation, and reflection—incorporate an examination of the target, method, and assessment elements of practice. For example, both design and implementation incorporate assessment. During reflection, the classroom assessment process takes a central role and becomes the point at which not only the validity of the lesson's targets and methods, but also the very method of student assessment, become the subject of scrutiny.

Whether or not the design–implementation–reflection cycle of educational activities becomes the cycle by which a teacher engages in practical research plays a part in teacher learning and growth (Ishii 2016). When the refinement or reframing of a teacher's philosophy, theories, or skills is stimulated, the reflection phase, in particular, does not merely stop with the assessment of student learning in the classroom, or problem-solving to improve subsequent classes. It is important, in addition to goals and assessment validity themselves, to be subject to investigation and for there to be the discussion that deepens understanding of how educational activities are conceived and executed and the steps by which children learn and create knowledge. Thus, following a cycle of design–implementation–reflection jointly managed with other people is effective in stimulating knowledge creation. These are aspects of lesson study in Japan which have been getting attention in other countries.

Practical Study Tools for Teacher Development Through Teaching

In Japan, in addition to informal learning by individual teachers in their everyday practice, multiple venues for formal learning exist for teachers:

1. Theoretical and methodological/pedagogical lectures and training available through boards of education and universities;
2. Independent external study groups such as nongovernment education research organizations and study circles (where teachers bring records or documents of their regular teaching practice and offer mutual critique); and
3. In-school teacher training focused on lesson study (publicly held classes inside or outside schools offering advance or follow-up conferences).

The purpose of 1 is mainly the acquisition of knowledge and skills, whereas the purpose of 2 and 3 is mainly to exchange practical experience, reflect upon it, and jointly come up with new/better practical theories and methods.

Since the 1990s, lesson study has been about stimulating consciousness and rethinking theory in practice (Schön 1983), which has suggested the importance of post-class case studies. This has gone in two directions, from different starting points: case studies for the study of learning and the study of teaching (Ishii 2014).

An example of the former, case studies for studying learning, can be found in "class conference" by Satō and Inagaki (1996). Sato came to emphasize the importance of pursuing the meaning and connections of learning, in preference to targeting the process of teachers' decision-making in teaching. Furthermore, these learning-centered approaches advanced the development of reflection tools to support teachers' reflection on past practical experience. An example is the card-constructing method developed by Fujioka (2000), in which classes are held and observed, and as many potential problems or concerns as can be thought of are written on cards, one issue per card. Then, the cards are stacked and divided into two groups, which are then subdivided into two again. The divided card groups are labeled, and then a structural diagram is created in which label–pair connections are indicated by lines, and reasons for them and realizations about the groupings are noted. This encourages classroom instructors to visualize how they see their classes, and to become conscious of a variety of things; that is, it fosters teachers' awareness.

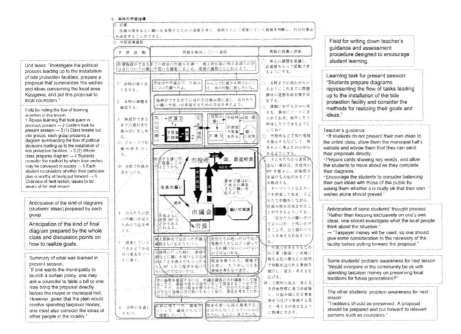

Fig. 8.5 Lesson Plan in Social Studies for 6th Grade Elementary School Students (prepared by Shoji Kawada, a teacher at Takamatsu Elementary School attached to Department of Education, Kagawa University. The boxes within the figure and the annotations are by the author)

Examples of the latter, case studies for studying teaching, are the "intervention class" by Saitō and the "stop-motion method" by Fujioka (1991). In the former, a supervising teacher takes over a class from the one normally instructing, asks the children questions, and intervenes in the class in response (Saitō 1977). In the latter, screening of the video record of a class is temporarily stopped, and a discussion is held on the teacher's teaching method, covering various aspects. The intention is to ask questions on points such as "Why was this approach taken with this subject?" and "What were you seeing regarding the children's learning at that time?" and thereby to investigate the intent of the teacher and the process by which they make judgments that inform their activities.

In addition, in lesson plans prepared in Japanese schools, interactions between teachers and students, particularly the teacher's expectations of the students' learning regarding speech, action, and cognition in response to teacher encouragement, are described in detail (see Fig. 8.5). In addition, blackboard plans visualizing and organizing such communication and thinking processes are often mentioned. Japanese teachers have traditionally stressed visualization processes for cultivating thinking in the classroom using blackboards (see Fig. 8.6). Using blackboards on which lesson material is left after the class has concluded, teachers can check the thinking processes of students and the conclusions drawn, and properly instruct them to put down their learning and thinking processes in their notebooks, deepening their think-

① "Is there a value that can be assigned to x in the equation $x^2=10$?": Question posed in present session.

② "If there exists a square whose area is 10 units, then there must also exist a number that can be squared to make 10.": First step in investigating the session question.

③ By thinking in simple terms, the existence of a square whose area is 10 units was confirmed.

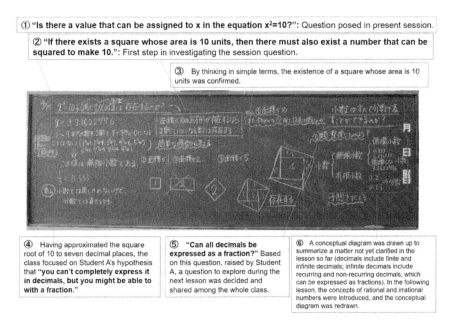

④ Having approximated the square root of 10 to seven decimal places, the class focused on Student A's hypothesis that "you can't completely express it in decimals, but you might be able to with a fraction."

⑤ "Can all decimals be expressed as a fraction?" Based on this question, raised by Student A, a question to explore during the next lesson was decided and shared among the whole class.

⑥ A conceptual diagram was drawn up to summarize a matter not yet clarified in the lesson so far (decimals include finite and infinite decimals; infinite decimals include recurring and non-recurring decimals, which can be expressed as fractions). In the following lesson, the concepts of rational and irrational numbers were introduced, and the conceptual diagram was redrawn.

Fig. 8.6 Example of a Blackboard in a Mathematics Lesson for 3rd Grade Junior High School Students (*Source* Kazuyuki Kambara, a teacher at Shinonome Junior High School attached to Hiroshima University. The boxes within the figure and the annotations are by the author)

ing and causing them to internalize lessons. The use of blackboards and development of techniques for teaching note-taking in Japan clearly reveals the Japanese classroom culture, in which an hour-long class takes on the aspect of a drama program and emphasis is placed on acquiring knowledge and deepening understanding during each hour of class. Blackboard-writing and note-taking are tools for making possible such creative whole-class teaching. Moreover, the notes carefully describing the learning process function as student portfolios and an everyday mechanism for nurturing continued learning.

Furthermore, lesson plans in Japan often include mention of the learning and living conditions of certain "sample students" to whom teachers wish to pay particular attention. In particular, some teachers have proceeded by noting details about individual students on seating charts: How is their thinking progressing about the topic of a teaching unit? How is each student in the class expected to think or express themselves? And how do they think and express themselves? (see Fig. 8.7) Thus, it is not simply a matter of taking the entire class as a group—each student is viewed as rich in their understanding, making for a class that is creative throughout.

In this way, Japan's teachers cultivate their assessment abilities for student learning in the lesson process, and the abilities relevant to the emergence of new learning in response, through opportunities to reflect on what happens in the classroom and during the decision-making process in post-lesson review meetings. This also takes

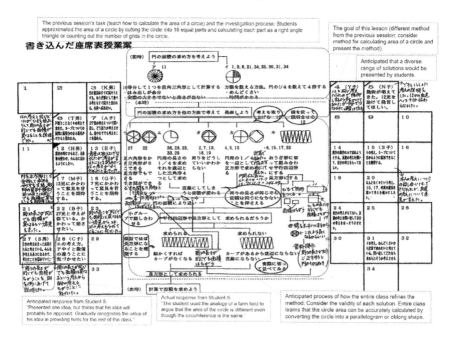

Fig. 8.7 Lesson Plan With Seating Chart (*Source* Kaoru Ueda, Ando Elementary School in Shizuoka City 1999, Ando shōhatsu ko o mitsumeru jyugyō [Ando Elementary School presentation: Lesson for discovering individuality], Meijitosho Shuppan Corporation, pp. 114–115. The boxes within the figure and the annotations are by this author)

place through opportunities to concretely imagine and envision pupil learning in the pre-lesson design stage. Therefore, because of the presence of the culture of teachers' practice research, a great deal of classroom assessment in Japan has not been a conscious application of tools but, instead, it has been inherent in the assessment abilities of teachers as a responsive art form, and has been implemented without being recognized as an assessment.

Conclusion

As put forward in this chapter, Japanese creative whole-class teaching that revolves around class-level activity, and especially the ideas of "teaching that builds on stumbles" and "stimulation", can provide clues for future assessment research when examined from the perspectives of assessment for learning and assessment as learning. If we strive to have assessment embedded in teaching and learning, formative assessment needs to be framed (1) not only as a closed reflective process but also as an open emergent process; and (2) not only as a visual and rational process whereby the teacher subject sees the student objects and tries to visualize their learning process, but also as a sensual and aesthetic process whereby the teacher naturally develops a sensitivity in the responsive relationship between teacher and students. There is a need to redefine the concept of formative assessment as "responsive and emergent assessment".

To realize this responsive and emergent assessment in the classroom, it will be necessary for teachers to improve their assessment ability—the art of leading the students in creative dialogue. Starting with lesson study, the culture, systems, and tools accumulated by the practical research of Japanese teachers provide clues for how to train teachers who can actualize formative assessment in their classrooms. Conversely, through the formative assessment embedded in creative whole-class teaching, which visualizes the dialogic process between teacher and children while facilitating thinking and communication, the teachers are given opportunities to grow as they learn from the reality of the children's thinking and communication processes.

References

Arani, M. R. S., Shibata, Y., Shibata, Y., Sakamoto, M., Iksan, Z., Amirullah, A. H., et al. (2017). How teachers respond to students' mistakes in lessons: A cross-cultural analysis of a mathematics lesson. *International Journal for lesson and learning studies, 6*(3), 249–267.

Archbald, D., & Newmann, F. M. (1988). *Beyond standardized testing: Assessing authentic academic achievement in the secondary school*. Reston, VA: National Association of Secondary School Principals.

Black, P., & Wiliam, D. (1998). Inside the black box: Raising standards through classroom assessment. *Phi Delta Kappan, 80*(2), 139–148.

Bloom, B. S., Hastings, J. T., & Madaus, G. F. (1971). *Handbook on formative and summative evaluation of student learning*. New York: McGraw-Hill.

Brookhart, S. M. (2007). Expanding views about formative classroom assessment: A review of the literature. In J. H. McMillan (Ed.), *Formative classroom assessment: Theory into practice* (pp. 43–62). New York: Teachers College Press.

Connelly, F. M., & Clandinin, D. J. (1988). *Teachers as curriculum planners: Narrative of experience*. New York: Teachers College Press.

Earl, L. M. (2013). *Assessment as learning: Using classroom assessment to maximize student learning* (2nd ed.). Thousand Oaks, CA: Corwin Press.

Eisner, E. W. (1979). *The educational imagination: On the design and evaluation of school programs*. New York: Macmillan.

Elbaz, F. (1991). Research on teachers' knowledge: The evolution of a discourse. *Journal of Curriculum Studies, 23*(1), 1–19.

Fujioka, N. (1991). *Sutop-pu moushon houshiki ni yoru jugyou kenkyuu no houhou* [Classroom research methods based on stop motion]. Tokyo: Gakuji Shuppan.

Fujioka, K. (2000). *Kakawaru koto he no ishi* [The will to engage]. Tokyo: Kokudosha.

Herbart, J. F. (1806). *Allgemeine Pädagogik aus dem Zweck der Erziehung abgeleitet*. Leipzig: Göttingen.

Ikuta, K. (2011). Waza no densho wa nani wo mezasunoka [What does the transmission of arts aim for?]. In K. Ikuta & K. Kitamura (Eds.), *Waza gengo* [Craft language] (pp. 3–31). Tokyo: Keio University Press.

Imaizumi, H. (1998). *"Areru" kodomotachi ni oshie rareta koto: Gakkou wo tanoshisa to anshin no ba ni* [What was taught by "roaring" children: To make the school a fun and comfortable place]. Tokyo: Hitonaru.

Ishii, T. (2011). *Gendai Amerika ni okeru gakuryoku keisei ron no tenkai* [Development of theories on educational objectives and assessment in the United States of America]. Tokyo: Toshindo.

Ishii, T. (2012). *Gakuryoku kojo* [Raising academic ability]. In K. Shinohara (Ed.), *Gakkou kaizen manejiment* [School improvement management] (pp. 136–150). Kyoto: Minerva.

Ishii, T. (2014). *Jyugyou kenkyuu wo toi naosu: Kyoujyugaku-teki kanshin no sai-hyouka* [Re-examining lesson studies: Re-evaluation of didactic interest]. In the National Association for the Study of Educational Methods (Ed.), *Kyouiku houhou 43: Jyugyou kenkyuu to kounai kenshuu* [Education method 43: Lesson study and in-school teacher training] (pp. 36–49). Tokyo: Tosho Bunka.

Ishii, T. (2016). Jugyou no kousou ryoku wo takameru kyoushi no jissen kenkyuu no houhouron [Teachers' practical research methodology for raising conceptual ability in teaching]. *Kyouiku Houhou No Tankyu* [Investigating Educational Methods], *19*, 11–21.

Ishii, T. (2017). Historical overview of lesson study. In K. Tanaka, K. Nishika, & T. Ishii (Eds.), *Curriculum, instruction and assessment in Japan: Beyond lesson study* (pp. 57–72). New York: Routledge.

Kawaji, A. (2005). *Toui Yoshio to mura wo sodateru gakuryoku* [Yoshio Toui and the academic skills to raise a village]. In K. Tanaka (Ed.), *Jidai wo hiraita kyoushi tachi* [Teachers who have pioneered an era] (pp. 75–86). Tokyo: Nippon Hyojun.

Korthagen, F. A. (2001). *Linking practice and theory: The pedagogy of realistic teacher education*. New York: Routledge.

Lampert, M. (2001). *Teaching problems and the problems in teaching*. New Haven, CT: Yale University Press.

McMillan, J. H. (2013). Why we need research on classroom assessment. In J. H. McMillan (Ed.), *SAGE handbook of research on classroom assessment* (pp. 3–16). London: SAGE publications.

Mukōyama, Y. (1985). *Jugyo no ude wo ageru housoku* [The laws and regulations that improve the classroom]. Tokyo: Meijitosho.

Saitō, K. (1958). *Mirai ni tunagaru gakuryoku* [Academic ability for the future]. Tokyo: Mugi.

Saitō, K. (1969). *Kyouikugaku no susume* [An encouragement of pedagogy]. Tokyo: Chikuma.

Saitō, K. (1977). *Kainyuujugyo no kiroku (Jou) [Record of an intervention class (top)]*. Tokyo: Ikkei.

Satō, M. (2010). *Kyouiku no houhou* [Educational methods]. Tokyo: Sayusha.

Satō, M., & Inagaki, T. (1996). *Jyugyou kenkyuu nyuumon* [An introduction to lesson study]. Tokyo: Iwanami Shoten.

Schön, D. A. (1983). *The reflective practitioner: How professionals think in action*. Aldershot, England: Basic Books.

Shibata, Y. (1967). *Gendai no kyoujyugaku* [Contemporary didactics]. Tokyo: Meiji Tosho.

Shulman, L. S. (1986). Those who understand: Knowledge growth in teaching. *Educational Researcher, 15*(2), 4–14.

Tanaka, K. (2008). *Kyouiku hyouka* [Educational assessment]. Tokyo: Iwanami Shoten.

Tanaka, K. (2017). Practices of leading educators: Yoshio Toi, Kihaku Saito, Kazuaki Shoji and Yasutaro Tamada. In K. Tanaka, K. Nishika, & T. Ishii (Eds.), *Curriculum, instruction and assessment in Japan: Beyond lesson study* (pp. 73–81). New York: Routledge.

Tōi, Y. (1987). *Inochinekko wo sodateru gakuryoku* [The academic abilities toward the growth of the roots of life]. Tokyo: Kokudosha.

Tulis, M. (2013). Error management behavior in classrooms: Teachers' response to student mistakes. *Teaching and Teacher Education, 33*(1), 56–68.

Tyler, R. W. (1949). *Basic principles of curriculum and instruction*. Chicago: The University of Chicago Press.

Ueda, K., & Ando Elementary School in Shizuoka City. (1999). Ando shōhatsu ko o mitsumeru jyugyō [Ando Elementary School Presentation: Lesson for discovering individuality]. Tokyo: Meijitosho Shuppan.

Wiggins, G. (1993). *Assessing student performance: Exploring the purpose and limits of testing.* San Francisco: Jossey-Bass.

Wiliam, D. (2011). *Embedded formative assessment.* Bloomington, IN: Solution Tree Press.

Yoshimoto, H. (1983). *Jyugyou no kousou ryoku* [The imagination of teaching]. Tokyo: Meiji Tosho.

Chapter 9
Professional Learning of Classroom Assessment in Singapore: Understanding Epistemic and Cultural Mediations of Practices Through the Case of Pei Pei

Wei Shin Leong

Abstract This chapter explores the professional learning episodes involved in classroom assessment through the case study of a Singaporean classroom teacher ('Pei Pei'), which was conducted by means of researcher-led interviews and observations. Such episodes encouraged this teacher to see and distil what she considers to be better classroom assessment practices in her English and music classrooms. Such findings from a teacher's reflections suggest that the explicit 'knowing about' that is inherent in classroom assessment is very different from the 'knowing that', which is disseminated through generic professional learning procedures. They also highlight the possibilities of how juxtapositions of seemingly incompatible beliefs and values of practices invite engagement in epistemic and cultural mediations of classroom assessment. The case study demonstrates that the spaces and boundaries of professional learning can be defined by a teacher, and that the facilitation of epistemic and cultural mediation ensures that professional learning and knowledge production are both personal and polycentric within different classrooms.

Keywords Beliefs and values · Classroom assessment · Singapore

Introduction

Classroom assessment, like many other aspects of a teacher's work, is particularly challenging. One reason for this is that classroom assessment resides in complicated intersections of fields (Brookhart 2004), which can span classroom pedagogy, classroom management, psychological assessment and, more recently, formative assessment and curriculum theories. Classroom assessment can mean different sets of

W. S. Leong (✉)
National Institute of Education, Nanyang Technological University, Singapore, Singapore
e-mail: weishin.leong@nie.edu.sg

© Springer Nature Singapore Pte Ltd. 2018   161
H. Jiang and M. F. Hill (eds.), *Teacher Learning with Classroom Assessment*,
https://doi.org/10.1007/978-981-10-9053-0_9

practices for different teachers: developing and administering class tests, selecting and adapting the appropriate classroom pedagogy, observing and responding to student's thinking and actions (including homework), policing undesirable student behaviour, and being accountable for students' learning to the authorities. This is a formidable list and, depending on how educators see such classroom practice as part of 'classroom assessment', it can mean different things in terms of defining classroom assessment, and consequently how related research and professional learning can even commence.

As early as the 1980s, teacher educators across the world highlighted that teachers have little or no training in classroom assessment, measurement and diagnostic practices (Stiggins and Bridgeford 1985; Trittel et al. 2014). Coupled with this inadequacy (given that classroom assessment can span several practices) across many education systems, there has been an increase in epistemic communities of classroom assessment in recent years advocating for teachers to raise their assessment literacies in realizing both formative *and* summative purposes of classroom assessment (Alonzo et al. 2015; Fullan 2001; Price et al. 2012; Stiggins 1991). In this chapter, classroom assessment is defined as the appropriate realization of formative and summative purposes in the design and implementation of assessment activities and the interpretation of assessment results in the classroom context. In Singapore, while summative assessment has dominated classroom assessment, teachers are invited to revisit their understanding of classroom assessment through policy initiatives such as 'holistic' and 'balanced' assessment (Primary Education Review and Implementation Committee 2009; Ratnam-Lim and Tan 2015). Singaporean teachers are consequentially asked to introduce classroom assessment more broadly, beyond the preparation of traditional examinations and tests to a set of assessment strategies to support students' learning. In the implementation of such policy initiatives, terms such as 'formative assessment' and 'assessment for learning' (AfL) are used interchangeably by teachers and school leaders (as in this chapter) and considered to be critical considerations of classroom assessment. These terms are also often assumed to be widely accepted and understood by local teachers.

Across the world, prospective and even experienced teachers have expressed their insecurities and concerns about their assessment competencies in the classroom (Klug et al. 2013; Spinath 2005). These take the form of the different 'reality shocks' that confront them as a result of the heterogeneous array of students' academic abilities, interests and motivations. This unfortunate convergence of a 'lack of assessment literacies' with an 'expected-to-be-more-competent' scenario in classroom assessment can result in the imposition of politically imposed professional learning sessions. Unfortunately, these sessions are not always well designed or culturally informed. The consequences of undesirable professional learning sessions are that teachers are left more cynical and no more assessment-literate or competent than before (Guskey 2001). This is a far cry from the calls for professional learning to be responsive to how individual teachers learn and thus have more influence on their classroom practice.

Professional Learning of Classroom Assessment

The research literature on classroom assessment suggests that its terms are neither always uncontested nor can they be easily understood. According to McMillan (2013), there is much to be done to establish a body of knowledge of classroom assessment, a field that is currently evolving and extremely fragmented. The notion rarely holds that the worth of, for instance, realizing formative assessment within classroom assessment practice is self-evident or guaranteed by a particular theory. Rather, it is only in learning about the mediating influences that we can understand how a particular practice thrives or is abandoned so that further theorization can take place. Classroom assessment has to be understood from a contextually grounded approach of seeing it in action: how any embedding of a new practice needs to be sensitive to the existing cases of indigenized and idiosyncratic practices (Black and Wiliam 2005). This is particularly the case in terms of formative assessment, which, unlike tests and exams, is embedded within the very fabric of classroom action.

Studies that have explored the professional development involved in supporting teachers to use formative assessment have been reviewed (Brookhart in-press) and conducted internationally, including in England (cf. Black et al. 2004; Marshall and Drummond 2006), Hong Kong (Carless 2005), Scotland (Hayward et al. 2004) and New Zealand (cf. Dixon and Haigh 2009; Hill 2016). These studies, among many others, examine the ways in which professional development can facilitate the implementation of formative assessment within the classroom. Traditional policy-led staff development, typically in the form of isolated workshops, has the inherent limitation of paying insufficient attention to the individual classroom teachers to enable them to mediate change themselves beyond the workshops. They focus, for instance, on passing down the 'knowing that' or codified procedural knowledge rather than learning in the sense of 'knowing about' becoming a practitioner—which includes not only codified knowledge but also how to decode and meaningfully apply it in the appropriate contexts (Bruner 1996; Duguid 2005). Brookhart (in-press) has highlighted how such workshops tend to help teachers replicate practical formative assessment procedures or strategies rather than helping them to reorientate beliefs about how different students (and themselves) learn.

Collaboration between university researchers/external experts and practitioners has been identified in several studies (Brookhart in-press; Hill 2011, 2016) as an effective way to blend educational research and professional development, providing teachers with the time, space and content necessary to increase their knowledge and foster meaningful change in their classroom practice (Birman et al. 2000). The visibility of such professional development in the studies indicates that teachers are being supported closely by researchers in universities. In the 'King's-Medway-Oxfordshire Formative Assessment Project' (Black et al. 2004), the 'Assessment is for Learning' programme in Scotland (Hayward et al. 2004), and the 'Learning How to Learn' development and research project (James et al. 2006), teachers worked with researchers to explore how ideas from AfL research might be translated into various contexts in different classrooms and schools. However, such a form of professional development is extremely labour and resource intensive, and the flow into classroom practice can be inhibited by different obstacles (Leong 2017). For instance, such efforts could, in fact, diffuse rapidly as support ceases as a result of inertia on the part of teachers, towards change, a lack of follow-up, funding cuts or changes in policy directives. An alternative to university or ministry-led professional development is to get teachers to act as their own agency of change, as the findings from the study 'Analysis and Review of Innovations in Assessment' (ARIA) suggest:

> This might come about through "picking up" relevant ideas from professional dialogue or from reading the professional and academic literature on the potential benefits of the proposed changes. They then seek support or have a go themselves. (Gardner 2010, p. 133)

What arguably appears to be the case throughout the projects examined under the auspices of ARIA is that, unless teachers are *first* committed through self-agency to any particular change, the chances of successful dissemination and professional learning, leading to a sustained practice of new classroom assessment, are likely to be slim. Other professional development models that draw on teachers' self-agency include learning teams, teacher networks and professional learning communities that accentuate collaborative, reflexive, site- and practice-based professional development within and between schools (Birman et al. 2000; Day and Sachs 2004; Hill 2016). These may provide a longer term solution to supporting teachers in sustaining the use of formative assessment or AfL practices in classrooms. In these alternative professional development methods, teachers can derive the impetus for change from their own professional reading, reflection and collegial interaction. The social networking of teachers within and across schools, particularly at transdisciplinary groupings, encourages 'cross-fertilisation and ideas' while resisting 'subject Balkanisation' (Hill 2016, p. 786).

Nevertheless, although knowledge can have a more extensive reach through scholarly writings, policy dissemination and formalized professional learning sessions, and changes to personal practice, can remain parochial (or tend to remain 'sticky'), as noted by scholars such as Duguid (2005). Acknowledging that the application of a teacher's professional learning is contextually related and highly dynamic, Opfer and Pedder (2011) conceptualized this from a complexity perspective. Their conceptualization shifted the focus from a cause-and-effect logic of teachers' learning (e.g., input from experts, output from trialling new practices) to a nonlinear model, thus enabling us to understand the different influences, reasons and ways in which individual teachers learn differently through their professional careers.

Methodology

The findings reported in this chapter come from interviewing and observing a single case-study teacher ('Pei Pei') regarding her classroom assessment in 2011–12. An important assumption underlying this study is that different experienced teachers have different trajectories of professional learning. It is very difficult to study such trajectories through limited encounters with large groups of teachers, especially in singular professional development workshops. Rather, I proceed from the premise that professional learning and classroom assessment practice cannot be divorced from the context in which they are developed, and need to be observed in situ on an individual basis. One way of seeing the relationship is through what Sellars et al. (2007) calls 'the space of reasons'—a reflection of a view of reality that suggests that an individual teacher exercises the agency of his or her own thinking and actions within a fast-paced context of reasoning based on different *epistemic* and *cultural* mediations. Epistemic mediations are the negotiations of evidentiary standards or determinants of learning in different subject(s). Such mediation involves asking, what constitutes learning and how do I know students have learnt in one subject versus another? Cultural mediations refer to the deliberation of personal and institutional beliefs, values and codes of conduct that exert a tacit, yet palpable control over classroom practices. They invite questions of whether certain beliefs, values or codes are more malleable than others in different contexts. As I engaged in the process of interview and lesson observation, I became more aware of the subjective, tentative and other potential qualities of these mediations of classroom assessment emerging from the data.

Pei Pei

Pei Pei was a lower secondary music and English teacher who had taught in the same secondary school for 8 years. She was deployed to teach music and English based on her specialization in these subjects at the pre-service training course. She was chosen as a secondary-school research participant (based on my preference for selecting experienced teachers with specific teaching subject combinations) in my Ph.D. study on classroom assessment, after she indicated her interest and was willing to be observed and interviewed for a period of a year.

The school was affiliated to a church and primary school. It accepted students with below-to-above-average academic performance in the year six national streaming examinations. The school is relatively well known in Singapore, particularly for its rich culture of sports and performing arts. In 2011–12 Pei Pei was asked to teach a Secondary 2 class for English and all the Secondary 1 and 2 classes for music. I sought permission to visit approximately once a month in the Secondary 2 English class and one music Secondary 1 class for 2 years. The English class was the smallest (15 students) of all the classes I observed (typically a class has around 40 students). This special arrangement was made because the students were 'banded together' after failing to do well overall in their Secondary 1 examinations. Pei Pei was assigned to teach the class in the hope of helping them do better the following year. Her Secondary 1 music class was a mixed-ability class.

Pei Pei's beliefs about teaching were shaped by her past experiences. In the following extract of a post-lesson interview, just after the students in her Secondary 2

English class were given a severe reprimand for shoddy work, she considered the importance of 'drilling' and 'scolding' in her English class.

> I liken their ability to my poor Chinese when I was in school. So I started learning Chinese when I was in primary school only. Never spoke or read much in Chinese before that…. Then I went to primary school; my teacher really drilled me through repeated *ting xie* [Chinese dictation test]. *Test, test, test, scold, scold, scold, drill, drill, drill, drill.* I survived till my O level Chinese – I got an A grade, okay via sheer rote-memorization…. I think it has an impact on the way I think and therefore the way I teach. (Post-lesson interview, 4 May 2011)

Pei Pei believed that 'drilling' and scolding had helped her to achieve a good grade in Chinese, so it could, therefore, work for her English students. Interestingly, she also acknowledged that such a learning approach was a very 'short-term' goal of getting a good grade, since she could no longer speak or write Chinese well. In contrast, she also shared her more positive music teaching and learning experiences:

> I don't scold as much in music… instead I give feedback, more maybe like the teachers who had taught me music here in Singapore and England…. Also looking back further, I was inspired by Janet… she was my choir conductor of Singapore Youth Choir… she is probably one of the best in Singapore because when she teaches music she teaches other things… like being responsible… I love the way she phrases her feedback and is very nurturing…. I always love the way she phrases her [feedback] and so I put that into how I teach music so that students can enjoy music as I still do now. (Post-lesson interview, 4 May 2011)

Pei Pei's other beliefs about teaching and learning were also gleaned from the frustration she experienced during the Secondary 2 English class. Pei Pei attributed her inadequacy in teaching them well to her inexperience and lack of knowledge about teaching such a class, and also of English in general. For instance, in this post-lesson interview, Pei Pei expressed her frustration at not being able to help the students to form a proper sentence:

> I cannot make it any simpler by breaking it down completely what a proper sentence is and how to write one. First of all, I don't know how to do it [break down the task of writing a simple sentence]…that's one thing – I may not have the skills … maybe if I was more experienced as a English teacher… or knowledgeable I would be able to find a solution. (Post-lesson interview, 14 April 2011)

She believed that the presence or absence of national examinations in the two subjects was a very important reason for the differences in her teaching:

> It's different in English because there is a high expectation for the boys to learn very specific items according to the examination…[this] doesn't mean that I have low expectations in music; it's more like… I just don't want to intimidate them in music lessons… what is the point of talking about very difficult musical terms when they don't understand it and if they don't… by telling them that they are wrong just shut them off from the music lessons. (Interview, 13 October 2011)

In contrast to her music classes, where she allowed her students to take their time to grasp listening and singing skills, Pei Pei felt she was always running out of time to mark and prepare for her English lessons and to get the boys ready for a specific part of the test and examination. 'Whatever I did, was already for the examinations'.

Pei Pei consistently referred to assessment in her interviews as the common tests and semestral examinations that recurred at the end of each term for her English class. When asked at the beginning of term whether assessment had a different meaning for her, Pei Pei clearly stated that assessment, as preparation for the tests and examinations, was a feature of her English classroom throughout the year:

> Other ways to think about assessment? Not really. I wouldn't know what to change to anyway and why there is a need to change...what I am teaching now, whatever I did, was already for the examinations. If I can, I would have started preparing them earlier like last year! (Interview, 10 March 2011)

In contrast, based on her seeing assessment as tests and examinations, Pei Pei responded that there was no assessment in her music lessons and she was interested in focusing more on teaching well.

> Yes, I don't have a formal assessment system in my music lessons because the school and parents don't expect me to do it...and secondly, I am not sure I want to carry out those assessments that I have done for 15 students for 700 students...yes I might get to see a lot of 'results'...but it would be only for me to know.... It wouldn't ever reach the school or parents...so I am not sure I want to waste time going through 1,500 sheets of homework for music, for instance...I might want to focus on exploring new ways of teaching that can help my students to learn better...all these clapping, singing and getting the boys to the board to notate...they are new to me. (Post-lesson interview, 14 April 2011)

> For music – it is non-assessable, no, I mean non-examinable. That is, no examination, therefore don't need to assess. Parents are not interested. So, no results to talk about it [assessment]. Don't have to report to school. No exam paper to set. I know I sound [a] very 'bad teacher'...but that's the truth. No assessment in music. (Interview, 4 May 2011)

In all these extracts, Pei Pei saw the word assessment as being synonymous with tests and examinations and as a separate event in the lesson. Her allusion in the last extract to what a 'good teacher' should do ('test regularly') highlighted how having a particular conception of assessment could influence her view of how she was a good teacher in the English class and a 'bad teacher' in the music class for not testing the students.

Pei Pei saw the benefits of tests and examinations—they helped to 'push' the students to work harder:

> These boys...they need the examination and tests...they only "wake up" when you tell them that what they are doing in their homework and for the examination and tests. Otherwise they don't see a value in doing it. Then for them because they cannot "see" their learning other than in [a] numerical sense, that is what marks they have got. So when they see their test results have dipped from twenty-five to twenty, then it's a clear indication for them that something is wrong. (Interview, 4 May 2011)

> As we got closer to their examinations...I found that assessment is a good bargaining chip for me...all I had to say is that "I am preparing you for examination," then you can tell that they are a bit more serious... especially for these boys who have been failing, examinations are motivating or [a] push factor to study. Especially these boys. Assessment does make them feel stressed...you might expect it only in a "brainier" class...but it does happen to them too. (Interview, 13 October 2011)

In the process of teaching the Secondary 2 students to prepare for tests and examinations, Pei Pei saw much wider differences in the attitudes and ability related to learning English in these 15 students, compared with over 700 Secondary 1 and 2 students in her music class. When asked how this was possible, Pei Pei responded that 'there would be differences in music, but it would be fewer and easier to manage as a whole as compared to that in English class' (Interview, 14 April 2011).

> It has to do with the caliber of boys...or the background they come [from]...you will find that only about five boys per class of about 40 have ever learnt [the] piano before...so I have the majority of the class without receiving formal music lessons at home, so I can teach more or less the same thing – start from the beginning and repeating when necessary, and they all seem to enjoy that process of trying to get at singing and listening. For the English class...they came with varying problems. (Post-lesson interview, 14 April 2011)

It seems that the 'problems' of 15 students in terms of learning English were greatly magnified, according to Pei Pei. The transcriptions of all her English lessons had coding related to preparation for tests and examinations or administering post-test activities to help these students overcome various learning problems. This included activities pertaining to Pei Pei explaining to students the requirements of the tests, the calculation of marks, the checking of files and also the specific 'drilling' of items in tests (e.g. spelling):

> Pei Pei went through the answers for the grammar section of the common test. She asked the students to write down the answers if they had got it wrong and went around to ensure every student did that. (Field notes, 9 March 2011)

> Pei Pei gave students empty 'study cards' to get them to write down the words they need to know the meanings [of] (taken from their textbook *More than Words*). She wanted them to memorize the words and meanings as they would be tested [on] these words in the mid-year examination. (Field notes, 6 April 2011)

> Pei Pei showed the class the data template for keying their marks for the Continual Assessment [CA] summative grade. She asked the students to check that the marks for their various homework activities were correctly filled in. She also went around to check that the students had filed all their work correctly for inspection. She walked over to me and shared that she wanted all her students to file their work for her to check, so that she can send the message of whatever they submitted to me for marking matters in [preparing them for] the tests and examinations. (Field notes, 4 May 2011)

Each time she returned their English tests and examinations to be filed, Pei Pei expressed her surprise or disappointment about the number of students who had achieved the goals of the numerical grades or marks set for them earlier. Even the reflection sheets for the students were directed at the performance of tests and examinations.

In contrast, there was no coding on the preparation for tests and examinations for her music lessons. Indeed, I did not observe the same anxiety to pursue a specific learning goal in Pei Pei's music lessons. In contrast with the English lessons, Pei Pei deliberately took her time introducing the fundamentals of musical skills. In this extract, she taught the students how to clap the rhythm of a new song before introducing the pitches and text:

Music Lesson Transcript (Pei Pei), 25 Feb 2011

[Pei Pei had just asked the class to clap a series of rhythms that were written on the board.]

Pei Pei: The first four rhythms were very good but I don't want you to clap like you are just reacting or following your friends. Try to read it well.

[Students clapped, but there were some variations in the clapping.]

Pei Pei: Not too bad... maybe about half of you have gotten it right. Let's go at [an] even slower speed.

[Students tried again and were more confident in their clapping.]

Pei Pei: Getting much better, everyone, now I want everyone to be steady now, don't gan cheong [dialect for rushing]...I can hear an extra beat at the end. Let's go even slower.

There was still some predictability in the music class, as in the English class, but in a different way. Pei Pei ensured that the students were able to demonstrate one task well before going on to the next at a comfortable pace. My field notes frequently captured this 'comfortable pacing'. Her reflection at the post-lesson interview was helpful in order to get to know this routine as part of her music assessment practices:

> Because there are no examinations or tests, like the boys are not expected to identify Beethoven's fourth or sixth symphony at the end of the course, I don't have to work towards a goal in terms of content...so I am able to start from the beginning...introducing music reading skills, music writing skills in the simplest form without the need to think we need to get THERE...because for sure...we can't get THERE with just one lesson a week. So, I can take my own time to build their skills slowly and in 'layers' upon 'layers.' The boys can be allowed to take *'own time own target'* [Singaporean slang for being able to take their own time to learn]. (Post-lesson interview, 14 April 2011)

In general, the atmosphere in the music class was very relaxed, as Pei Pei responded to the students in a light-hearted manner, often making use of localized jokes. Possibly the students felt it was safe to make mistakes and to ask questions. On those occasions when students did not clap or sing correctly, Pei Pei was observed to be sensitive not to embarrass them, or, as she termed it, 'masking assessment':

> I was trying to explore masking assessment then, like, you know, Bermuda Triangle...it's there but it isn't there? Yeah, I know some boys don't get it during the music lesson...but I don't want to embarrass by pointing it out so directly...so I will try to get those students to sing or clap by themselves without stating anything yet...then to get the others to sing or clap...I think most times they get to hear the differences and figure out how to get it through such peer support...fortunately it has worked out usually...otherwise I will have to find other ways to help them. (Post-lesson interview, 29 September 2011)

In contrast, the English class was visibly directed at the inability of students to hand in work or 'score' well. Her frustration was evident in a number of lessons where she was visibly upset when reprimanding students, to the extent of calling up the parents in class. In one of the lessons (23 March 2011), Pei Pei was seen throwing students' files across the floor and also ordering half the class to stand outside the classroom to complete their homework. She assured me, upon viewing the video playback the following week, that this was 'formative anger' that she had scripted into her lesson to wake the students from their dormancy and lackadaisical attitude towards learning.

> I wouldn't scold the boys publicly if I know that the boy has some sensitive issue or that it is not typical of him to hand up such low quality of work – I would go to speak to him privately. The boys know me well...and so they could take my scolding and reprimand. From my conversation with their parents now, I know some of the boys are really having some communication gaps with family. For the last lesson on checking of files, I have purposely made it a little dramatic...I actually make myself crush paper and throw file...all of it is calculated...otherwise the boys really cannot seem to 'wake up' and learn important lessons of being a responsible and organized person. (Post-lesson interview, 30 March 2011)

The public reprimanding and shaming of students for not handing in or for doing shoddy work, as a means to motivate students, was a regular feature of Pei Pei's English classes, in sharp contrast with her music classes. Given the differences in conceptions and practices of classroom assessment in English and music, I asked Pei Pei whether she thought there were aspects of conception and practice in each of the subjects that could be related or even applied to each other. For instance, in this extract, Pei Pei wondered whether the way in which she gave encouraging feedback and 'second chances' in her music lessons could work in her English lessons.

> It is more natural in music...there is no push factor.... There is no such thing as if you don't [do] this well, you will fail for [the] exam...it's like if you don't do this well...can you not try it again and I can try it again next week...For English...perhaps it's possible...just that I need to think through carefully...if I was more aware about it...and now that you have brought my attention to it, I will have to see whether it is possible right from the beginning. It is certainly true that how I teach is colored by what assessment is about...So right from the start for English if I can focus on values of learning like "Is this the best you can do...How can you make it better?" more than like "You are doing it wrong, I am only going to give you 18 marks"...Maybe if my feedback is more like qualitative...no marks.... Then maybe it will be different...the reason I need to give a grade now is that I need to key in the marks for English.... If I can change the way of assessment, then it will be very different. (Interview, 13 October 2011)

Pei Pei concluded that the stresses of a national examination for subjects such as English would invariably affect her conceptions and practices in the classroom. From this extract, she was not optimistic about making changes in the near future because of the requirements of the national examination; at least she conceded there was a possibility that her English class could be more like her music class. She also acknowledged that she needs to be more diligent in recording evidence of learning in her music classes, to get closer to a summative judgment. This, she acknowledged, was an area for improvement, because, unlike English, there was no one reviewing her students' music assessment results. To me, it was a significant professional learning outcome that Pei Pei could see the possibility for change in her classroom assessment by drawing upon her own experiences of teaching two different subjects.

Pei Pei's conceptions of classroom assessment centred on the presence (or absence) of expectations such as tests and examinations for the subjects. Therefore, whatever she did for English lessons (homework, tests, classwork) was done to prepare the students for the examinations. In the total absence of any exams or tests in music, Pei Pei could explore new ways of teaching that focused on student mastery of learning musical concepts, singing and understanding. She was also seen to be more nurturing and to encourage good efforts (rather than perpetually reprimanding for unacceptable work). To me, this is an assessment that supports genuine learning, although Pei Pei did not make use of any explicit or formalized formative assessment terms in the interview. Throughout the research, Pei Pei did not mention any specific training on formative assessment. This was probably due to the fact that, at the point of research, formative assessment was relatively new to secondary-school teachers in Singapore.

Discussion

This study has contributed to assisting a particular teacher in examining the conceptions permeating her day-to-day classroom assessment work. A cycle of reflection, grounded in examining their practices of classroom assessment, could stimulate teachers to ask and respond to difficult questions, which would otherwise remain tacit (Feiman-Nemser 2001; Pope et al. 2009). This study has shown that the process of rendering the tacit explicit is not likely a singular encounter with a revelation that has been known (i.e., conceptions and practices exist a priori); it is a dialectical one in which teachers' familiar and tacit knowing interacts with, and is reshaped by, newly explicit knowing prompted by an external party. The experiences of being involved in such research made more visible to Pei Pei what classroom assessment is and how it could change, consistent with conclusions from other researchers such as Bell and Cowie (2001) and Hill (2016). Reflecting on the interview questions and her own practices helped Pei Pei to become more aware of the limits of her professional knowledge and skills and to think about improving classroom assessment practices on her own.

For Pei Pei, the pressure of the summative assessment tasks was very important in her English class, as she was determined to help her students do better than they had done previously. This pressure drove her to distil and drill down into the very details of exactly what words the students should memorize and the kinds of question they could tackle in order to achieve a better grade. This sort of pressure might have helped students raise their test scores, but whether it was an *educational* or even *ethical* practice is open for debate. The motivation for teachers to raise test scores through unfair and maybe even unethical ways, such as excessive drilling and testing, has been reported by researchers (Pope et al. 2009), as has the evidence that improvement in scores does not necessarily translate into improved student learning (Koretz 2003; Pope et al. 2009; Stobart 2008). Such practices present ethical issues because they may lead to misrepresentation of students' actual mastery level of the assessed knowledge and skills. In the music classroom, Pei Pei, however, was enacting formative assessment naturally, where the mastery of musical skills could be privileged *without* the pressure of a performativity agenda. In doing so, mastery of learning takes on a natural kind of 'layering' that is not excessively hurried or imposed through acts of force. Yet, this current indigenous formative lens and enactment of her classroom assessment (perhaps partly due to the large number of students she needs to teach in music classes) may also have blinded her to possible differences in evidence of music learning in her music class. It is worth noting that Pei Pei saw much wider differences in ability and attitudes towards learning English in these 15 students, in comparison with over 700 Secondary 1 and 2 students in her music classes.

Comparing Pei Pei's conceptions of classroom assessment in two different subjects, I can appreciate the difficulties that she experienced reconciling the different expectations of teaching, learning and assessment. The presence of high-stakes summative assessment in English classes meant that it was difficult for her to promote student independence and autonomy of learning within the classroom setting; she was compelled to teach students to 'get it right' in the classroom before they went away to work on their homework. A teacher-centred style of teaching and instruction then became inevitable (Marshall and Drummond 2006). This clearly contrasted with her music lessons, where she gave autonomy to students to help one another, while she took the backstage role of encouraging them to self-correct. Her deeply contrasting practices of classroom assessment in two different subjects are mediated by epistemic commitments underpinned by examination or non-examination requirements. I have to question whether Pei Pei's judgment of students' learning has been compromised because she has focused excessively on summative and formative assessment in her English and music classes, respectively. In being tied down by summative assessment requirements in English classes, Pei Pei believed she had to commit herself to a more transmissive form of teaching, with the students needing to be fully compliant with her demands and with little opportunity to explore on their own. The students could be fully involved in learning (rather than just being compliant with requirements) in music classes; however, without any clarity regarding the standard of performances expected at the end, the learning process and outcome could also be compromised.

Such findings also highlight a possible disjunction between the Western cultural and intellectual ideals of an 'autonomous learner' and the Confucian-heritage values of 'teacher authority' over 'student autonomy' in different subject classes for a single teacher. Pei Pei had had a challenging time learning the Chinese language locally, whereas she was more successful learning music under the tutelage of her music teachers in Singapore and England. Many researchers have highlighted how teachers' cultural mediation of classroom assessment can act as a filter to either facilitate or impede learning (Dixon et al. 2011). Pedder and Opfer (2012) highlighted the importance of attending to teachers' cultural orientations, in particular, the degrees of dissonance between their values and their practices of teaching. The higher they value certain practices of assessment (likely as a result of past experiences and maybe the context of the presence/absence of high-stakes assessment), the higher the likelihood that they will prioritize them and *re-enact* these practices. Pei Pei's memory of past experiences as a student of Chinese and music encouraged her to replicate certain classroom assessment practices in her English and music classrooms. Having been taught and assessed as a student in different ways, it is likely she has also acquired different cultural orientations towards the learning and assessment of English and music, manifested in the sharp contrast in her practices.

Educators facilitating professional learning should recognize that teachers are not necessarily free to change their classroom assessment conceptions and practices, even if they wish to do so. While the sharing of 'new knowledge' of alternative classroom assessment practices through professional workshops can facilitate a certain 'knowing *that*', such knowledge is also likely to remain 'sticky' as just-codified knowledge lying in print or on PowerPoint slides. Access to such knowledge does not confer the ability to put it to use appropriately. No amount of such 'sharing' will necessarily bring about actionable knowledge. What is critical is the knowing *how* embedded in current practices already, wrapped around certain epistemic and cultural commitments that resist change. The reality of teachers' classroom assessment work may, for example, still require students to be given tests in certain subjects, and these realities need to be taken into account when helping teachers to see the perils of the current reality and the possibility of change. Such a reality has been widely reported by counterparts in many Asian countries recently (e.g. Tan 2016; Hui et al. 2017). It is particularly critical, in such challenging circumstances, to create conversations to help teachers see any potential convergence of values and recognize the utility of changing certain intentions of classroom assessment. Such conversations help them to engage with new thinking and activities of classroom assessment without needing to impose new knowledge on them at this stage.

Helping teachers to tap into their self-agency is a powerful device in fostering learning and change, and is considered one of the most important elements in ensuring successful professional learning and the development of teachers' classroom assessment (Gardner et al. 2010). The concept of 'relational agency' (Blackler and Regan 2009; Edwards 2011) is equally useful in understanding that any form of professional learning resides not only in individual cognition of a singular episode of practice, but also in the resources found through comparing and relating to differences in practice within the self across episodes. The relational agency in this study helped me to understand Pei Pei's progressive negotiation and possible re-creation of conceptions and practices of classroom assessment with different epistemologies. When the assessment practices of two subjects are different, epistemic and accountability barriers develop to the extent that productive sharing and learning becomes challenging—even when the different practices actually belong to the same teacher. Such is the professional 'blindness' to oneself even though the enactment of practices may take place every day.

Teacher educators also need to be sensitive to professional blindness, such as that described above, caused in part by the lack of opportunities to critically observe, review and reflect on teachers' actual classroom practice. Teachers may not need to be 'filled by' new principles of classroom assessment nor should they be 'empowered to change' without introducing new insights or practical ideas. By seeking an appropriate balance between presenting new information and reflecting through a critical expert friend, both can benefit from new insights of knowing how. In considering what this balancing may entail, I am reminded of what Richardson (1992) labelled the agenda-setting dilemma: A teacher educator may want to see teachers' practices change in a particular way while empowering the teachers themselves to be meaningfully involved in determining the changes. However, I argue that there is a great deal for teachers to learn, from and by themselves. Having noted this, I also acknowledge that it is critical for leaders in schools to provide safe spaces, support and resources for such professional learning. This will involve helping teachers to build individual and collective capacities to advance all students' learning (Hill 2016), while at the same time modelling how teachers can negotiate between interests in learning and grappling with the administrative responsibilities of reporting grades, performances and other results (Brookhart in-press). The spaces for conversation and experimentation need to become a 'safe haven' for individuals and groups of teachers to deliberate about the possibilities and also to contextualize the appropriate teaching, learning and assessment within different classrooms.

In this study, Pei Pei was able to pick up ideas about summative and formative assessment from my promptings and discussion, and through reflecting on her own practices. While there was no deliberate attempt to change her conceptions and practices, she was able to see the *possibilities* for change. This suggests that professional learning is not necessarily always situated within a formalized and organized setting. Instead, it may first be 'sparked off' by informal professional dialogue before being further taken up through more formalized, school-based professional learning such as lesson study and professional learning communities (Eraut 2004; Hill 2016; Putnam and Borko 2000). In this way, professional knowledge production for a teacher is not simply *a* space bounded by the formalized professional learning plan of a school or the ivory tower of academia. The spaces and boundaries of professional learning can be defined in different ways by a teacher as he/she works with a facilitator to challenge and change assessment approaches, especially so since these are epistemically and culturally mediated.

Notes

Having returned to Singapore from my Ph.D. study in 2014, I have been supporting the Ministry of Education and the National Institute of Education's efforts to design and run assessment literacy workshops for teachers. I have made extensive use of the findings from this case-study teacher to begin informal conversations with teachers, before facilitating further formalized discussion and reflection of their conceptions and practices of classroom assessment. The case study of Pei Pei can also be viewed in this YouTube clip: https://youtu.be/4vqlmzUL2Ak.

References

Alonzo, D. A., Lee, J., & Davison, C. (2015). *A teacher's assessment for learning competency framework: Development and application.* Paper presented at the annual meeting of the American Educational Research Association, Chicago.

Bell, B., & Cowie, B. (2001). The characteristics of formative assessment in science education. *Science Education, 85*(5), 536–553.

Birman, B. F., Desimone, L., Porter, A. C., & Garet, M. (2000). Designing professional development that works. *Educational Leadership, 57*(8), 28–33.

Black, P., Harrison, C., Lee, C., Marshall, B., & Wiliam, D. (2004). Working inside the black box: Assessment for Learning in the classroom. *Phi Delta Kappan, 86*(1), 8–21.

Black, P., & Wiliam, D. (2005). Lessons from around the world: How policies, politics and cultures constrain and afford assessment practices. *The Curriculum Journal, 16*, 249–261.

Blackler, F., & Regan, S. (2009). Intentionality, agency, change: Practice theory and management. *Management Learning, 40*(2), 161–176.

Brookhart, S. (2004). Classroom assessment: Tensions and intersections in theory and practice. *The Teachers College Record, 106*(3), 429–458.

Brookhart, S. (in-press). Functions of formative assessment in teacher education. In D. J. Clandinin & J. Husu (Eds.), *The Sage handbook of research on teacher education.* London: Sage.

Bruner, J. S. (1996). *The culture of education.* Cambridge: Harvard University Press.

Carless, D. (2005). Prospects for the implementation of assessment for learning. *Assessment in Education: Principles, Policy & Practice, 12*(1), 39–54.

Day, C., & Sachs, J. (2004). Professionalism, performativity and empowerment: Discourses in the politics, policies and purposes of continuing professional development. In C. Fay & J. Sachs (Eds.), *International handbook on the continuing professional development of teachers* (pp. 3–32). Berkshire: McGraw-Hill International.

Dixon, H. R., & Haigh, M. (2009). Changing mathematics teachers' conceptions of assessment and feedback. *Teacher Development, 13*(2), 173–186.

Dixon, H. R., Hawe, E., & Parr, J. (2011). Enacting Assessment for Learning: The beliefs–practice nexus. *Assessment in Education: Principles, Policy & Practice, 18*(4), 365–379.

Duguid, P. (2005). 'The art of knowing': Social and tacit dimensions of knowledge and the limits of the community of practice. *The Information Society, 21*(2), 109–118.

Edwards, A. (2011). Building common knowledge at the boundaries between professional practices: Relational agency and relational expertise in systems of distributed expertise. *International Journal of Educational Research, 50*(1), 33–39.

Eraut, M. (2004). Informal learning in the workplace. *Studies in Continuing Education, 26*(2), 247–273.

Feiman-Nemser, S. (2001). From preparation to practice: Designing a continuum to strengthen and sustain teaching. *The Teachers College Record, 103*(6), 1013–1055.

Fullan, M. (2001). *Leading in a culture of change.* San Francisco: Jossey Bass.

Gardner, J. (2010). What is innovative about teacher assessment? In J. Gardner, W. Harlen, L. Hayward, & G. Stobart (Eds.), *Developing teacher assessment* (pp. 71–84). Berkshire: Open University Press.

Gardner, J., Harlen, W., Hayward, L., & Stobart, G. (Eds.). (2010). *Developing teacher assessment.* Berkshire: Open University Press.

Guskey, T. R. (2001). Professional development and teacher change. *Teachers and Teaching: Theory and Practice, 8*(3), 381–391.

Hayward, L., Priestley, M., & Young, M. (2004). Ruffling the calm of the ocean floor: Merging practice, policy and research in assessment in Scotland. *Oxford Review of Education, 30*(3), 397–415.

Hill, M. F. (2011). 'Getting traction': Enablers and barriers to implementing assessment for learning in secondary schools. *Assessment in Education: Principles, Policy & Practice, 18*(4), 347–364.

Hill, M. F. (2016). Assessment for learning community: Learners, teachers and policy makers. In D. Wyse, L, Hayward, & J. Pandya (Eds.), *The Sage handbook of curriculum, pedagogy and assessment* (Vol. 2, pp. 772–789). London: Sage.

Hui, S. K. F., Brown, G. T., & Chan, S. W. M. (2017). Assessment for learning and for accountability in classrooms: The experience of four Hong Kong primary school curriculum leaders. *Asia Pacific Education Review, 18*(1), 41–51.

James, M., Black, P., McCormick, R., Pedder, D., & Wiliam, D. (2006). Learning how to learn, in classrooms, schools and networks: Aims, design and analysis. *Research Papers in Education, 21*(2), 101–118.

Klug, J., Bruder, S., Kelava, A., Spiel, C., & Schmitz, B. (2013). Diagnostic competence of teachers: A process model that accounts for diagnosing learning behavior tested by means of a case scenario. *Teaching and Teacher Education, 30,* 38–46.

Koretz, D. (2003). Using multiple measures to address perverse incentives and score inflation. *Educational Measurement: Issues and Practice, 22*(2), 18–26.

Leong, W. S. (2017). Contextualising assessment for learning in Singaporean classrooms. In K. H. Tan, M. A. Heng, & C. Ratnam-Lim (Eds.), *Curriculum leadership by middle leaders: Theory, design and practice* (pp. 88–103). Abington: Routledge.

Marshall, B., & Drummond, M. J. (2006). How teachers engage with assessment for learning: Lessons from the classroom. *Research Papers in Education, 21*(02), 133–149.

McMillan, J. H. (2013). Why we need research on classroom assessment. In J. H. MacMillan (Ed.), *Handbook of classroom assessment* (pp. 3–16). Thousand Oaks, CA: Sage.

Opfer, V. D., & Pedder, D. (2011). Conceptualizing teacher professional learning. *Review of Educational Research, 81*(3), 376–407.

Pedder, D., & Opfer, V. D. (2012). Professional learning orientations: Patterns of dissonance and alignment between teachers' values and practices. *Research Papers in Education, 1*(1), 1–32.

Pope, N., Green, S. K., Johnson, R. L., & Mitchell, M. (2009). Examining teacher ethical dilemmas in classroom assessment. *Teaching and Teacher Education, 25*(5), 778–782.

Price, M., Rust, C., O'Donovan, B., & Handley, K. (2012). *Assessment literacy: The foundation for improving student learning.* London: Oxford Brookes University Press.

Primary Education Review and Implementation Committee. (2009). *Report of the primary education review and implementation committee.* Singapore: Ministry of Education.

Putnam, R. T., & Borko, H. (2000). What do new views of knowledge and thinking have to say about research on teacher learning? *Educational Researcher, 29*(1), 4–15.

Ratnam-Lim, C. T., & Tan, K. H. (2015). Large-scale implementation of formative assessment practices in an examination-oriented culture. *Assessment in Education: Principles, Policy & Practice, 22*(1), 61–78.

Richardson, V. (1992). The agenda-setting dilemma in a constructivist staff development process. *Teaching and Teacher Education, 8*(3), 287–300.

Sellars, W., Scharp, K., & Brandom, R. (Eds.). (2007). *In the space of reasons. Selected essays of Wilfrid Sellars.* Cambridge: Harvard University Press.

Spinath, B. (2005). Akkuratheit der Einschätzung von Schülermerkmalen durch Lehrer und das Konstrukt der diagnostischen Kompetenz: Accuracy of teacher judgments on student characteristics and the construct of diagnostic competence. *Zeitschrift für Pädagogische Psychologie, 19*(1/2), 85–95.

Stiggins, R. J. (1991). Assessment literacy. *Phi Delta Kappan, 72*(7), 534–539.

Stiggins, R. J., & Bridgeford, N. J. (1985). The ecology of classroom assessment. *Journal of Educational Measurement, 22*(4), 271–286.

Stobart, G. (2008). *Testing times: The uses and abuses of assessment.* Abingdon: Routledge.

Tan, C. (2016). Tensions and challenges in China's education policy borrowing. *Educational Research, 58*(2), 195–206.

Trittel, M., Gerich, M., & Schmitz, B. (2014). Training prospective teachers in educational diagnostics. In S. Krolak-Schwerdt, S. Glock, & M. Böhmer (Eds.), *Teachers' professional development* (pp. 63–78). Rotterdam: Sense Publishers.

Chapter 10
Challenges and Opportunities in Implementing Formative Assessment in the Classroom: A Dutch Perspective

Kim Schildkamp

Abstract This chapter comments on the Asian-Pacific case studies in this volume and connects to the contexts in Europe. It is found that the experiences presented in these case studies provide valuable insights about key factors that impact on teacher learning and classroom assessment practices, highlighting the differential impact of national and local policies, teacher agency and beliefs, performativity, and accountability systems, and the context within which schools function.

Keywords Accountability, (in)formal data · Data literacy · Formative assessment · Student involvement, Professional development

Introduction

The chapters in this volume all describe different types of (formative) assessment approaches in the classroom, and have identified several challenges and opportunities in their specific contexts. Several of these challenges and opportunities have also been identified in a European/Dutch context. In this commentary, I focus on the following aspects as these have also arisen frequently in European and/or Dutch studies on formative assessment: accountability pressure, the use of formal and informal assessment data, data literacy, student involvement, and professional development in the form of teacher collaboration.

K. Schildkamp (✉)
University of Twente, Enschede, Netherlands
e-mail: k.schildkamp@utwente.nl

© Springer Nature Singapore Pte Ltd. 2018   177
H. Jiang and M. F. Hill (eds.), *Teacher Learning with Classroom Assessment*,
https://doi.org/10.1007/978-981-10-9053-0_10

Accountability Pressure

Accountability pressure shapes the process of formative assessment in schools. The results from a study conducted in China (Zhao, Yan, Tang, and Zhou, this volume) show, for example, that although a new curriculum was implemented, including paying attention to (formative) assessment, the focus for most teachers was still on summative assessment in terms of teaching to ensure that students get high scores on their tests. Another example comes from the chapter from India (Ratnam and Tharu, this volume). Although it was specified in the Indian curriculum renewal that teachers needed to implement formative assessment practices, the focus for teachers seemed to be more on keeping a record of students' real-time performance in the classroom, rather than on using the information to support student learning. Furthermore, the high-stakes summative assessment context in Singapore (Leong, this volume) prevented teachers from using formative assessment practices in a way that promotes student independence and autonomy of learning within the classroom. The focus seemed to be on raising test scores and not on student learning. A counterexample seems to come from the Australian chapter (Willis and Klenowski, this volume). In 2008, national testing was introduced in Australia, and since 2010 test results for individual schools were released publicly through the media. This put a lot of pressure on schools and created a focus on summative assessment. Yet, the teachers described in this chapter were implementing different formative assessment approaches in their classroom. This led to increased learning, and will ultimately also probably lead to increased achievement scores on the national tests.

The examples mentioned above are probably recognizable for many other countries. For example, in an EU study focused on the use of (assessment) data in the Netherlands, England, Germany, Lithuania, and Poland, we found that using data for accountability was common in all five countries (Schildkamp et al. 2014). In most of these countries, the focus seemed to be more on accountability than on school improvement. Although it is important to hold schools accountable for their functioning, this should not be the most important aspect of using (assessment) data. This can come with negative side effects, such as focusing only on a specific type of student who can help improve your status on those accountability indicators deemed to be important by the government, teaching to the test, cheating, and excluding certain students from a test (Ehren and Swanborn 2012; Sach 2013). Therefore, it is recommended to combine pressure from the accountability system with support, for example, in the form of professional development in the use of (assessment) data with a focus on school improvement (Schildkamp et al. 2014; Schildkamp and Lai 2013). As Earl and Katz (2006) state: "Accountability without improvement is empty rhetoric, and improvement without accountability is whimsical action without direction (p. 12).

Formal and Informal Assessment Data

Formative assessment includes the use of different kinds of assessment results, collected formally (systematically) and informally (often collected as teachers notice things). Some chapters focus more on the use of formal assessment results, such as performance assessments, examinations, standardized tests, and portfolios (Lam, this volume; Leong, this volume; Willis and Klenowski, this volume; Zhao et al. this volume). Some chapters focus more on the use of informal data, such as observations and dialogue in the classroom (Dixon and Hawe, this volume; Ishii, this volume). Some chapters focus on the combination of formal (e.g., examinations) and informal assessment (e.g., observing students engaging in various classroom activities, oral discussions in the classroom; Ratnam and Tharu, this volume; Smardon and Serow, this volume).

Van der Kleij et al. (2015) stress the importance of the use of various assessment approaches, involving the collection of formal and informal data, as these have different relevancies at various stages in the learning process. They state that different types of assessment methods are needed if teachers want to fully grasp the complexity of learning at all levels. Decisions should be based on multiple data sources gathered from multiple perspectives at different aggregation levels. As a result, teachers can continuously provide feedback at the school, class, and individual levels, to guide and enhance student learning. The assessment methods mentioned in the different chapters of this volume can form an inspiration for teachers all over the world with regard to collecting valuable formal and informal data on student learning. However, to be able to use formal and informal data, teachers need data literacy.

Data Literacy

Several chapters (Dixon and Hawe, this volume; Ishii, this volume; Lam, this volume; Zhao et al. this volume) discuss the importance of knowledge and skills needed with regard to the use of assessment data. The teachers in the China study (Zhao et al. this volume), for example, had developed their assessment literacy, but there was still room for improvement, for example, concerning technical knowledge and skills (e.g., with regard to the quality of assessments), specifying teaching objectives, developing more diverse assessment methods, and feedback. What also becomes clear from this volume is that specific types of (formative) assessments require specific types of knowledge and skills. For example, the concept of "teaching that builds on children's stumbles or mistakes," introduced in the Japanese chapter (Ishii, this volume), requires specific assessment knowledge and skills with regard to leading students in a creative dialogue. The use of assessment portfolios as discussed in the Hong Kong chapter (Lam, this volume) requires an in-depth understanding of concepts such as self-assessment, learning reflection, and self-regulated learning.

All of these different types of knowledge and skills can be summarized under the term *data literacy*. This is a complex term, involving many different aspects, such as developing, implementing, and using a range of assessment types and tools to gather a comprehensive evidence base about student learning; collecting, analyzing, and interpreting different types of data about student learning; identifying problems and possible causes of poor performance based on the analysis of data; and making instructional and/or curricular improvements based on data, for example, instructional differentiation based on assessment results (Hoogland et al. 2016). In the study conducted by Hoogland et al. (2016), teachers indicated that they recognized the importance of having data literacy, but they also indicated that they struggled in this area, as one of the interviewed teachers stated when talking about the competences needed: "When I read all of these competences, if I match them all, I should wear a t-shirt that says 'super teacher!' That teacher does not exist" (p. 382).

Another important aspect of data literacy is teachers' pedagogical knowledge (PK) and content knowledge (CK). Both are needed to provide students with useful feedback (Ní Chroinín and Cosgrave 2013), and to engage students in the process of formative assessment. The latter is another competence needed for the use of formative assessment: How to involve students in the process of formative assessment.

Student Involvement

The importance of student involvement in the process of formative assessment is stressed in several chapters of this volume. The New Zealand chapter (Dixon and Hawe, this volume), for example, focuses on a course on assessment for learning (AfL). At the beginning of the course, teachers were mainly focused on the role of the teacher. However, after the course, the teachers realized the importance of student involvement and defined AfL as "an everyday practice with students, teachers, and peers seeking, reflecting upon and responding to information from discussion and interactions in order to reach goals" (p. 9).

The Japanese chapter (Ishii, this volume) also stresses the importance of student involvement. The concept of "teaching that builds on children's stumbles or mistakes" is introduced in this chapter as a way to involve students. Whole-class teaching is used, and through the exchange of ideas, children make new discoveries and construct new knowledge. Students in the classroom receive opportunities to look at mistakes together in order to build joint knowledge. The children who stumbled or made the mistake can learn from their mistake, the children who know the correct answer can learn from expressing their answer, including the reasons behind it. This way, students' meta-cognition is fostered, and students' self-assessment capability is strengthened. Important here is that an open classroom climate exists, where students can express themselves without the fear of making mistakes. The Australian chapter (Willis and Klenowski, this volume) presents another way to involve students, by the use of peer-assessment. Teachers in this chapter decided to engage students in a peer-review process, which allowed students to receive timely feedback from their peers, and also learn how to self-assess to improve the quality of their own work. Teachers played an important role in this process, as they had to teach students how to give feedback and how to make suggestions for improvement.

However, the teachers described in the Indian chapter struggled with involving students. For these teachers, this did not match their ideas about good teaching, as the following quotation from the Indian chapter demonstrates: "They say that students can learn on their own, how is this possible?" (Ratnam and Tharu, this volume, p. 11). Although several teachers in the Indian chapter tried to adapt to new ways of teaching, and tried to involve students in interactions and dialogue in the classroom, their teaching could still be characterized as continuous noticing and correcting, making their classroom interaction primarily teacher generated. A similar situation can be found in Nauru (Smardon and Serow, this volume), where a teacher-directed approach existed, as the following quote demonstrates: "children ask what they do, and you have to tell them what to do" (Smardon and Serow, this volume, p. 15). However, the teachers described in this chapter were aware of this and were trying to move toward a more student-directed approach.

Other studies also demonstrate how important it is to involve students in the process of formative assessment Teachers can, for example, engage in discussion with students about their answers, expertise, or feedback (Gamlem and Smith 2013; Hargreaves 2013; Havnes et al. 2012). These discussions can give teachers insight into students' thinking, which they can use in adjusting instruction and providing feedback (Heitink et al. 2016). However, the results of two Dutch studies also show that involving students in the process of formative assessment is not easy. For example, on average, peer- and self-assessment techniques are only used in 0–25% of the lessons. Although teachers indicated that they find it very important to involve students in the process of formative assessment, they lacked the knowledge and skills to actually use these techniques in their classrooms (Kippers et al. 2016; Wolterinck et al. 2016).

Important questions that need to be answered, following from the chapters in this volume, are: How can teachers involve all of the students in their classroom in the process of formative assessment? How can teachers create the open climate which is needed for formative assessment, where it is okay for students to make mistakes, and discuss and learn from these mistakes? How can we support teachers in developing the knowledge and skills needed to involve students in the process of formative assessment? The latter will probably require some form of professional development.

Professional Development in the Form of Teacher Collaboration

The chapters from Australia (Willis and Klenowski, this volume), China (Zhao et al. this volume), Hong Kong (Lam, this volume), Japan (Ishii, this volume), Nauru (Smardon and Serow, this volume), and Singapore (Leong, this volume) all stress the importance of on-the-ground professional development in the form of teacher collaboration and inquiry. Teachers can learn from their colleagues, from collegial interaction and reflection. For example, from one of the cases in the chapter from Hong Kong (Lam, this volume), it becomes clear that teachers can learn a lot from regular co-planning meetings to discuss, review, and develop pedagogical/assessment ideas. This is crucial, as assessment training can provide teachers with domain-specific input, but teachers still need to trial, develop, and evaluate these assessment ideas in their own classrooms.

As has become evident from the chapters in this volume, professional development in the use of (formative) assessment is urgently needed. Several studies indicate that professional development is crucial for the successful implementation of formative assessment, including aspects such as teaching strategies, basic principles of good feedback, effective questioning, and also instructional resources, materials, and examples (Ní Chroinín and Cosgrave 2013; This is the case in several countries around the world, including the Netherlands (Kippers et al. 2016; Wolterinck et al. 2016).

An example of such a professional development intervention in the form of a professional learning community is the data team intervention. This intervention has been implemented and studied in the Netherlands, Belgium, England, and Sweden (for example, see Lai and Schildkamp 2016; Schildkamp et al. 2017). A data team consists of a team of three to six teachers, one or two school leaders, and a data expert, who work together to solve a specific educational problem at the school (e.g., low language achievement) based on (assessment) data. The teams follow an eight-step systematic procedure: (1) problem definition, (2) formulating hypotheses, (3) data collection, (4) data quality check, (5) data analysis, (6) interpretation and conclusions, (7) implementing improvement measures, and (8) evaluation. The teams are supported by an external coach, who guides the teams through the eight steps (Schildkamp et al. 2017). Studies show that the intervention has led to professional development in terms of an increase in data literacy (Ebbeler et al. 2017) as well as increased student learning and achievement (Poortman and Schildkamp 2016). The latter should be the goal of using (formative) assessment in education: increasing student learning and achievement in the classroom. Professional development in professional learning communities focused on the use of formative assessment is a great opportunity to realize both teacher and student learning.

References

Earl, L. M., & Katz, S. (2006). *Leading schools in a data-rich world. Harnessing data for school improvement*. Thousand Oaks: Corwin Press.

Ebbeler, J., Poortman, C. L., Schildkamp, K., & Pieters, J. M. (2017). The effects of a data use intervention on educators' satisfaction and data literacy. *Educational Assessment, Evaluation and Accountability, 29*(1), 83–105.

Ehren, M. C., & Swanborn, M. S. (2012). Strategic data use of schools in accountability systems. *School Effectiveness and School Improvement, 23*(2), 257–280.

Gamlem, S. M., & Smith, K. (2013). Student perceptions of classroom feedback. *Assessment in Education: Principles, Policy and Practice, 20,* 150–169.

Hargreaves, E. (2013). Inquiring into children's experiences of teacher feedback: Reconceptualising assessment for learning. *Oxford Review of Education, 39,* 229–246.

Havnes, A., Smith, K., Dysthe, O., & Ludvigsen, K. (2012). Formative assessment and feedback: Making learning visible. *Studies in Educational Evaluation, 38,* 21–27.

Heitink, M. C., Van der Kleij, F. M., Veldkamp, B. P., Schildkamp, K., & Kippers, W. B. (2016). A systematic review of prerequisites for implementing assessment for learning in classroom practice. *Educational Research Review, 17,* 50–62.

Hoogland, I., Schildkamp, K., Van der Kleij, F. M., Heitink, M. C., Kippers, W. B., Veldkamp, B. P., et al. (2016). Prerequisites for data-based decision making in the classroom: Research evidence and practical illustrations. *Teaching and Teacher Education, 60,* 377–386.

Kippers, W. B., Wolterinck, C. H., Schildkamp, K., & Poortman, C. L. (2016). Strategieën voor formatief toetsen in de lespraktijk: onderzoek en concrete voorbeelden [Strategies for formative assessment in the classroom: Research results and examples]. In D. Sluijsmans & R. Kneyber (Eds.), *Toetsrevolutie: naar een feedbackcultuur in het voortgezet onderwijs [The assessment revolution]* (pp. 113–125). Culemborg, The Netherlands: Uitgeverij Phronese.

Lai, M. K., & Schildkamp, K. (2016). In-service teacher professional learning: Use of assessment in data-based decision-making. In G. T. Brown & L. R. Harris (Eds.), *Handbook of human and social conditions in assessment* (pp. 77–94). New York: Routledge.

Ní Chroinín, D., & Cosgrave, C. (2013). Implementing formative assessment in primary physical education: Teacher perspectives and experiences. *Physical Education and Sport Pedagogy, 18,* 219–233.

Poortman, C. L., & Schildkamp, K. (2016). Solving student achievement focused problems with a data use intervention for teachers. *Teaching and Teacher Education, 60,* 425–433.

Sach, E. (2013). An exploration of teachers' narratives: What are the facilitators and constraints which promote or inhibit 'good' formative assessment practices in schools? *Education, 3–13: International Journal of Primary, Elementary and Early Years Education, 43,* 322–335.

Schildkamp, K., Handelzalts, A., Poortman, C. L., Leusink, H., Meerdink, M., Smit, M., et al. (2017). *The data team procedure: A systematic approach to school improvement.* Dordrecht: Springer.

Schildkamp, K., Karbautzki, L., & Vanhoof, J. (2014). Exploring data use practices around Europe: Identifying enablers and barriers. *Studies in Educational Evaluation, 42,* 15–24.

Schildkamp, K., & Lai, M. K. (2013). Data-based decision making: Conclusions and theoretical framework. In K. Schildkamp, M. K. Lai, & L. Earl (Eds.), *Data-based decision making in education: Challenges and opportunities* (pp. 177–191). Dordrecht: Springer.

Schildkamp, K., Smit, M., & Blossing, U. (2017, online pre-publication). Professional development in the use of data. From data to knowledge in data teams. *Scandinavian Journal of Educational Research.*

Van der Kleij, F. M., Vermeulen, J. A., Schildkamp, K., & Eggen, T. J. (2015). Integrating data-based decision making, assessment for learning and diagnostic testing in formative assessment. *Assessment in Education: Principles, Policy & Practice, 22,* 324–343.

Wolterinck, C. L., Kippers, W. B., Schildkamp, K., & Poortman, C. L. (2016). *Factors influencing the use of formative assessment in the classroom.* Paper presented at the AERA Conference, April 9, 2016, Washington, D.C.

Chapter 11
Curriculum and Policy Reform Impacts on Teachers' Assessment Learning: A South African Perspective

Anil Kanjee

Abstract The chapters in this volume provide a fascinating and very detailed overview of experiences regarding the development and application of assessment knowledge, skills and practice across different education contexts within the Asia-Pacific region. At a time when many countries the world over, and especially within sub-Saharan Africa, have embarked on key curriculum and assessment policy reforms (Sayed and Kanjee in Assess Educ Princ Policy Pract 20:373–384, 2013), the specific focus on teacher learning through classroom assessment is both timely and relevant. More important, the experiences presented provide valuable insights about key factors that impact on teacher learning and classroom assessment practices, highlighting the differential impact of national and local policies, teacher agency and beliefs, performativity and accountability systems, and the context within which schools function. In addition, the social, economic and cultural factors that need to be considered when developing and practicing classroom assessment for use in supporting student learning are also highlighted across the chapters. A number of key insights extracted from the different chapters are noted below as these insights are especially useful for scholars, researchers, policymakers as well as teachers and school leaders, across both developing and developed nations, grappling with similar challenges related to teacher professional development and improving student learning.

Keywords Classroom assessment · Formative assessment
Teacher professional development

A. Kanjee (✉)
Tshwane University of Technology, Tshwane, South Africa
e-mail: kanjeea@tut.ac.za

© Springer Nature Singapore Pte Ltd. 2018   185
H. Jiang and M. F. Hill (eds.), *Teacher Learning with Classroom Assessment*,
https://doi.org/10.1007/978-981-10-9053-0_11

Introduction

The chapters in this volume provide a fascinating and very detailed overview of experiences regarding the development and application of assessment knowledge, skills and practice across different education contexts within the Asia-Pacific region. At a time when many countries the world over, and especially within sub-Saharan Africa, have embarked on key curriculum and assessment policy reforms (Sayed and Kanjee 2013), the specific focus on teacher learning through classroom assessment is both timely and relevant. More important, the experiences presented provide valuable insights about key factors that impact on teacher learning and classroom assessment practices, highlighting the differential impact of national and local policies, teacher agency and beliefs, performativity and accountability systems, and the context within which schools function. In addition, the social, economic and cultural factors that need to be considered when developing and practicing classroom assessment for use in supporting student learning are also highlighted across the chapters. A number of key insights extracted from the different chapters are noted below as these insights are especially useful for scholars, researchers, policymakers as well as teachers and school leaders, across both developing and developed nations, grappling with similar challenges related to teacher professional development and improving student learning.

Willis and Klenwoski (this volume) describe the assessment strategies teachers in Brisbane use to support student learning and how these practices are used to engender the development of new assessment knowledge and skills. The authors contextualise change in teacher practice within the curriculum reform process, foregrounding teacher agency and teacher reflection as critical factors impacting on how they engage with students and peers in addressing issues of assessment. The authors demonstrate how teachers enhance their own learning as well as learning among students through two processes. The first is the innovative use of technology (Turnitin program) to implement peer assessment activities. Through this process, the teachers provide relevant feedback that addresses the specific learning needs of students while at the same time facilitating deeper conversations among themselves. In these conversations, they clarify the meanings of criteria used, and the strategies applied for suggesting improvements in student learning. The second is their practice of sharing their understandings and expectations with other teachers as well as their students when exploring notions of what quality work should look like. In this regard, the authors argue that 'collaborative critical inquiry with peers and academics led to positive classroom assessment innovations that have the potential to inform system innovation'. Thus, we see the influence on teachers' learning through the introduction of new technology and practices changing how teachers approach their assessment practice. Introducing digital tools can assist teachers to turn what might previously have been summative information to formative use. Even when reform-oriented curriculum and assessment policy encourages teachers towards more formative practices, access to such technology requires resources which may not be available in many educational settings internationally.

In China, Zhao, Yan, Tang and Zhou (this volume) reflect on how changes in teacher classroom practices to more formative, student-centred assessments have been achieved as part of a comprehensive curriculum reform process. The authors attribute these to reform initiatives that emphasise changes in both curriculum and assessment, through the provision of relevant materials, promotion of school-based professional development opportunities as well as efforts to minimise the negative effect of examinations on students. Zhao and his colleagues list five core requirements for teachers to develop more formative classroom assessment practices: (i) reducing emphasis on screening and ranking and focussing the developmental role of assessment; (ii) placing greater emphasis on critical thinking, as well as on students' creative, cooperative and practical abilities; (iii) making assessment more interactive and collaborative between teachers and students; (iv) exploring new methods like portfolio and performance assessments; and (v) shifting the focus from results to process in both summative and formative assessments. The authors, however, note that key challenges working against the appropriate use of assessment in the classroom, and in particular the provision of effective feedback to students, can be the limited assessment knowledge and skills among teachers, high workloads, and limited and poor school-based professional development opportunities for teachers. These findings also foreground the complexity of effective change in teacher practice, despite national and local efforts implemented for supporting teachers. In their conclusion, the authors summarise their efforts by noting that 'What to assess determines *what* teachers teach and *what* students learn. Likewise, *how* to assess determines *how* teachers teach and what students learn' (*emphasis added*). The system accountability goals and processes, here as everywhere, tend to impact and override even serious attempts to shift teaching in the formative directions.

In his account of how two Hong Kong teachers developed their writing assessment knowledge and skills, Lam (this volume) highlights the importance of accounting for various micro-, meso- and macro-level factors that impact on schools, teachers and students. Given the critical impact of meso-level (school level) factors on teacher learning, as well as the dearth of research at this level, the author focuses his study on the schooling context within which these language teachers develop new assessment knowledge and skills. Lam highlights three school-level factors that constrained or facilitated the classroom assessment practices of the two teachers in his study. First, the prevalence, and focus of teacher evaluation systems, and their impact on the teachers' career advancement; second, the dominant culture prevalent within the school regarding opportunity for innovation and improvement within the classroom, and third, opportunity for collaboration in developing new knowledge and skills for supporting learners improve learning. Notwithstanding the different learning trajectories reported for each teacher, Lam acknowledges that teacher learning extends beyond formal training programmes and highlights the difficulty teachers experience, within schools, in transferring knowledge into practice, even in instances where teachers are willing and possess the necessary capacity. This finding lends weight to using the school and classroom context as a site for teacher assessment learning, especially when curriculum reform is occurring and external professional development is available (Kanjee 2017).

Ratnam and Tharu (this volume) also outline how teachers in the Indian state of Karnataka responded to a curriculum reform initiative, the Continuous and Comprehensive Evaluation (CCE) scheme, to develop their classroom practices for the effective use of assessment to support student learning. The authors highlight the challenges of effecting relevant reform within an education system subjugated by a strong examination culture that engenders the dominance of teacher-centred practices, especially when combined with high workloads that mainly comprise non-teaching activities, and a culture of top-down training provided to teachers. The emphasis of the curriculum reform initiative on shifting classroom assessment practices to more formative assessment approaches is considered critical in changing teacher practices, albeit that this might be in a routinized manner. Paradoxically, however, the authors report that these routines did create some opportunities for teachers to interact with learners in different, and novel ways that facilitated more 'formative assessment like' practices, i.e. emerging classroom dialogue, thus ensuring greater 'active involvement of both teachers and students in listening to and responding to the other as mindful people engaged in evaluation' (p. 20). Wiliam (2011) notes that teacher practices that engineer effective classroom discussions, activities, and learning tasks that elicit evidence of learning is one of the key formative assessment strategies for improving student learning. For Ratnam and Tharu, the assessment demands of the curriculum reform process required teachers to engage in new self-learning practices that was not only qualitatively different from the prescribed top-down training that characterise teacher professional development within the education sector, but also more effective in 'fostering spontaneous and situation learning in both teachers and students (p. 20).

In his account of teacher learning about assessment in Japan, Ishii notes that assessment is embedded in teachers' daily practice, and exemplified by the creative whole class teaching style that characterises lessons in Japanese classrooms. This teaching style requires lessons to be creative and dramatic where teachers can use student stumbles (errors) to facilitate learning by engaging students through meaningful dialogue and student self-reflection. This process, which Ishii notes as the design–implementation–reflection cycle, characterises the nature of professional development for Japanese teachers and requires them to think reflectively, regulate their practice and engage with peers to create opportunities for self-study. Ishii provides exemplars of practical study tools used by Japanese teachers to learn from their classroom practice. These include the card construction method, used to increase awareness among teachers of key issues that may impact their teaching. This is done by peers who observe lessons, and record all possible challenges and concerns on cards, and each of these is then followed up by in-depth teacher discussion. Another is the intervention class where the supervising teacher (or Head of Department) presents a lesson which the teacher observes, followed by an in-depth discussion. A third approach is the stop motion method, a process where lessons are recorded on video and reviewed with colleagues. In each of these approaches, the purpose is to review the teaching methods applied, the decisions made while presenting lessons and how these impact on students' learning. This process, according to Ishii, implies that teachers are inherently using assessment as well as a reflection as they learn from their engagement with students while also supporting their students to improve learning. In this regard, Ishii calls for a definition of formative assessment as 'the art of leading the students in creative dialogue' (p. 15). This call is an interesting one although the approach might well depend on cultural and societal factors that would make it more appropriate in some contexts than others.

One very different culture from the Japanese context is Nauru. Smardon and Serow (this volume) exemplify the impact of colonization on teachers' classroom assessment practice. This, according to the authors, is manifested in the use of English as a language of instruction, and the Western perspectives within which the Nauru Quality School Standard Framework was developed. Working within this context, Smardon and Serow argue that teacher agency, as well as in-depth knowledge and consideration of their students' background, was critical for the two teachers in their study to resist the impact of colonization in their classroom and daily practice. The authors demonstrate how the two teachers worked to develop their own professional learning of classroom assessment by translating their formal theoretical knowledge gained in Western settings into practical strategies for supporting student learning in their cultural context. In particular, Smardon and Serow highlight the contradictions when addressing issues of teacher–student power relations, an issue that impacts teachers across many developing nations, especially in instances where classroom practices clash with cultural expectations. By promoting learner-centred strategies in her classroom, one teacher in the study required her students to demonstrate greater levels of autonomy, at least within the classroom context, while knowing that these same students simultaneously function within communities that expect greater levels of compliance. Another teacher tackled these issues differently, deliberately integrating Nauruan stories and legends, and drawing on her students' cultural capital to enhance their learning. In addition, the benefits of working with other teachers prompted one of the teachers to establish a professional learning community for teachers in her school to support each other to improve their own assessment classroom practices. However, in addition to these cultural issues, the authors also acknowledge the impact of large class sizes that limit what teachers can do to effect more formative assessment approaches in their practice, and the negative impact large numbers of students has on teacher learning in such contexts. These effects have also been encountered in the African context in schools with high student–teacher ratios, and where it is difficult to release teachers to spend time on their own professional learning (Sayed et al. 2014).

In a contrasting example, Dixon and Hawe describe how they supported teachers in New Zealand to examine their beliefs about the roles and responsibilities towards learners and teachers in the assessment process using reflection, modelling and practical experiences of assessment for learning. The authors highlight two key issues that impact on teacher learning: the national policy, which in New Zealand advocates for the development of assessment capable teachers and students as well as for the adoption of assessment for learning (AfL) principles and practices; and, teacher self-efficacy, which the authors define as 'the generalized expectation a teacher has in regard to his or her ability to influence students, as well as beliefs about their ability to perform the professional tasks that constitute teaching, such as assessing student learning' (p. 3). In their tertiary assessment course, Dixon and Hawe utilised complementary approaches in developing teachers' AfL knowledge and skills that not only integrated relevant theory and practice of the AfL strategies, but also facilitated active engagement of participating teachers across the different lecture sessions. The key strategies applied in the delivery of the course included: modelling the application of AfL strategies and techniques as it would be applied within the teachers' classrooms, supporting teachers to reflect on their knowledge and practice; and, creating opportunities for teachers to observe, and experience, the application of the new assessment knowledge and skills that they were expected to develop, by functioning both as students studying towards a formal qualification, and as students (learners) in a school classroom. This dual role, according to the authors, is what provided teachers with 'a compelling argument for change as well as a concomitant vision for AfL practice' (p. 16).

In the final case, studying how one teacher in a Singapore school developed her assessment knowledge and skills, Leong highlights the value of teacher self-agency, teacher reflection, the creation of a safe space and provision of support for facilitating professional learning and sustained change in classroom practice. The author argues that new knowledge about classroom practices are inadequate if teachers are unable to affect this in their daily practice, where teachers often face constraints that impact on what, and how, any assessment knowledge and skills are implemented. Using experiences of the teacher in her English and Music classes, Leong demonstrates how different subject requirements regarding summative assessment facilitate or hinder a teacher's ability to experiment and develop new classroom assessment practices. To counter this, Leong argues for creating conversations among teachers that support new thinking and activities about their assessment practices that do not require additional theoretical knowledge. A key message of Leong is that spaces and boundaries of professional learning cannot only be confined to moments of learning that occur in workshops and training sessions but also in schools and classrooms through personal conversations and interactions between colleagues.

The messages in these case studies strongly resonate with several studies in developing countries regarding assessment professional development initiatives. Specifically, in education systems where policy reform towards integrating assessment to improve learning are desired but where regular external testing is still dominant, teachers face significant difficulties in changing classroom practices. While there may be a will to change, and professional development might provide encouragement and support to use formative practices, large classes, limited resources, cultural expectations and external testing, among other factors, place the teacher in a web of competing demands. Ultimately, sustained and relevant reform in teacher's assessment practices can only be attained through appropriate changes in policy, effecting specific support for enhancing teacher learning at the school and classroom level, and teacher agency regarding the effective use of assessment for identifying and addressing learning needs of all students.

References

Kanjee, A. (2017). Using formative assessment to address the challenge of equity and quality in schools: Preliminary findings from a randomised control trial. Paper presented at the 35th African Association of Educational Assessment, August 5–11, 2017, Kampala, Uganda.

Sayed, Y., & Kanjee, A. (2013). Assessment in Sub-Saharan Africa: Challenges and prospects. *Assessment in Education: Principles, Policy & Practice, 20*(4), 373–384.

Sayed, Y., Kanjee, A., & Rao, N. (2014). Assessment of and for learning. In *Learning and education in developing countries: Research and policy for the post-2015 UN development goals* (pp. 91–109). Palgrave Macmillan: US.

Wiliam, D. (2011). *Embedded formative assessment*. Bloomington, IN, USA: Solution Tree Press.

Chapter 12
Classroom Assessment for Teacher Learning and Student Learning

Mary F. Hill, Kelvin Tan and Heng Jiang

Abstract In this concluding chapter, we use the guiding questions for the book as a framework to examine what the case studies tell us about what and how teachers learn as they wrestle with classroom assessment, pushing the boundaries of their practice while finding ways to work within the constraints of their context. We then address themes that cut across the cases, highlighting the impact of the contexts in which these teachers work and learn.

Keywords Accountability · Classroom assessment · Cultural beliefs and expectations · High stakes assessment · International assessment discourses Teacher learning

Introduction

The case studies in this volume are rich in details of the many different contexts and classrooms they describe and the ways teachers understand and approach their practice. As we stated early in the book, dual themes are at play here: teachers using and adapting assessment practices to foster students' learning, and learning, in the process, how to develop and use classroom assessment tools for this inquiry purpose. In this sense, the teachers in these contexts are shown to be learning through using assessment, not just learning about or how to use it in the service of their students'

M. F. Hill (✉)
Faculty of Education and Social Work, The University of Auckland, Auckland,
New Zealand
e-mail: mf.hill@auckland.ac.nz

K. Tan (✉) · H. Jiang
National Institute of Education, Nanyang Technological University, Singapore, Singapore
e-mail: kelvin.tan@nie.edu.sg

© Springer Nature Singapore Pte Ltd. 2018
H. Jiang and M. F. Hill (eds.), *Teacher Learning with Classroom Assessment*,
https://doi.org/10.1007/978-981-10-9053-0_12

learning. In many different ways, the authors of the case study chapters have shown how teachers learn in each individual context and how they put this learning into action. In constructing each chapter, three main questions were either explicitly or implicitly addressed, namely:

1. How do Asia-Pacific teachers practice classroom assessment?
2. Why do they practice such classroom assessment strategies?
3. What do teachers learn from practicing classroom assessment in these ways?

In this concluding chapter, first, we use these questions as a framework to examine what these cases tell us about what and how teachers learn as they wrestle with classroom assessment, pushing the boundaries of their practice while finding ways to work within the constraints of their context. We then move to address themes that cut across the cases, highlighting the impact of the contexts in which these teachers work and learn. Within each, for example, teachers face various school climates and cultures, accountability demands, and societal norms, as well as the international assessment discourses at play across the Asia-Pacific region.

Classroom Assessment Practices and Teacher Learning

Reading across the chapters from each country in this text, it is clear that the authors have focused their gaze on what teachers are doing in their classrooms in the name of assessment and learning. In contrast with examinations mandated outside the classroom (even if they take place within the classroom from time to time), the goals of classroom assessment within and across these cases lie on a continuum of practices ranging from what might be described as relatively formal teacher-implemented assessment tasks for accountability purposes at one end, through to interactive formative assessment processes at the other. We move along this continuum to discuss the classroom practices across the cases according to their major purposes: making judgments, monitoring progress; diagnosing learning status to plan teaching; and, informing learning, and teaching through assessment as an embedded process. Of course, this approach is just one way to "see" classroom assessment practices. There are other ways in which the practices across the case study chapters might be examined. For example, it would be possible to use a different continuum such as the extent to which the assessment is focused upon and applied to individuals rather than a whole class. Another analysis approach might be the extent to which students are at the center of the process. Although the purpose dimension is used here to explore the classroom assessment practices across the region, in the latter half of the chapter the practices are revisited against historical, societal, and cultural dimensions, and in relation to international trends.

A full range of purposes for classroom assessment appear across the chapters. The authors have described how and why teachers met accountability demands, conducted tests and used the results, and introduced portfolio assessment, and the ways in which they worked to embed assessment into teaching and learning as a dialogic and interactive process. Across these contexts are many contrasts in purposes and practices, sometimes even within the same school. For example, in Singapore, the case of Pei Pei clearly indicates the effects of accountability measures on one teacher, and, in Nauru, teacher education effects clearly contrast with local cultural expectations and play out as competing drivers for each teacher within the classroom. It is of course relatively simplistic to use purposes as the frame of reference to organize such a discussion because, as just mentioned, multiple purposes can be driving teachers' practices at any one time. Therefore, we use this continuum more as a heuristic to guide the discussion rather than a set of fixed indicators. Our discussion starts with the *making judgments* end of the continuum and moves stepwise through the purposes listed earlier towards classroom assessment embedded in teaching and learning as a *formative interactive process*.

In several of the case study chapters teachers demonstrate clearly that an important aspect of their work is to make consistent and important judgments with respect to the progress and achievement of their students. Clearly, in Australia, there is a trend towards closer auditing of student achievement that requires teachers to learn more than before about making judgments to meet national, state and local education goals while at the same time actively engaging in making decisions about classroom assessment (Willis and Klenowski this volume). As in all the case studies in this volume, Willis and Klenowski focus on the particular to provide views into classrooms, and, while, as they say, the purpose is not to homogenize the concepts of teacher agency and informed professionalism, these views do show how agentic teachers productively engage in both implementing and amplifying student learning through assessing but may also resist assessment requirements, or misunderstand or be overwhelmed by conflicting demands. In one case, when presented with new national and state expectations, two Queensland teachers showed how engaging in deep professional conversations between themselves and with facilitators about these practices, and how they related to curriculum, helped them learn a great deal about assessment and their own knowledge and assumptions. These two teachers were trying to reach some agreement about the standards reached by their students from evidence in their work. While teacher judgments about how well their students are meeting such standards might be seen as preferable to national tests, the case of these two teachers clearly demonstrates that this is no easy or straightforward task. These teachers learned much about how to work together when some of their assumptions differed, develop a shared language of assessment, record what evidence of achievement might look like, design curriculum and teaching plans based on the information, and clarify assessment standards and expectations. Thus, whilst policies for assessing standards through teacher judgments might at first glance appear straightforward, these cases demonstrate this is far from the case. Making judgments prompts, and can sustain, extensive teacher learning about assessment, but also about curriculum, instruction, their students, and about themselves.

In contrast with the professional learning prompted in this Australian case, but still connected with making judgments, Ratnam and Tharu consider the washback effects of a centrally controlled examination system which curtails teachers' flexibility in using everyday classroom assessments. Challenged to introduce a curriculum initiative, continuous and comprehensive evaluation (CCE), this case clearly demonstrated the struggles that teachers face caught in the nexus of external examination pressures and pressure to implement continuous process-centered formative assessment. In this ethnographically oriented case, while the teachers faithfully attempted to implement the new formative practices by following the training manuals and could articulate ways in which they had implemented the approach, observations showed how this was so much more difficult to do in practice. Their learning was impeded by many factors, not the least of which were the practical aspects: teacher overload; training issues; and the external examination demands, which determined how the year ran and was organized, curtailing time to learn to use new practices. These issues resonated with other cases in this volume where external testing and challenging teaching conditions were apparent, such as in Nauru and even, to some extent, the Singapore and Hong Kong cases. As Lam (this volume) sums up, "teacher learning is a slippery, complex and multi-levelled concept." In his chapter, Lam demonstrates clearly how learning to use new approaches in assessment is a personally driven, career-long process and certainly beyond "the provision of initial teacher education, short-lived professional development and participation in school-based collaborative projects among colleagues and/or with university researchers" (p. 18, this volume). As other authors in this collection have also demonstrated, with institutional support and backing, each teacher has both the opportunity and responsibility to learn continuously to improve their own practices in the service of enhancing student learning.

Diagnosing learning status to plan and design learning, an intermediary point along the assessment purposes continuum was also a theme running through the cases in this text. A case in point is China, where education reform since 2005 has included urging teachers to minimize screening and deepen the developmental function of assessment to realize "evaluation's role in improving students' development and teachers' teaching" (Zhao, Yan, Tang, and Zhou this volume). The findings of Zhao et al.'s study indicated a clear preference for the diagnosis, motivation and development functions of assessment. In this context, formative assessments were seen as helpful for discovering students' problems, analyzing teaching and improving teaching quality.

Integrating assessment into classroom teaching as an embedded process was proposed by Benjamin Bloom as *formative classroom assessment* (cited in Guskey 2005), as a way to "reduce variation in students' achievement and to have all students learn well" (quoted in Guskey 2005, p. 1). A key element in achieving this, Bloom argued, was to "increase the variation in instructional approaches and learning time" (p. 1), and central to this is the need understand what students know, their conceptions and misconceptions, in order to differentiate teaching to account for such variation. As well as the China case above, this approach is exemplified in this book by the historical cases of classroom assessment in Japan. While, clearly, the classroom assessment practices are embedded within the instruction, in this context excellent teaching and learning are characterized by dialogic interactions within creative whole-class lessons. As Ishii illuminates, a fundamental idea within Japanese primary classrooms is for the teacher to elicit students' conceptions, reasoning, and knowledge and build on their "stumbles or mistakes" in a safe and supportive climate in ways that involve the class collaboratively discussing and solving problems together. Opportunities to look at mistakes are given regularly and this kind of responsive teaching is aimed at students finding their mistakes for themselves and learning, with support, to achieve a deeper level of understanding through challenge and explanation, discussion and feedback. This "art of teaching" resonates with more recent Western discourses of assessment for learning and assessment as learning, featured in the cases from New Zealand and Nauru, in particular, although they are also echoed in Pei Pei's music classes in Singapore.

The cases in this text, however, mostly included classroom assessment for all the purposes along the continuum but with particular points of emphasis, as examined above. In most cases it is a matter of emphasis where the focus lies with teachers and this is constrained by the context and the agency teachers have within the policies and practices available to them. The case of New Zealand is instructive because, although there is a clear set of national standards against which students in Years 1–8 are regularly compared, with their achievement against these reported on to parents, and by the schools to the Ministry of Education, there has been a long-term assessment for learning policy which balances the summative standards agenda with a much more formative one. As Dixon and Hawe (this volume) argue, probably due to the lack of an external testing regime and an enduring emphasis on the importance of formative assessment supported by formal and informal assessment tools, New Zealand primary school teachers emphasize formative purposes. But even with this formative history and culture of assessment, many teachers struggle to fully realize the full potential of assessment for learning, where the aim is to have assessment capable students who can actively participate in assessing their own learning, and be self-regulating learners. As the New Zealand case demonstrates, it was not until the teachers themselves experienced an assessment for learning approach within their own professional learning that they could see the full extent of the approach. In contrast with the use of discrete formative assessments, these teachers came to understand how embedded within the assessment decision making students must be in order for them to become assessment capable.

The Impact of Context on Teacher Learning and Their Classroom Assessment Practices

The cases included in this volume show that the complexity of teachers' classroom assessment practices is not only represented by the multiple purposes and formats of assessment per se, but is also due to the situated nature of assessment in certain social-cultural contexts. Teachers are appropriating various cultural resources to develop their assessment practices, not only in terms of technical procedures of implementing assessment, but also actively constructing their interpretations on what they can learn from the process. As introduced earlier in this chapter, several contextual factors at play in all of these cases influence what teachers believe they can (and cannot do) and it is to some of these we now turn.

Accountability and High Stakes Summative Assessment

Increasing focus on international assessment results across countries, such as the PISA and TIMMS programs, limit and curtail expectations about how and how well teachers should practice assessment in their classrooms. Such high stakes international assessments lead to active comparisons of academic achievement between countries, in turn increasing pressure and the stakes of the national assessment. Classroom assessment practices offer a microcosmic glimpse of how teachers balance the pressures of accountability for high stakes summative assessment with formative uses of assessment for supporting and enhancing students' learning.

In Chap. 3, Smardon and Serow observed that "in the Nauruan context, classroom assessment practices combined assessment for both summative and formative purposes." However, they argued that the teachers interviewed about their classroom assessment practices "had the opportunity to extend their understanding and use of assessment into more formative approaches" beyond "simply measuring student achievements." Such classroom assessment discourse frames summative assessment in the classroom as a limited endeavor from which teachers were encouraged to shift beyond to a more formative approach—"enabling teachers to view students' understanding, provide feedback, assist in making informed decisions concerning the next steps to take in the teaching/learning sequence, or as a component within the sequence of classroom activities."

Likewise, the Japan case in this book alludes to the negative effects of standardized tests and summative assessment serving as "a tool to rank and control children, teachers, and schools." Classroom assessment, in contrast, is heralded as "part of grassroots initiatives to reconfigure 'assessments' as a tool to improve schools and identify quality and fairness in education."

Such distrust of summative assessment amongst teachers raises an interesting question, and opportunity, for classroom assessment discourse—which prevailing and primary purpose for learning should teachers direct classroom assessment practices to achieve? Should teachers always privilege formative assessment purposes in their classrooms and assume high stakes summative assessment to be the purview of external parties? Or should teachers also understand summative assessment practice as an equally important part of classroom assessment in interaction (and not opposition) with formative assessment practice? Perhaps this largely depends on what teachers view their "classroom" to be as the site and context for their *classroom* assessment practices.

Cultural Beliefs and Expectations of 'the Classroom' in Classroom Assessment

Various chapters in this book have understood 'the classroom' to embody and represent cultural expectations of teachers in teaching, assessment, and curriculum. For example, Smardon and Serow describe Nauruan *classroom* teachers as being charged with the "responsibility of delivering *local* curriculum through pedagogy that reflects the *cultural* basis of the students' community" (emphasis added). The classroom is the domain of teacher agency performing the role of "cultural mediators" between "children in their classrooms and the wider Nauruan community." As Smardon and Serow note, the Nauruan teachers are not oblivious to this, and show that they may struggle to use new assessment practices in which students have a role. They note that it may take several generations for Nauruan students to accept this new assessment role, given the cultural expectations that strongly shape what is possible.

In the case of Japan, "the classroom" is vitally important for containing and encapsulating "hourly lessons as a complete experience." In opposition to "technologies developed *outside of the classroom*," the emphasis for teachers is observed to be the creation of "activities with the child *in the classroom*." As such, the classroom would seem to provide, for Japanese teachers, a sanctuary for exclusive interaction with students through activities. In turn, this may constrain and limit classroom assessment practices to only teaching activities during lessons for "creative whole-class teaching." While it might appear that limiting assessment practices in the classroom to whole-class teaching activities might not include formative assessment practices that emphasize assessing and supporting individual students, identifying their achievement gaps and providing individual students with feedback on how to close the gap, individuals can also be the source of class action. This draws our attention to ways in which a specific cultural practice, class teaching supported through lesson study, can also incorporate more global assessment themes. As Ishii demonstrates, the act of assessment can be seen embedded in the teaching process "in the creative dialogue between teacher and children" (p. 1, this volume). Through this discussion and other means such as observations, it appears that teachers develop a detailed understanding and categorization of individual students' thinking/misconceptions, enabling them to create a new plan or approach through which to take the learning further. This is explicitly tackled in Ishii's chapter, explaining that whole-class teaching "is not simply a matter of taking the entire class as a group—each student is viewed as rich in their understanding, making for a class that is creative throughout" (p. 12, this volume).

Finally, the "possible disjuncture between Western cultural and intellectual ideals of an 'autonomous learner' and the Confucian-heritage values of 'teacher authority' over 'student autonomy' in different subject classes" was observed by Leong in his case study of a Singapore teacher's classroom assessment practices. The teacher in question, Pei Pei, responded to the pressures of summative assessment in the English language by adopting a regimental approach, which dictated what students should memorize and their choice of questions, "in order to achieve a better grade." In contrast, the same teacher practiced formative assessment "naturalistically *without* the pressure of a performativity agenda" in her music lessons, which is a subject that does not suffer from summative assessment pressures. Such a contrast challenges the notion that both summative and formative assessment practices can be practiced at the same time, for all subjects in the classroom.

Whilst the notion of 'the classroom' constructs classroom assessment discourse, the contrast in Pei Pei's assessment practices reveals how prevailing assessment agendas influence the notion of how and what should be learnt in the classroom in the first place. This raises another interesting question for classroom assessment—is there a risk that some classroom assessment practices may unduly emphasize teaching activities for the whole class to the detriment of supporting the learning needs of individual students?

Conclusion

This collection of case studies from China, Australia, Nauru, New Zealand, Hong Kong, India, Japan, and Singapore reveals how teachers develop and use classroom assessment strategies for student learning, and undertake their own professional learning, in these different countries. The international collection of authors brings to the book a breadth of knowledge and experience about classroom assessment and a depth of analysis across a number of comparative dimensions, such as between centralized and decentralized education systems, developing and developed countries, and between Eastern and Western cultures in the Asia-Pacific region. The nuances represented in each case raise our awareness of significant variety within the collective regional identity in Asia-Pacific, and the ways in which these ebb and flow across the region. As discussed in this chapter, very different forces are at play in shaping classroom assessment, and teachers weave their practices within and sometimes against these forces. While they might well be aware of, and open to, alternative approaches, the material circumstances in which they live and work constrain and enable what is possible.

Despite the contextual constraints, however, similar discourses about classroom assessment do cross jurisdictional boundaries and influence the classroom assessment practices of teachers across the region. For example, as these cases demonstrated, as well as the desire to ensure students meet certain standards, teachers strive to use formative practices to understand and build on students' understandings and abilities. These practices might shift shape as they encounter accountability requirements, local conditions, and cultural norms, but the formative intent is recognizable across the region. These cases show that the complexity of teachers' assessment practices is not only represented by the multiple purposes and formats, but also due to the situated nature of assessment in certain social-cultural contexts. Teachers are appropriating various cultural resources to develop their assessment practices, not only in terms of technical procedures of implementing assessment but also by actively constructing their interpretations on what they can learn from the process.

Reference

Guskey, T. R. (2005, April). *Formative classroom assessment and Benjamin S. Bloom: Theory, research and implications.* Paper presented at the annual meeting of the American Educational Research Association, Montreal, Canada.

Printed by Printforce, the Netherlands